MasterChef
EVERYDAY

CONTENTS

JOHN TORODE

"Fantastic flavours, wonderful textures, creating really beautiful plates of food... that takes practice. And, as any MasterChef contestant will tell you, the real trick is to always keep cooking – every day."

We have tasted some absolutely incredible food over the years on MasterChef and seen a host of amazing contestants journey from triumph to disaster and back again. That's a lot of great food and a lot of great memories – and it's wonderful to see some of the stories from the people behind the food, as well as the really, really superb recipes, in this book.

MasterChef is about truly talented chefs all committed to creating really sensational food. I feel very lucky to be a part of that. And to work alongside Gregg with his wonderful knowledge of ingredients, and how they work together on the plate and on the palate, is a total joy. As judges on the show, we know that every forkful we taste is loaded with imagination, talent, hard work, and care. That's a real responsibility as a judge – and one that Gregg and I both take very seriously. But cooking is also about having fun, about giving expression to a part of yourself, about letting yourself go and seeing where things take you. It should make you feel good! Really good food day to day is about really good ingredients cooked from the heart, and about the joy of sharing that food with family and friends.

All of the brilliant recipes in this book are dishes you can create at home – you can choose whatever you want and be as adventurous as you want. There are some incredibly original ingredients, some moments of awe-inspiring technical genius, some totally show-stopping examples of presentation – without that, it wouldn't be MasterChef! But to help you along the way, Gregg and I take some of those great MasterChef recipes and give them a bit of an "every day" spin. We keep the essence of the original dishes – their flavours, their personalities – and give you a few tips, tricks, and shortcuts to save you time at home. With a little know-how and a bit of variation, you can cook and eat that wonderful food every day of the week. What better way to feed your loved ones – and your creativity?

Fantastic flavours, wonderful textures, creating really beautiful plates of food... that takes practice. And, as any MasterChef contestant will tell you, the real trick is to always keep cooking – every day.

GREGG WALLACE

"Great food, delivered with love from great contestants – here for you to create yourselves at home. Cook, eat, enjoy. A prize for whoever does the best Gregg Wallace-style tasting!"

I am a very fortunate man – as you've seen on television I get to stick my spoon or fork in some truly delightful dishes. I will never tire of good food. I will always delight in the simple pleasure of good eating. Not all of my favourite MasterChef dishes are complicated – a lot of the time it is the clever use of ingredients handled with care that produces the best results. Watch MasterChef closely and you'll notice that as the competition develops and the food gets better, so my spoonfuls get bigger. I can't help it! You know you've got a great dish as a judge when you reach the point when you are no longer tasting, you are eating.

So many of my favourite MasterChef dishes are contained within these pages. That pleases me a great deal, and what also pleases me is that all of these dishes are achievable and all of them deliver splendid results. Whether you've just started to cook or are a seasoned galley-hand, you'll find much here that will tickle your taste buds. I really like the straightforward layout of this book – this is a book meant for cooks. Split into three sections – Starters, Mains, and Desserts – the pages are packed with cooking tips, ingredient information, comments from John and me taken straight from the show, and of course, knock-out recipes. I particularly like the recipes that have been simplified for every day by John and me. John is a great chef and a good mate, and I've always loved his approach to food. His passion and knowledge jump from the page. My tips can of course all be found in the Desserts section. Come on, guys, you didn't expect anything else from me, did you? My love of the sweet and sticky is well known, and I urge you while using this book to leave a little bit of room for pudding.

It's really nice to read comments from previous MasterChef contestants, finalists, and winners. It brings back happy memories of triumph, skill, and determination from fantastic people who were born to cook. It's pleasing to hear them talk about food again in these pages and fascinating to hear their comments about participating in a competition that has pretty much been my life for the last seven years. It's wonderful to know as I look at the photographs in this book that I've tasted each and every dish. Great food, delivered with love from great contestants – here for you to create yourselves at home. Cook, eat, enjoy. A prize for whoever does the best Gregg Wallace-style tasting!

PEOPLE

I grew up in Wisconsin, where the food was good, fill-you-up Midwestern fare, but not quite so fancy. When I was 16 I discovered the Japanese cooking show *Iron Chef* and it completely blew my mind. The food was completely new and exciting. I was immediately enthralled by Japanese food, and seeking out new food in general, and that has been what's driven me to become a more serious cook.

Tim Anderson

former food buyer turned chef, MasterChef 2011 CHAMPION

I entered MasterChef because I was a fan of the show and I thought it looked like fun. I thought I was a pretty good cook and it was something I really enjoyed doing. I'd always toyed with the idea of cooking professionally, plus, I felt I'd never had a truly satisfying job in my life. I remember that around the time I applied for MasterChef, I was working from home and would too often just stop working at 3 o'clock in the afternoon to go into the kitchen and cook. I think I needed a change.

Throughout the series, I got to work with some amazing chefs; those experiences were dreams come true in their own right. Unmoulding the croquembouche that Michel Roux had just taught us to make was a moment of particular joy. It was also an enormous thrill to work with Paco Roncero, Wylie Dufresne, and John Campbell. Incredible cooks with incredible minds, all of them, and I learned so much in just one day working with each of them.

There were a couple of anxious moments in the competition: I messed up some soufflés in Australia, as I recall, and on the same occasion I was provided with the world's worst ice cream maker, which refused to set a batch of ice

"Taking risks is what's taken me this far and I think it can get me further. I'm very interested to see where this will take me because I think it will take me somewhere awesome."

cream after more than 2 hours of churning. I completely ruined the entire dessert and I genuinely thought I could not win the competition after that. Since winning MasterChef, **I've worked at the Fat Duck and Le Gavroche**, I've brewed my own beer at two different microbreweries, I was invited to speak at the Japanese Embassy, and in between I've been cooking for a living, doing private dining, demos, and pop-ups. In short, **I've been living the dream.**

I was raised in a traditional Italian family, where both my parents were passionate about food. It has always been a big part of my life but gaining a place on MasterChef provided the skills, the confidence, and the right platform for me to launch a new career and turn my culinary dream into a way of life.

Sara Danesin Medio
former Intensive Care Sister turned chef, **MasterChef 2011 FINALIST**

My **childhood memories in Italy** include seasonal outings with my dad foraging for mushrooms, wild asparagus, dandelions, and radicchio, and days spent in the kitchen with my mother creating beautiful meals for the whole family.

I was an ICU nurse at York Hospital when I applied for MasterChef. **After a bad day at university, I decided to go for food: my great passion!** I suppose it was to prove to myself and the rest of the world that I can cook under pressure and under any circumstances. My favourite moments were working with three of my all-time favourite chefs (Michel Roux, John Campbell, and Tom Kitchin) and making those amazing cocoa and partridge ravioli. And discovering that yes, **indeed, I can make puddings!** But at times it was stressful and I feared that I would not be able to combine my work, family commitments, and MasterChef.

I now cook at two cookery schools, am collaborating with Garofalo Pasta to promote better quality pasta in the UK, as well as doing private catering. In July 2011, **I launched Sara@ StJohn's Dining Club** in York with my husband David, with whom I share a great love of food and who has been my mentor throughout. Our private dining club has now hosted more than 1000 people, with visitors coming from all the major UK cities. We have also had guests from Canada and The Netherlands!

"I've put my heart and soul into this, I really have."

MasterChef for me was always a way in to working as a chef. It was also about finding out whether my food was good enough from people who really knew what they were talking about. It's fine for your friends to tell you what a great cook you are but it's a bit different when John Torode says it!

Tom Whitaker

former account director turned chef, **MasterChef 2011 FINALIST**

I was brought up in Oxfordshire by parents who loved good food. **I learnt to cook as a child** but I really turned a corner when I moved to Italy, where I witnessed first hand what true food obsession was. The pride that they take in their regional dishes and ingredients is wonderful, and when I moved back to the UK **I really wanted to take that ethos into British food**.

There were so many great experiences on MasterChef but two main ones stand out for me. The first was Australia; I hadn't been there before, and it was such a great thing to have that opportunity, especially cooking for John's family. **It felt great that he had enough confidence in us as cooks** to let us loose on his nearest and dearest. The other experience I really loved was cooking with John Campbell. I felt like I learned a huge amount from him and was really in awe of his food. He has kindly allowed me to go back for a stage soon, which I cannot wait to do. However, I didn't particularly enjoy the vegetarian task, that sort of food isn't really my strong point and I think it showed.

Things have been nuts since I finished the show. I have launched my private dining company, but I've been doing stages with various chefs, food festivals, pop-ups, and private events non-stop since I left my old job. I see this period as a chance to enjoy the opportunities that MasterChef offers to its alumni!

"I'm proud that my food was good enough to put me in the last three."

ELIZABETH ALLEN
former architecture student turned chef and **2011 CONTESTANT**

My family has always been my inspiration for cooking. I come from a mix of Singaporean and British backgrounds, and food is our shared passion. I entered MasterChef because **I felt I could achieve so much more** than being an architecture student and the programme gave me the opportunity to show and express my passion for cooking. The highlight was cooking my own dishes for John and Gregg: the crab tortellini and my version of roast duck. **Since MasterChef, I have begun working as a chef** in Windsor and started my own website, "The Modern Chef". I've worked in Michelin-starred restaurants, performed at food festivals, met some great chefs, and continue to work towards my goal of becoming a female Michelin-star chef.

ANNIE ASSHETON
food writer and 2011 **FINAL 6**

I started cooking when I was very young (if you count making up strange caramel concoctions!), but it was helping my mother prepare for dinner parties that inspired me most. I was hooked from then on. When I did MasterChef, having been a mother at home, **I felt very ready for a bit of adventure** and a challenge more stimulating than the housework. It would be hard for anything to beat **the thrill of the audition** when I was finally given one of those aprons. My lowest point was when I unmoulded my caramel parfait only to see it collapse in a very unfrozen puddle on the plate; it was too late in the competition to survive that kind of disaster. So much has happened since MasterChef: launching a cookery school, working at the amazing L'Ortolan just outside Reading, media work. **It has all been fabulous** and looks set to continue that way. Entering the competition was definitely one of the best decisions I've ever made.

NEIL BALDWYN
former materials analyst turned baker and **2011 CONTESTANT**

I've been cooking for as long as I can remember. My mum is an amazing cook and it was through years of watching and helping her that I learnt to cook. My dad also does a mean beans-on-toast! I was accepted into catering college at the age of 18 and bought all the chef whites and everything, but at the last minute I couldn't go through with it – I just didn't have the confidence. I went into MasterChef to **prove to myself that I could do it**. Since leaving the series I have opened my own bakery, so now I get to bake every day!

SERENA CRUMP
sheep farmer and 2011 CONTESTANT

I am a sheep farmer from Herefordshire, where we produce top-quality lamb. **I entered MasterChef as a challenge for myself**, encouraged by a friend, not quite realising how much pressure I would be under – apart from the odd Young Farmers cooking challenge, I had never cooked for anyone other than family and friends! **I loved being part of the whole MasterChef experience**, from thinking outside of my cooking box to meeting all the other people and contestants. Basically, the excitement of it all! The lowest point was, of course, going home but I knew I played too safe among very talented cooks. Since being on MasterChef I have, together with my friend Sue, who is Cordon Bleu trained, started The Cookery Club @ The Woodhouse. We really enjoy sharing our passion for food and cooking, using in-season and local produce, and **the club is going from strength to strength**.

MATTHEW DRIVER
editor and 2011 CONTESTANT

The challenge of pitting myself against incredibly talented people to impress the tough MasterChef judges seemed like a really fun thing to do, not to mention the chance of working with some of the best chefs. I also wanted to **demonstrate and develop my cooking skills**, in order to help achieve my ambition of setting up my own food business. And, of course, I wanted to win! My highlight was the first time we stepped into the brand new MasterChef HQ – a remarkable space – after coming through the audition rounds, with John and Gregg standing at the front welcoming us in. The **anxiety and nerves were immense** but so was the excitement. It was quite tough going out of MasterChef. I didn't stop cooking, though, and **it really inspired me to hone my craft**. Afterwards, I had a fabulous experience on internships at Sam and Sam Clark's Moro and Morito in London, and I am currently working towards starting my own business.

PAUL ELDER
healthcare worker and 2011 CONTESTANT

My **love of cooking** probably started from the caravan holidays we used to take in France when I was a child. You had all this amazing food in vans at the side of the road, such as roast chickens, rabbits, and ducks. I didn't take MasterChef seriously at first but **once the ball started rolling I wanted to go as far as I could**. The low point was plating up my invention test dish, only to realise I'd left the cling film on the egg. I waited to be judged by John and Gregg, frantically trying to think of a good excuse. Since the show, I've been helping MasterChef: The Professionals winner Claire Lara on a range of events and functions. My **next food challenge** is setting up a farmers' market stall selling French and English pâtisserie.

NICKY FRENCH
medical writer and **2011 CONTESTANT**

I fell in love with food 30 years ago when my mum made chilli con carne for the first time. I learned to cook at uni, with my best friend, Mags. No pot noodles for us. Why did I enter MasterChef? Why not? **You've got to live your dreams** – life is very short. The high point was being with my family and friend Jo, **when I got into the final 20 – WOW!** And the low point? That damn mayonnaise! Never mind, I still love cooking, and still do it regularly for friends and family. But I always avoid egg-based dishes!

ONDINE HARTGROVES
contact centre team leader and **2011 CONTESTANT**

I began cooking when my eldest son was a baby – opportunities to dine out were limited, so I started to cook. I found that I really enjoyed it and my friends loved eating it, and from there **I was bitten by the cookery bug.** The highlight of the MasterChef series for me was being told at the London auditions that John and Gregg were there and would be deciding who would go through. It was **so terrifying and wildly exciting at the same time.** The low point was when I realised that my idiotic, childish mistake would mean that I was going to lose my place in the competition – stupid potatoes! After MasterChef, I gave birth to my baby boy, Faron, with whom I was pregnant at the time. I've also started a part-time professional chef course, and in the near future I'll be starting my own business catering dinner parties for people in their own homes. So even though I did not get as far as I would have liked, **I am still following my dream.**

CLAUDIA HUXTABLE
fashion lecturer and **2011 CONTESTANT**

I guess I've been cooking from the age I could stand on a chair and start mixing and making things! To me, **food is the centrepiece of a family occasion**; it goes hand in hand with love and laughter. As a child I was mesmerised by MasterChef and NEVER missed the show on a Sunday evening. My first ambition was to enter MasterChef when I was older. Making it through **the first filmed audition was such a buzz.** Competitive cooking in front of an audience was the ultimate challenge…I loved it! But I had a feeling in the pit of my stomach when I was next to leave – I knew my food that day just hadn't made the grade before I was even told. Since the show, I've cooked for private customers and have run a charity café. **I will be launching a school meal initiative** in the New Year and still plan to open my community café eventually.

JACKIE KEARNEY
former research analyst turned chef and **2011 FINAL 4**

My food inspiration comes from travelling around Asia. **I fell in love with the ingredients and flavours**, and with the street food dining culture. I wanted to see if I have what it takes to make a living from it. When you're older and have a secure career, it's difficult to make that leap. **MasterChef gave me that opportunity**. Cooking for (and then later working for) Yotam Ottolenghi was a huge highlight as he's one of my food heroes. My lowest point was missing out on a place in the final. A piece of my heart broke that day and that disappointment will never go away. After realising current times would make it difficult to open my street food café, I took Sara's advice and started The Hungry Gecko Dining Club at my home. I'm also **buying a classic van and turning it into a food truck** so I can take my street food to the streets!

ANNELIESE KIELY
food writer and 2011 **FINAL 6**

I'm half Spanish and half Irish and **come from a family of excellent cooks** on both sides. We are a very close-knit family and it was inevitable that at least one of us would become a chef. I entered MasterChef because **I thought I could win it**. I was nearly four months pregnant by the second challenge and, unfortunately, I was so preoccupied by my pregnancy that I couldn't concentrate, so my standards suffered as a consequence. Since the show, apart from having a beautiful baby boy, I have set up a little business, La Cala Catering, and I also run a market stall in Winchester High Street on Saturdays selling Spanish delicacies. It is really hard to prepare for, but **I love my Saturdays – I love selling out** and customers coming back for more!

KENNEDY LEITCH
cellist and **2011 CONTESTANT**

I have always been a fan of television cooking shows. Watching them, I decided to improve my food and just grew to love constructing different dishes and entertaining my friends. As a cellist in the Royal Scottish National Orchestra, **I love to entertain playing the cello; through food and cooking, I get the same thrill!** My MasterChef highlight was cooking for the previous winners – people who had gone through similar experiences and could judge my food in the context of the competition. The low point was definitely when I chopped the top of my finger off in the middle of a field in Scotland. Thankfully, after a couple of months, I was able to play the cello again, and I'm currently back with the RSNO. I still love to cook at home for friends and I've tried to take on board everything I learnt. MasterChef really was **a wonderful experience that will live with me forever**.

FIONA LUCK
legal secretary turned caterer and **2011 CONTESTANT**

I was raised by my father, a naval officer, who travelled all over the world and was a superb cook. He introduced my palate to a variety of exotic flavours from an early age. When I was very young, **I started cooking to spoil him** when he came home on leave, but I think he spent more time bandaging my cut fingers than he did forcing down my culinary offerings with an appreciative smile and valiant stoicism! The highlight of the entire show was being given **the opportunity to dedicate a dish to my father**. He died very suddenly seven years ago so, when I was asked for an interpretation of the perfect roast, I created the roast I would cook for my father if I could cook for him one last time. It was an incredibly emotional day but **his inspiration helped me** win the challenge. Since the show, I have launched my own catering company and am working hard to develop a reputation for culinary excellence and exclusivity.

POLLY OXBY
housewife and caterer and **2011 CONTESTANT**

I started cooking, really, with my Granny. The first recipe I remember learning by heart was a Victoria sponge, and it is the first thing I taught my children to cook, too. I had been watching MasterChef for 6 years and just thought, "I'll fill in the application form". I had no expectations beyond that, just that I would love to have all those opportunities the programme offered – **never in a million years did I think I'd get as far as I did!** My highlight during the series was going to Scotland. We had become quite a close group by then, and to go away and cook in such an alien environment with new friends was just brilliant. I totally understand why I left the show when I did, but I would have loved to have had a go at the subsequent challenges! **I'm now cooking professionally** and have my own catering business doing private dining, which I am loving. Without sounding cheesy, MasterChef has changed my life and I am very happy about that!

JAMES PERRY
carpenter and chef and **2011 FINAL 5**

I am a 25-year-old carpenter. Cooking has always been my way of showing my creative side; like carpentry, it allows me to use my hands and build something from nothing. I had **thought about entering MasterChef for some time** but I didn't think I would get too far. After most of my friends urged me to do it, I thought, "why not?" Besides, I **didn't want to be 35 years old and sat there thinking, "what if?"** The highlight for me was cooking for Michel Roux Jnr – he is a food hero of mine. I would love to have the chance one day to cook for him again, showing how much I've learnt. Since leaving MasterChef I have been regularly **working at the Michelin-star Paris House** restaurant, and I feature on the Morning:MK radio show "Foodie Tuesday".

PETER SEVILLE
former lecturer turned chef and **2011 CONTESTANT**

My love of food was kick-started in a charming restaurant in the middle of Paris. I had almost no idea what I ordered, but **what came out of the kitchen was a revelation** – taste buds that I had long since forgotten were reawakened, and my vegetarian status quivered. Since then, I have never looked back but I take steps to maintain my ethical stance by buying free-range, organic, sustainably sourced produce wherever possible. When I entered MasterChef, I wanted to find out whether my dreams of cooking in my own gastro pub could eventually become a reality. I also wanted to **see whether it's true that cooking doesn't get tougher than this!** For me, the highlight of the competition was getting to cook my own food for the past winners of MasterChef – how many people can claim they've done that? In September 2011, my partner and I took over a beautiful old country pub in Worcestershire, and I have been cooking every day since!

ALICE TAYLOR
model and **2011 CONTESTANT**

Eating was probably my favourite pastime when I was growing up! But I didn't start cooking seriously until I was dating my partner, now hubby, Chris. He would slap up the same dish of what I'm told was "food" every time he asked me over for dinner: fillet steak brutally pan-fried for about an hour, microwaved sweet potato, and a bland ready-made cauliflower cheese. After three nights of this meal **I decided to explore my long buried love of food**… and to cut a long story short, Chris hasn't cooked for me in nearly 5 years now, and long may that last! My favourite part of MasterChef was probably cooking in Scotland for the Highland Games…despite losing the challenge, it was such fun working as a team and being out in The Highlands in the brisk temperatures. Since leaving MasterChef, life has pretty much gone back to normal, but **I do intend to follow the food dream** when my 3-year-old son is older and starts full time school.

As a rugby player, I won the 2003 World Cup with England, and captained England to the final of the 2007 tournament in France. But the Celebrity MasterChef final was probably one of the most nerve-wracking challenges I've ever faced. I gave it everything, though, and that makes me feel really proud of myself. I gave it every ounce of the big man's effort.

Phil Vickery MBE

England rugby player and Celebrity MasterChef 2011 CHAMPION

I retired from playing rugby because of injury at the end of 2010 and was looking around for new projects to keep me occupied. I've always been a fan of MasterChef – **I love British food and produce**, and it was something I was really keen to get involved in.

I started cooking as a kid – food was always around me when I was growing up and I would help my mum and nan with their baking days and the Sunday roasts. I was the peeler and chopper back then! On Celebrity MasterChef, I had **the chance to cook the food that means something to me**; the Cornish junket was a pudding from my childhood, and cooking the neck of lamb with merguez sausage also brought back really good thoughts as it was inspired by something I ate on my honeymoon with Kate, my wife.

All my experiences of Celebrity MasterChef were incredible, but a personal highlight of the show was cooking with Michael Caines at Gidleigh Park. It was one of the most exciting things I have ever done. He introduced us to new **tastes and flavours that I could never have dreamed of** – it was truly magical. On the other hand, one of the final challenges was cooking on set for the cast of Spooks – I must

"It'll mean an awful lot to my family, but more than anything, I'm proud of being here and what I've done. When you've cooked something well, it's the best feeling in the world."

have spent nearly two hours just chopping carrots and spuds...it definitely wasn't my finest or most enjoyable time!

Winning Celebrity MasterChef was up there with receiving my MBE. **I'm so excited to see what I can do in the world of cooking.** I grew up on a farm and am really passionate about British agriculture and the countryside in general. MasterChef has taught me so much about cooking and I'm really keen to take it further!

I'm best known for playing Tony Hutchinson in the Channel 4 television soap *Hollyoaks*, which I've been appearing in since 1995. I've always been a massive fan of MasterChef, so when I was contacted and asked if I wanted to go on the show I said I'd love to – it was as simple as that.

Nick Pickard
actor and **Celebrity MasterChef 2011 FINALIST**

I first started cooking when I was 19. I'd just left home and moved to Liverpool, and it was the first time I'd really had to look after myself. I was living in a house with three other guys and I very quickly **became sick of all the microwave meals**. So I started experimenting; simple things at first – curries, meatballs, stuff like that. I was also playing a lot of football at the time and I was often cooking for the team as well.

I'd **never sweated so much as I did** doing this programme – I'd never been under so much pressure in all my life! My lowest point was definitely the Bakewell tart. I saw early on that the pastry was going wrong but I couldn't start again – I realised I'd just have to carry on even though I knew it wasn't going to work, and that wasn't a great feeling.

If I had to choose my proudest moment, I'd say it was the Cockney Pie and Mash, because I'd wholly come up with the idea, and **it was one that meant a lot to me**. Sadly, a couple of years ago I lost my dad, and he was larger than life. He loved his food and one of his favourite dishes was pie and mash. But we never made it at home because we'd always go down the pie and mash shop. I loved that **my pie and mash was 100% me**, not simply me cooking a recipe from somewhere else.

"It's absolutely taken over my life, to be honest!"

In my day job, I'm a journalist and broadcaster, presenting programmes such as *Newsnight*. I wanted a new challenge and MasterChef was certainly that. I found the experience exhilarating and stressful, but working with the other contestants and the production team was terrific fun.

Kirsty Wark

journalist and presenter and **Celebrity MasterChef 2011 FINALIST**

One of my earliest culinary memories is helping my mum make pancakes when I was quite little – certainly before I started school. **I always loved being in the kitchen**, whether at home or when I stayed with my Aunt Anna. She showed me how to make beef tea, which I adored, and which was regarded as a nourishing remedy for colds and flu. Mum always had a sheaf of handwritten recipes – "Mary's stroganoff" or "Edith's scones" – so **I identified cooking and baking with friendship**. I still do now, and my friends all give gifts of chutney or jam, just as their mothers did. My husband Alan makes marmalade each year – as his own mother does!

During Celebrity MasterChef, John and Gregg were supportive and funny, and **it was rewarding seeing my cooking improve**. There were lots of highs, including cooking lobster ravioli for a very exacting group of diners at Gidleigh Park, but I loved making my simple fresh pasta with tomato and mussels most. My low point was the WI criticizing my mother's recipe for wild mushroom soup – or at least my interpretation of it!

I'm delighted to be hosting a new culinary quiz on BBC 2 in the new year, called *A Question of Taste*. It is going to be both entertaining and actually pretty informative, but it will be great because the audience at home can play along too!

"It's just a great adventure and I really don't want it to stop."

DARREN CAMPBELL MBE
Olympic champion and CELEBRITY 2011 CONTESTANT

I've always cooked quite a bit. I am a sprinter, a former Olympic, European, and Commonwealth Champion, and when I was training I had to be self-sufficient as I would be out of the country for months at a time on warm weather camps. As athletes, we would have our own "special ways" to cook or season dishes, so we would quickly pick up different recipes from each other. When I was back home again, I would often cook for myself as my dietary requirements to fuel training were a bit different to those of my family of small children. After my father passed away last year, I spent a bit more time at home and I found myself experimenting in the kitchen more. I thought taking part in Celebrity MasterChef would give me the opportunity to takeon a new challenge. I hope it also demonstrates to the young people I mentor that it is good to try something new! My best moment had to be at the Brit School when my jerk-flavoured chicken was the first of all the dishes on offer to sell out. Having to cook in such vast quantities was a real challenge for myself and Linda, so when the dish was so well received by the young people – who are so often the harshest critics! – it was really rewarding. The crab soup, though, that was my lowest point – but also most amusing. I wasn't sure where to start, and in hindsight it probably shouldn't have been with water.

MARGI CLARKE
actress and CELEBRITY 2011 CONTESTANT

I'm an actress and TV Presenter – or Tyrone's mum from *Coronation Street*, if you don't already know! Being as my skills are – I'm a "mum" cook – Celebrity MasterChef comes only once in a showbiz lifetime and I loved my chance to up skills with the dynamic best! Although I'm a "home bird", I'm a pretty disorganised cook – as you may have noticed in the programme, I had the scruffiest work station on the set – but somehow managed to get through to the second round. My late beloved mother Francis was a great, resourceful cook – and rearing a family of ten in the 1960s, she had to be. One of us kids always helped out peeling spuds. It was on the days of the rota that I played kitchen partner to Mam that I picked up the skills to cook and be creative in the kitchen. Once a week, it would be my favourite: Scouse. I loved the savoury smell warming the kitchen. I was delighted that my "International Gourmet Scouse" on the show lived up to the name. Another highlight for me was opening the lid of the invention test box and a baby octopus jumping out! My decision to fry up the suckered, tentacled sea creature nice and crispy won positive critiques from John and Gregg and gave me the edge in that round. But when we were taken to a Thai restaurant in London's West End, my downfall (my nemesis!) was a wok: it went up in flames. MasterChef has always been a must-see in our house. Working with such esteemed chefs as John and Gregg was a brilliant experience, and one that has benefited my family as I'm now a better cook with an enlivened repetoire.

DANNY GOFFEY
musician and **CELEBRITY 2011 SEMI-FINALIST**

I like doing things with my hands – I'm best known for being the drummer in the band Supergrass – and as **I'm always cooking for my family** (we have 4 children), I've been getting a passion for it. Music has been such a huge part of my life that concentrating on cooking for the programme felt like a new chapter. I like being creative, although **cooking on MasterChef was just as nerve-wracking as playing on Top of the Pops!** I'd never cooked an escalope before, and that was pretty terrifying, as I didn't know how the ingredients were meant to go together. When John initially thought I'd done it wrong, and then both of them admitted I had done well, that was a nice moment. I was really pleased to get as far as I did. It got tougher with every challenge and I had to think a lot harder about doing things that were really different, things I hadn't done before. **It was such a buzz cooking totally new things** – it was tricky, but you've got to conquer your worries a bit with stuff like that. Something new is always good to learn.

RUTH GOODMAN
social historian and **CELEBRITY 2011 CONTESTANT**

I'm a historian best known for appearing in historical documentaries, where I demonstrate my interest in the ordinary, the domestic, and the practical side of the past. I wanted to go on MasterChef because I love sharing my interest in food. Because I'm possibly "stuck in the past" when it comes to my cooking, **it was great to share different styles of food with people**, and spend time with people with more modern styles. My low point was the stressfulness of the competition – I'm not the sort of person who enjoys competing against people, and I didn't really find that side of things pleasant. My high point was cooking the squirrel; not that it was difficult, but because **it was nice to get the opportunity to try something few people have**. Yum!

RICKY GROVES
actor and **CELEBRITY 2011 CONTESTANT**

Readers will know me best for the 9 years I spent playing Gary Hobbs in *EastEnders*. Before I started acting, **I was a trainee chef and worked in several hotels** and restaurants, so I started cooking at an early age. As someone who loves cooking, MasterChef is a great place to learn some new things and be around people who love food. It was disappointing not making it through to the next round, but meeting and **getting to know all the other contestants was great**, especially meeting Phil Vickery in the first rounds and seeing him go on to win the competition.

SHOBU KAPOOR
actress and **CELEBRITY 2011 CONTESTANT**

I'm an actress, probably best known for my role playing Gita Kapoor in *EastEnders*. **My mother was a fantastic cook**: she would take ingredients from all over India and transform them into delicious and healthy meals. I didn't dare step into her kitchen until I was twenty. I remember making *basin ke laddoo* (an Indian sweet made with gram flour, ghee, and sugar) under her watchful eyes, convinced I was murdering her recipe!

I took part in MasterChef as a challenge for myself. The highlight for me was presenting a two-course meal – a mix of Indian and Italian cuisine – which was in keeping with my mother's tradition of eclecticism. But the lows? Sealing ravioli with butter, creating a sticky toffee pudding that looked somewhat like a concave monster...I could go on!

TIM LOVEJOY
television presenter and **Celebrity 2011 SEMI-FINALIST**

I am a TV presenter and producer, and have worked in live weekend TV for 15 years. I'm probably best known for producing and presenting *Soccer AM*, and now present *Something For The Weekend* alongside Simon Rimmer. I first started cooking when I left home in my late teens – I always ate well but the food was pretty basic. **I'm what you would call a "meat-and-two-veg" man**. I decided to go on MasterChef purely for the challenge; I really wanted to see how good I was. **I love cooking for my two daughters**, and it really was a case of, "Let's see how far I can go". The low point was the first episode, where we had to cook ravioli. We were just presented with the ingredients and basically told to get on with it – at that moment, I felt completely out of my depth and that my little knowledge wouldn't be enough. My high point was the challenge in Aura, a high-end London Thai restaurant, where we were cooking with woks: it was a proud moment **when the head chef said I'd done a perfect job** of cooking his signature dish.

LINDA LUSARDI
actress and **CELEBRITY 2011 SEMI-FINALIST**

I am an actress and former model. It wasn't until I got married and had my two beautiful children that my love for cooking started. **I jumped at the chance** to take part in MasterChef as I felt it would take my cooking to a whole new level. My high point was watching back the early shows and **hearing John and Gregg say that I was a good cook** and that I presented my food very well. The low point was when my treacle tart turned out like a rock-hard, dry old biscuit! I am so glad I took part in the show as **my family has really enjoyed the improvement** in my cooking.

AGGIE MACKENZIE
journalist and **CELEBRITY 2011 SEMI-FINALIST**

I'm probably better known for cleaning, but the truth is **I'm far happier with my hands in the mixing bowl** than in the washing-up bowl. I started cooking when I was 20. I realised the route to sophisticated suppers was not via tins of mince so I joined a Cordon Bleu evening class (it was the 70s!). It was like falling in love, and **I've been mildly obsessed with cooking** ever since. I've managed to weave food into my career; my last editorial job was overseeing the Good Housekeeping Institute. Why MasterChef? I was asked – well it seemed rude to refuse. Weeping on the first task was not so good, but **making the tortellini was a definite high**.

SHARON MAUGHAN
actress and **Celebrity 2011 SEMI-FINALIST**

I've been an actress for over 40 years, and am possibly best known for appearing in *Holby City*. I had always been a really basic, functional cook, mainly making stews and casseroles. On Celebrity MasterChef, I enjoyed the chance to cook more sophisticated versions of what I normally cook. On the programme, I was shocked at how nervous I was. **It was like an opening night at the theatre** – the nerves are 10,000 times worse when you're standing in the wings, but once you're on the stage you take a deep breath and get on with it. It was the same in the kitchen. It was a disappointment not being able to take part in the second two tests in the first episode, due to illness. I was worried that not being there to show Gregg and John what I could do might be a disadvantage, but when I came back I found that I liked working with Danny, and our meatballs seemed to go down really well. **I was really proud of my vegetable bake** that I made for the hospital canteen. John said that he'd eat the whole thing, which coming from him was definite praise.

COLIN MCALLISTER
property developer and **CELEBRITY 2011 CONTESTANT**

I'm one half of Colin & Justin: we're interior designers, journalists, and all-round global style warriors. I started cooking when I was 12 years old; I used to knock out cake mixes every other day. **I think we should continually be challenged in our lives** and the thought of being on Celebrity MasterChef under the kitchen microscope of Gregg and John really did freak me out! Being in a real, working kitchen when we catered for the staff at the Royal Free Hospital was an absolute blast. It was **manic and nerve-wracking but very satisfying**, too. The low was my slightly tongue-in-cheek take on the Scottish deep fried Mars Bar. At home the night before, I made Bounty Bar tempura, fresh mango ice cream, and raspberry coulis with dark chocolate shavings. It looked and tasted superb then, but **on the day it all went horribly wrong**, and it ended up looking like a real dog's dinner!

MICHELLE MONE OBE
entrepreneur and **CELEBRITY 2011 CONTESTANT**

I'm an entrepreneur and creator of Ultimo, a leading designer lingerie brand. I thought I'd be able to cope with MasterChef pretty well – **I'm always under pressure in business** – but I'll admit that I was out of my comfort zone. I couldn't believe how much pressure there was in the kitchen, or how tiring it was. I hoped that appearing on MasterChef would **help me to be a more adventurous cook**. I didn't enjoy the competition at first because I was so nervous, but as I relaxed, I really began to love it. The best moment was when John said that my Saddle of Rabbit looked so good that it could have come out of a restaurant – that was **a real high point for me**. I was really hoping to impress them after some earlier mistakes, so it really meant a lot.

JUSTIN RYAN
property developer and **CELEBRITY 2011 CONTESTANT**

I'm the other half of Colin & Justin: we're known for shows like *The Million Pound Property Experiment*, *How Not to Decorate* and *Colin & Justin's Home Heist*. **My mum is an excellent cook and I thought I'd inherited her skills**, but working under John and Gregg showed me I have a lot to learn. As a viewer, I knew that doing MasterChef would be a real challenge; as a contestant it was ten times more stressful than I ever imagined. A highlight was when I was in the Italian restaurant: I made an asparagus gratin with truffles and managed to take more orders, and make more, than anyone expected. **It was a truffle triumph!** But without a doubt the low point, wholly and unequivocally, was my attempt at making a pork escalope. **I do actually know how to do an escalope**, but that's MasterChef for you; I simply lost my bottle with nerves.

STARTERS

PIGEON BREAST WITH APPLE AND BLACK PUDDING, AND A CIDER JUS

Phil Vickery MBE England rugby player and 2011 Celebrity champion

PREPARATION TIME
10 minutes

COOKING TIME
30 minutes

SERVES 4

4 EATING APPLES, ideally British Cox's
2 tbsp DUCK FAT, at room temperature
20g (¾oz) BUTTER
SALT and freshly ground BLACK PEPPER
200g (7oz) BLACK PUDDING, diced

4 PIGEON BREASTS
250ml (8fl oz) DRY CIDER

TO GARNISH
50g (1¾oz) PEA SHOOTS
50g (1¾oz) WATERCRESS

British black pudding is made from blood (usually pig's), pork, cereal, and seasonings. It is sold already cooked, but is usually sautéed or grilled before serving.

1   Preheat the oven to 180°C (350°F/Gas 4). Peel and core the apples, and chop them into 8 pieces each. Place a frying pan over medium to high heat and add 1 tbsp of the duck fat and the butter. Season the apple wedges with salt and pepper, add them to the pan, and fry for 2 minutes until they start to turn golden. Remove them from the pan with a slotted spoon and transfer to a non-stick baking tray. Bake in the oven for 10 minutes until just tender, ensuring that they don't lose their shape.
2   Add the black pudding to the pan and fry for 5–6 minutes until crisp. Remove and drain thoroughly on kitchen paper, then spread out on a baking tray and bake for 10 minutes in the oven until very crisp.
3   Using the same pan, heat the remaining duck fat over high heat. Season the pigeon breasts, add them to the pan skin-side down, and sear for 1 minute. Turn the breasts over and add the cider to the pan. Cook for a further 2 minutes, then remove the pigeon breasts from the pan and rest on a warm plate.
4   Boil the cider until reduced by half, then remove from the heat.
5   To serve, slice the pigeon breasts as thinly as possible. Place 8 pieces of the apple on each plate and then lay the slices of pigeon breast on top. Finally, sprinkle the plates with the black pudding, the pea shoots, and the watercress, and finish with a drizzle of the cider jus.

Simplify for **EVERY**DAY

• You could simply fry the apple slices on each side for 2–3 minutes in butter and olive oil, instead of using duck fat, then sauté the black pudding, and omit the oven stage. • Try using chicken or duck mini fillets instead of the pigeon breasts (you may need to cook the chicken 1–2 minutes longer).

COCOA AND PARTRIDGE RAVIOLI WITH DEMIGLACE, BEURRE NOISETTE, AND PARMIGIANO

Sara Danesin Medio MasterChef 2011 finalist

PREPARATION TIME
1 hour 30 minutes,
plus chilling

COOKING TIME
2 hours 15 minutes

SERVES 4

FOR THE FILLING
2 tbsp OLIVE OIL
½ CARROT, chopped
½ CELERY stick, chopped
1 ONION, chopped
3 DRIED PORCINI MUSHROOMS,
   rehydrated in boiling water
2 BAY LEAVES
small sprig of ROSEMARY
small sprig of THYME
SALT and freshly ground
   BLACK PEPPER
2 JUNIPER BERRIES, crushed
LEGS and CARCASSES of 2
   FRENCH RED-LEGGED
   PARTRIDGES
2 tbsp finely grated
   PARMESAN CHEESE
2 tbsp RICOTTA CHEESE

½ EGG YOLK
knob of UNSALTED BUTTER

FOR THE PASTA DOUGH
175g (6oz) TYPE '00' FLOUR, sifted
4 tsp SEMOLINA FLOUR, sifted
4 tbsp COCOA POWDER
2 EGGS, beaten
1 EGG YOLK
1 tsp EXTRA VIRGIN OLIVE OIL
1 EGG WHITE, whisked

FOR THE BEURRE NOISETTE
60g (2oz) UNSALTED BUTTER

TO SERVE
3 tbsp finely grated
   PARMESAN CHEESE
1 tsp THYME leaves

1 To make the ravioli filling, heat the olive oil in a large casserole and sauté the carrot, celery, onion, porcini mushrooms, bay leaves, rosemary, thyme, salt, pepper, and juniper berries until the onion is softened and golden brown.
2 Add the partridge legs and carcasses and brown them, then cover with boiling water to a depth of 5cm (2in) above the pan's contents. Bring to the boil, then simmer gently for 2 hours, partially covered, until the leg meat falls easily away from the bone.
3 While the partridge is cooking, make the pasta dough. Place the flours and cocoa on a clean, flat surface. Make a well in the centre, add the beaten eggs, egg yolk, and olive oil, and knead to a smooth dough. Wrap in cling film and rest in the fridge for 30 minutes.
4 Remove the partridge legs from the casserole. While they are still warm, pick the meat off the bone and chop it to a pulp, ensuring there is no shot in it. Mix it with the Parmesan and ricotta cheeses. Season to taste and add the egg yolk.
5 Strain all the stock through a fine sieve into a clean pan and reduce until syrupy and thick (a demiglace).
6 Work the pasta through a pasta maker to a fine sheet and use an 7.5cm (3in) round cutter to cut out 12 circles of pasta.

Wet the edge of a disc of pasta with egg white and place a teaspoon of filling in the centre. Fold the circle in half and close the ravioli, making sure that no air remains trapped inside. Repeat with the remaining discs. Cook the pasta in a large pan of boiling salted water for 3 minutes and then drain.

7 While the pasta cooks, make a beurre noisette by placing the unsalted butter in a heavy pan and heating until it turns nut-brown. Remove from the heat and strain through a sieve lined with muslin cloth.

8 To serve, add the beurre noisette to the drained ravioli along with the grated Parmesan cheese. Toss gently, and place at the centre of the serving plates. Just before serving, add a knob of butter to the demiglace and whisk to emulsify. Garnish the ravioli with the demiglace and thyme and serve immediately.

JOHN TORODE

"I think it's a beautiful looking thing and I think it delivers on every single level."

PAN-FRIED CHICKEN LIVERS WITH RED ONION AND MANGO MARMALADE, SERVED WITH A BABY LEAF SALAD AND HARD DOUGH BREAD

Claudia Huxtable MasterChef 2011 contestant

PREPARATION TIME
30 minutes

COOKING TIME
1 hour 15 minutes

SERVES 4

"The taste will speak for itself."

FOR THE BREAD
3 tbsp CASTER SUGAR
1 sachet of DRIED YEAST
175ml (6fl oz) warm WATER
1 tbsp GROUNDNUT OIL
1 tbsp melted BUTTER or
  MARGARINE
1 tsp SALT
350g (12oz) PLAIN FLOUR
MILK, for brushing

FOR THE MARMALADE
2 RED ONIONS, finely sliced
2 tbsp LIGHT BROWN
  MUSCOVADO SUGAR
15g (½oz) BUTTER
1 large RIPE MANGO, finely diced

2 tbsp RED WINE
splash of BALSAMIC VINEGAR
1 large sprig of THYME

FOR THE CHICKEN LIVERS
400g (14oz) CHICKEN LIVERS,
  trimmed of any sinew
½ tsp PAPRIKA
SALT and freshly ground
  BLACK PEPPER
PLAIN FLOUR for dusting
2 tbsp GROUNDNUT OIL

FOR THE SALAD
60g (2oz) LAMB'S LETTUCE
¼ CUCUMBER, sliced
a few sprigs of RED AMARANTH

1 In a small bowl, dissolve the sugar and yeast in the water. Let it stand for about 10 minutes until creamy. In a large bowl, combine the yeast mix with the oil, margarine, salt, and 300g (10oz) flour. Stir well. Mix in half the remaining flour, beat well, then mix in the remainder. When the dough has pulled together, turn out onto a floured surface and knead for about 8 minutes until smooth and supple. Oil a large bowl, place the dough in it, and turn to coat with oil. Cover with a damp cloth, and leave in a warm place until doubled in volume, about 45 minutes.

2 Preheat the oven to 180°C (350°C/ Gas 4). Deflate the dough and turn out onto a floured surface. Divide into 12 portions, then shape into flat ovals. Brush with milk and bake for 12–14 minutes or until golden brown. Transfer to a wire rack and leave to cool.

3 Combine the onions, sugar, and butter in a pan, and cook over medium heat for about 5 minutes until the onions caramelize. Add the mango and stir for 3–4 minutes until softened. Add the wine, vinegar, and thyme and stir regularly on low heat until thickened. Leave to cool and remove the sprig of thyme before serving.

4 Season the chicken livers with paprika, salt, and pepper, and dust with flour. Heat the oil in a pan until just smoking. Fry the livers in batches for 1 minute on each side until they start to brown around the edges. Transfer to a warm plate to rest for 2 minutes, then serve with the marmalade, bread, and salad.

CHICKEN SHANK WITH PUMPKIN CROQUE MONSIEUR, AND A PECAN AND FLOWER SALAD

Tim Anderson MasterChef 2011 champion

PREPARATION TIME
40 minutes

COOKING TIME
35–40 minutes

SERVES 4

FOR THE SHANKS
4 CHICKEN LEGS
SALT and WHITE PEPPER
pinch of SMOKED PAPRIKA
pinch of GROUND CORIANDER
1 tbsp AVOCADO OIL
knob of UNSALTED BUTTER

FOR THE SAUCE
150g (5½oz) CHERRIES, pitted
300ml (10fl oz) CHICKEN STOCK
4 tbsp BOURBON or RYE WHISKEY
3 tbsp DRY WHITE VERMOUTH
3 tbsp RED VERMOUTH
4 tsp ORANGE JUICE

FOR THE CROQUE MONSIEUR
350g (12oz) PUMPKIN, peeled,
  deseeded, and diced
1 tbsp AVOCADO OIL
4 slices WHITE SANDWICH BREAD
2 slices of IBERIAN HAM

2 slices PONT L'ÉVEQUÊ cheese
25g (scant 1oz) UNSALTED
  BUTTER, softened

FOR THE CRACKLING
250g (9oz) LARD
reserved CHICKEN LEG SKINS

FOR THE SALAD
50g (1¾oz) ROASTED PECANS
small handful CHERVIL
small handful DILL
small handful SAGE
small handful EDIBLE FLOWERS
2 tsp AVOCADO OIL
1 tsp LEMON JUICE

1 Preheat the oven to 200°C (400°F/Gas 6). Skin the chicken (reserving the skins) and trim to reveal the bottom portion of the bone. Rub the salt, spices, oil, and butter into the chicken. Bake for 15 minutes or until browned and just cooked through. Remove from the oven and leave to rest.

2 For the sauce, put the cherries and stock in a saucepan, bring to the boil, and reduce by half. Press through a fine sieve.

3 Combine the whiskey and vermouths, heat in a small pan, and flambé until the flames die down. Add the orange juice and reduce by two-thirds. Combine the whiskey mixture with the stock mixture and reduce by a further one-third until glossy.

4 Make the croque monsieur. Toss the pumpkin in the oil and season with salt. Roast for 20–25 minutes, or until completely tender. Blitz in a food processor into a thick purée, leaving some chunks.

5 Make sandwiches with the ham, cheese, and pumpkin purée, buttering both sides of the bread with the softened butter. Trim the crusts from the sandwiches and preheat a griddle over high heat. Griddle the sandwiches for 2 minutes on each side until golden, and the cheese has melted and is beginning to ooze out round the edges.

6 Cut each sandwich into 4 small triangles and serve 2 triangles per person.

7 Prepare the crackling. Melt the lard in a saucepan. Fry the reserved chicken leg skins until crisp and golden. Drain on kitchen paper, then break into small pieces.

8 When ready to serve, make the salad. Halve the pecans and roughly tear the chervil, dill, and sage, then combine in a bowl with the edible flowers.

9 Toss with the avocado oil and lemon juice and season with a little salt.

10 To assemble the dish, spoon a ring of sauce on to 4 serving plates. Place a triangle of croque monsieur in the middle of each plate and place the chicken on top of it. Scatter tiny bits of salad and crackling around the edge in a delicate pattern.

CHERRY CHICKEN

JOHN TORODE CAPTURES ALL OF TIM'S EXCITING FLAVOURS WITH THIS EASY VARIATION

PREP: 30–35 MINS + OVERNIGHT MARINATING • COOK: 45 MINS

CHICKEN 'N' PUMPKIN

SERVES 4

4 CHICKEN THIGHS, trimmed
150ml (5fl oz) BUTTERMILK
3 tbsp OLIVE OIL
generous pinch of sweet
  smoked PAPRIKA
2 GARLIC cloves, bruised
SALT and freshly ground
  BLACK PEPPER

25g (scant 1oz) BUTTER
250g (9oz) PUMPKIN, peeled,
  deseeded and diced into
  2.5cm (1in) cubes
1 tsp freshly chopped RED
  CHILLI (optional)
1 tbsp freshly chopped SAGE

1 Place the chicken thighs in a freezer bag. Mix together the buttermilk, 1 tbsp of the oil, paprika, garlic, and seasoning and pour into the bag. Squash together until well coated, then zip up the bag and leave to marinate, ideally overnight, or for at least 4 hours in the fridge.
2 Preheat the oven to 200°C (400°C/Gas 6). Place the butter and remaining olive oil in a roasting tin and heat in the oven for a few minutes until melted and well combined. Add the diced pumpkin. Season, stir until well coated in the oil and butter, then cook in the oven for 35 minutes. Remove from the oven and stir in the chilli, if using, and sage, then return to the oven for a final 10 minutes.
3 Meanwhile, remove the chicken from the marinade, shaking off any excess. Place in a lightly oiled roasting tin and roast for 30–35 minutes or until golden and cooked through. Serve with the pumpkin, and the sauce spooned over.

"The fruitiness of the cherry against the nuttiness of the pumpkin gives this dish a real richness of flavours. A guaranteed taste sensation – and so easy to do!"

RED WINE AND CHERRY SAUCE

1 tbsp OLIVE OIL
½ small SHALLOT, finely chopped
150ml (5fl oz) CHICKEN STOCK
100ml (3½fl oz) RED WINE
25g (scant 1oz) DRIED CHERRIES
SALT and freshly ground

BLACK PEPPER
½ tbsp softened BUTTER
½ tbsp PLAIN FLOUR

1 To make the sauce, heat the oil in a small saucepan, add the shallot and sauté for 1–2 minutes or until softened. Add the chicken stock, red wine, cherries, and seasoning to the pan, bring to the boil, then simmer for 10 minutes.

2 Mix the softened butter together with the flour until you have a paste. Add the paste to the sauce a little at a time and stir until it has melted into the sauce and thickened it.

TRI-CITY SLIDERS
Tim Anderson MasterChef 2011 champion

PREPARATION TIME
2 hours, plus soaking
and proving

COOKING TIME
1–2 hours

SERVES 4

Preparation

FOR THE DASHI
1 sheet KONBU SEAWEED
2 litres (3½ pints) STILL
  MINERAL WATER
80g (2¾oz) KATSUOBUSHI
  FLAKES

FOR THE BUNS
1 tsp FAST-ACTION DRIED YEAST
500g (1lb 2oz) STRONG WHITE
  BREAD FLOUR
½ tsp SUGAR

25g (scant 1oz) BUTTER, melted
½ tsp SALT
1 EGG
100ml (3½fl oz) PILSNER

FOR THE MAYONNAISE BASE
1 EGG YOLK
2 tbsp RICE VINEGAR
pinch of WHITE PEPPER
pinch of SALT
200ml (7fl oz) RAPESEED OIL

DASHI

To make the dashi, place the konbu and water in a large pan, and soak for 10 minutes. Bring to the boil, then reduce the heat and simmer for 10 minutes. Add the katsuobushi and leave to infuse until all the flakes have sunk, then strain through muslin and keep warm. There will be more dashi than you need for this recipe, but you can store the remainder in the fridge for several days, or freeze it in convenient quantities for up to 6 months.

BUNS

Preheat the oven to 200ºC (400°F/Gas 6). Put all the ingredients, plus 150ml (5fl oz) water, in a bowl and mix until well combined, then turn the mixture out on to a floured surface and knead for 5 minutes to a smooth dough. Transfer the dough to a large bowl, cover with cling film, and set aside to prove for about 2 hours. When the dough has risen and doubled in size, portion it into 3cm (1¼in) balls, set them in small metal rings, and bake on a lightly greased baking sheet for 14 minutes. Remove from the oven and allow to cool before cutting in half horizontally.

MAYONNAISE BASE

Beat the egg yolks, rice vinegar, and seasoning together in a large bowl. Set the bowl over a pan of simmering water, making sure the bowl is clear of the water, and gradually whisk in the oil until well combined. Continue to whisk for 3–4 minutes until the mayonnaise has thickened. Remove from the heat and set aside.

The Los Angeles Slider

FOR THE MARMALADE
5 tsp GERMAN SMOKED BEER
1 tsp LAPSANG SOUCHONG
   TEA LEAVES
½ green JALAPEÑO PEPPER,
   deseeded and finely sliced
zest and juice of 2 LIMES
zest and juice of 1 ORANGE
30g (1oz) SUGAR
¼ tsp POWDERED PECTIN
¼ tsp GROUND CINNAMON

FOR THE PATTY
200g (7oz) WAGYU HANGER
   STEAK, trimmed and
   finely chopped

SMOKED SEA SALT and WHITE
   PEPPER

FOR THE MOUSSE
½ very ripe AVOCADO, stoned
30g (1oz) cooked BUTTER BEANS
3 tbsp AVOCADO OIL
juice of ½ LIME
pinch of XANTHAN GUM

TO SERVE
4 leaves of LITTLE GEM LETTUCE
1 SHALLOT, finely sliced
4 sprigs of CORIANDER

1 For the marmalade, combine the beer, 5 teaspoons of water, and tea leaves, and infuse for 5 minutes. Strain and discard the tea leaves. Put the liquid with the remaining ingredients in a small saucepan and cook for 15 minutes or until thick and jammy. Transfer to a small bowl, cover, and set aside until needed.
2 For the patty, season the steak with the salt and pepper, then form into 4cm (1½in) diameter patties. Cover and chill.
3 For the mousse, blitz all the ingredients in a food processor until smooth. Quenelle onto the burger and charge with nitrous oxide just before serving.
4 To serve, stack in this order: bun, marmalade, lettuce, patty, shallot, mousse. Garnish with coriander and extra mousse.

The Tokyo Slider

FOR THE JELLY
3 tbsp DASHI
3 tbsp MIRIN
3 tbsp pure YUZU JUICE
3 tbsp SOY SAUCE
2 tbsp AGAR-AGAR FLAKES

FOR THE PATTY
200g (7oz) MONKFISH
   LIVER, trimmed
100g (3½oz) PANKO
   BREADCRUMBS
pinch of WHITE PEPPER
pinch of SALT

1 EGG, beaten
RAPESEED OIL, for frying

FOR THE KETCHUP
1 tbsp UMEBOSHI PURÉE
2 tbsp WORCESTERSHIRE SAUCE
1 tbsp CASTER SUGAR

FOR THE MATCHA MAYONNAISE
20g (¾oz) prepared MAYONNAISE
   BASE
1 tsp MATCHA GREEN
   TEA POWDER
½ tsp WASABI POWDER

TO SERVE
small piece of DAIKON, sliced into
    4 paper-thin discs
small handful of SHISO CRESS

1 tsp SEVRUGA CAVIAR
2 tsp SALMON ROE
2 GREEN SHISO LEAVES, halved
8 ENOKI MUSHROOMS

1 Put the dashi, mirin, yuzu juice, and soy sauce in a small pan and bring to the boil. Add the agar-agar and boil for 2 minutes until dissolved. Pour into a small plastic container to a depth of 3mm (⅛in), then chill in the fridge to set. Just before serving, cut out 4cm (1½in) circles of the jelly with a round pastry cutter.
2 Using a pastry cutter, cut out four 4cm (1½in) circles of liver. Season the breadcrumbs. Dip one side of the liver in egg, then dredge in the breadcrumbs. Heat a little oil in a pan and fry for 1 minute on each side until golden. Drain on kitchen paper.
3 To make the ketchup and the mayonnaise, mix all the ingredients.
4 To serve, stack in this order: bun, mayonnaise, daikon, jelly, patty, ketchup, shiso cress, caviar, salmon roe. Garnish with mayonnaise, half a shiso leaf, and 2 mushrooms.

The London Slider

FOR THE PATTY
40g (1¼oz) extra MATURE
    CHEDDAR CHEESE
100g (3½oz) lean LAMB MINCE
½ tsp GARAM MASALA
small pinch of ASAFOETIDA
small pinch of CHILLI POWDER
pinch of SALT
RAPESEED OIL, for frying

FOR THE CHUTNEY
1 GRANNY SMITH APPLE, peeled,
    cored, and grated
¼ RED ONION, grated
5 tsp ANGOSTURA BITTERS
5 tsp MALT VINEGAR

30g (1oz) SUGAR
small pinch of POWDERED PECTIN
pinch of SALT
pinch of NUTMEG

FOR THE MAYONNAISE
3cm (1¼in) piece of CUCUMBER,
    finely diced
3 leaves of MINT, shredded
4 tsp prepared MAYONNAISE BASE
2 tsp PLAIN GREEK YOGURT

TO SERVE
BABY CHARD and MINT leaves
30g (1oz) RHUBARB, diced very
    small (brunoise)

1 Cut the cheese into 3cm (1¼in) squares no more than 3mm (⅛in) thick. Season the lamb with the spices and salt and form into 4cm (1½in) patties, wrapping it around the cheese. Fry in a little rapeseed oil for 2 minutes on each side.
2 For the chutney, combine all the ingredients in a saucepan and cook, stirring, over medium heat for 10–12 minutes or until thick and jammy. Transfer to a small bowl and leave to cool.
3 To make the mayonnaise, combine all the ingredients.
4 To serve, stack in the following order: bun, mayonnaise, chard, patty, chutney. Garnish with mint, chard, and diced rhubarb.

TIM'S TRI-CITY SLIDER SIMPLIFIED FOR **EVERY**DAY... ▶ PAGE 48

KING-SIZE SLIDER

JOHN TORODE RE-CREATES TIM'S SLIDERS FOR EVERYDAY EATING – GO LARGE AND GO EASY

PREP: 20–25 MINS • COOK: 16–20 MINS

SERVES 4

THE PATTY

85g (3oz) CHEDDAR CHEESE
400g (14oz) lean LAMB MINCE
¼–½ tsp GARAM MASALA
large pinch of ASAFOETIDA
large pinch of CHILLI POWDER
large pinch of SALT
RAPESEED OIL for frying

1 Cut the cheese into four 3cm (1¼in) squares 3mm (⅛ in) thick.
2 Mix the lamb with the spices and salt, divide into quarters and flatten. Place the cheese in the centre and shape the meat around it to make burgers of about 4cm (1½in).
3 Heat the oil in a pan, add the burgers and cook for 8–10 minutes, turning frequently until cooked. Remove from the heat.

THE CHUTNEY

2 GRANNY SMITH APPLES, peeled and cored
½ RED ONION, peeled
3 tbsp ENGLISH BITTER
3 tbsp MALT VINEGAR
60g (2oz) GRANULATED SUGAR
1 tsp powdered PECTIN
pinch of SALT
pinch of freshly grated NUTMEG

1 Coarsely grate the apple and onion into a saucepan and add the bitter, vinegar, sugar, pectin, salt, and nutmeg.
2 Stir together until the sugar has melted, then cook over moderate heat for 8–10 minutes, stirring frequently until thick, jammy and chutney-like. Remove from the heat.

THE CUCUMBER MAYONNAISE

60g (2oz) MAYONNAISE
20g (¾oz) GREEK YOGURT
6cm (2½in) length of CUCUMBER, finely diced
6 MINT LEAVES, chopped
SALT and freshly ground BLACK PEPPER

1 Whisk the mayonnaise and yogurt together.
2 Fold in the cucumber and mint. Season to taste.

"Great flavours; irresistibly pick-up-able. The kids will love digging into these!"

THE BUN

4 plain BURGER BAPS
1 EGG, beaten
2 tsp CUMIN SEEDS, ground in a pestle and mortar
2 tsp CORIANDER SEEDS, ground in a pestle and mortar
BABY CHARD and MINT LEAVES, to serve

1 Preheat the oven to 190°C (375°F/Gas 5). Brush the top of each bap with a little egg, scatter the crushed cumin seeds on top and bake in the oven for 2 minutes or until just browned.

STACK THE BURGER

To assemble the king-size slider, cut the baps in half then divide the cucumber mayonnaise between the bun bases. Place a few leaves of the chard on top, add a patty, and then a layer of the chutney. Place some mint leaves on the chutney, and then top each stack with a lid, and serve immediately.

PEA AND MINT SOUP WITH PROSCIUTTO
Justin Ryan property developer and 2011 Celebrity contestant

PREPARATION TIME
10 minutes

COOKING TIME
15 minutes

SERVES 4

"What is really
nice today is
being told that my
cooking is coming
on in leaps
and bounds."

1 tbsp OLIVE OIL
2 slices of PROSCIUTTO
600ml (1 pint) CHICKEN STOCK
8 sprigs of MINT, leaves only

450g (1lb) FROZEN PEAS
100ml (3½fl oz) CRÈME FRAÎCHE
SALT and freshly ground
  BLACK PEPPER

1 Heat the oil in a large saucepan and fry the prosciutto until crisp. Remove from the pan and drain off excess fat on kitchen paper, then crumble into small pieces and set aside until needed. Wipe the pan out with kitchen paper.

2 Heat the stock in the wiped-out pan and add the mint and peas. Cover and boil for 5 minutes then drain, reserving the stock.

3 Transfer the peas, mint, and half the stock to a food processor. Add 60ml (2fl oz) crème fraîche and blend to a smooth paste, gradually adding the remaining stock through the funnel of the processor. Return to the pan, adding a little more stock if you prefer a thinner soup. Season to taste. Reheat but do not boil.

4 To serve, pour the soup into warm soup bowls, and garnish with a swirl of the remaining crème fraîche and the reserved pieces of prosciutto.

Mint is one of the most popular flavours in the world. It is at once cooling and warming, with a sweet fragrance. When dried, the aroma is pungent and concentrated although it lacks the sweetness of the fresh herb.

ENTREMÉS OF EMPANADILLA, SALMOREJO, AND FLAMENQUIN

Anneliese Kiely MasterChef 2011 contestant

PREPARATION TIME
45 minutes, plus chilling

COOKING TIME
1 hour

SERVES 4

FOR THE PASTRY
300g (10oz) PLAIN FLOUR
100ml (3½fl oz) OLIVE OIL
1 EGG, beaten
3 tbsp DRY WHITE WINE
pinch of SALT

FOR THE EMPANADILLA
2 ONIONS, finely sliced
1 GREEN PEPPER, deseeded
 and finely sliced
1 RED PEPPER, deseeded
 and finely sliced
4 tbsp OLIVE OIL
150g (5½oz) COOKING
 CHORIZO, skinned
175g (6oz) PORK LOIN STEAK,
 finely chopped
1 GARLIC clove, crushed
1 tbsp TOMATO PURÉE
100ml (3½fl oz) RED WINE
pinch of SAFFRON
freshly ground BLACK PEPPER
1 EGG, beaten

FOR THE SALMOREJO
1 GARLIC clove, crushed
500g (1lb 2oz) fresh PLUM
 TOMATOES, skinned
 and deseeded
3 tbsp OLIVE OIL
75g (2½oz) stale BREAD,
 torn into chunks
good pinch of SALT
2 slices of SERRANO HAM,
 shredded (even better would
 be cubed Serrano or Iberico
 ham, if easy to find)
⅓ CUCUMBER, finely diced
3 SPRING ONIONS, finely chopped
1 hard-boiled EGG, finely chopped

FOR THE FLAMENQUIN
2 PORK LOIN STEAKS, 200g (7oz)
 each, trimmed of fat
4 slices SERRANO HAM
75g (2½oz) PLAIN FLOUR
1 EGG, beaten
75g (2½oz) BREADCRUMBS
4 tbsp OLIVE OIL

1 For the pastry, put all the ingredients into a food processor, with 3 tablespoons of cold water. Pulse until the mixture starts to form a dough. Knead gently on a floured surface until smooth. Wrap the dough in cling film and chill in the fridge for 1 hour.
2 Make the filling for the empanadillas. Fry the onion and peppers in olive oil until soft. Transfer to a bowl. Add the chorizo to the pan and fry gently for 5 minutes, breaking up the meat as it fries. Drain off excess oil, then add the chorizo to the vegetables.
3 Add a little olive oil to the pan and fry the pork and garlic for 5 minutes until just cooked. Return the chorizo mixture to the pan. Add the tomato purée, red wine, and saffron. Simmer for 10 minutes until thick. Season to taste. Leave to cool.
4 For the salmorejo, put the garlic, tomatoes, oil, and bread into a blender with a good pinch of salt and blitz until smooth. Pour into a jug and chill.
5 Preheat the oven to 180°C (350°F/Gas 4). Roll out two-thirds of the pastry thinly to 3mm (⅛in) and use it to line four 8–10cm (3½–4in) tartlet tins. Roll out the remaining pastry and cut 4

circles for lids. Spoon the cooled filling into the tins. Brush the pastry edges with water, place the lids on top, and press well together to seal. Chill for 15 minutes, then bake in the oven for 12 minutes. Remove the tarts from the oven and brush the tops with the beaten egg. Prick the pastry with a skewer and return to the oven for a further 5 minutes until golden brown. Remove from the oven and leave to cool for 5 minutes on a wire rack.

6 For the flamenquin, beat the pork steaks with a meat mallet (or rolling pin) until thin. Cut each piece in half to make 4 thin pieces of pork. Top each one with a slice of Serrano ham and roll up tightly (you may need to secure the rolls with cocktail sticks). Dip each parcel in the flour, shake off the excess, then dip into the beaten egg. Finally coat each piece in breadcrumbs. Heat the olive oil in a frying pan, shallow fry the flamenquin until crisp and golden, then transfer to the oven for 8–10 minutes to cook through. Drain on kitchen paper.

7 To assemble the dish, divide the salmorejo between 4 small bowls and top with the Serrano ham pieces, cucumber, spring onion, and egg. Serve with the flamenquin and empanadilla.

Semi-dried and dried Spanish chorizo are generally made from pork and pork fat spiced with smoked paprika. The casing is usually removed before cooking.

SAVOURY TOASTS
Ruth Goodman social historian and 2011 Celebrity contestant

PREPARATION TIME
10 minutes

COOKING TIME
10 –15 minutes

SERVES 4

4 slices of SOURDOUGH BREAD
  for toast
½ tbsp OLIVE OIL
1 whole LAMB'S LIVER, deveined
  and cut into small cubes
1 tsp FENNEL SEEDS

SALT and freshly ground BLACK
  PEPPER
50g (1¾oz) BUTTER
3 tbsp DOUBLE CREAM
tiny sprigs of THYME LEAVES,
  to garnish

"I never know
whether I'm going
to impress or
not, I find it nigh
impossible to
second guess
what other
people's opinion
of my food is."

1 Preheat the oven to 190°C (375°F/Gas 5). Drizzle the sliced bread with the olive oil and lay out on a baking tray. Place in the oven and bake for 5–8 minutes, checking regularly until the slices have turned golden brown. Remove from the oven and place on the serving plates.
2 Place the pieces of liver in a bowl. Add the fennel seeds and a generous grinding of black pepper. Mix together.
3 Melt the butter in a frying pan over medium to high heat. When the butter begins to foam, add the liver and spice mix. Fry for 2–3 minutes, turning so that all sides are browned evenly. (If you do not have a large frying pan, this may need to be done in batches.)
4 Once the liver is browned, add the cream to the pan, bring to the boil, and simmer for 2–3 minutes. Taste and season if necessary.
5 Serve the liver on the toast, and garnish with fresh sprigs of thyme.

CRAB TORTELLINI WITH SINGAPORE CHILLI CRAB SAUCE AND TEMPURA SAMPHIRE

Elizabeth Allen MasterChef 2011 contestant

PREPARATION TIME
40 minutes

COOKING TIME
1 hour

SERVES 4

FOR THE CRAB AND STOCK

2 CARROTS, chopped
2 ONIONS, chopped
1 large BOUQUET GARNI – thyme, bay leaf, and parsley stalks, wrapped in a piece of leek
1½ tsp SALT
2 tsp BLACK PEPPERCORNS
750ml (1¼ pints) DRY WHITE WINE
250ml (8fl oz) WHITE WINE VINEGAR
1 large LIVE CRAB

FOR THE SAUCE

4 tsp GROUNDNUT OIL
1¼ tsp GINGER PASTE
1¼ tsp GARLIC PASTE
1 tbsp minced RED ONION
2 tsp CHILLI PASTE
5 tbsp TOMATO KETCHUP
5 tbsp CHILLI SAUCE
200ml (7fl oz) reserved CRAB STOCK
1 EGG

FOR THE TORTELLINI

175g (6oz) reserved WHITE CRABMEAT
1 RED ONION, finely chopped
1 SPRING ONION, finely chopped
½ RED CHILLI, deseeded and finely chopped
½ tsp SALT
½ tsp freshly ground BLACK PEPPER
24 fresh, 9cm (3½in) WONTON or TSUI GAO SKINS

FOR THE TEMPURA

VEGETABLE OIL, for deep-frying
75g (2½oz) RICE FLOUR
250ml (8fl oz) ice cold WATER
150g (5½oz) SAMPHIRE

TO GARNISH

4 tsp SALMON ROE
100g (3½oz) CHERRY TOMATOES, halved
sprigs of herbs, such as CHERVIL and RED AMARANTH

Male brown crabs are preferred to females as they have larger claws with succulent white meat. Once cooked, crab can be kept in the coldest part of the fridge for up to 4 days.

1 First make the stock for the crab. Put the carrots, onions, bouquet garni, seasoning, white wine, and 2.5 litres (4½ pints) of water in a large pan. Bring to the boil, then simmer uncovered for 15–20 minutes. Add the vinegar and simmer a further 5 minutes.

2 To humanely kill the crab, put it in a bag in the freezer for 2 hours so that it is dormant. Lay the crab on its back, lift the tail flap and insert a skewer into the small dent in the shell. Push down until it reaches the back shell and move it side to side. Remove the skewer. Now push it through the mouth area, below the eyes, pushing upwards towards the back shell. Move it side to side again. Quickly weigh the crab and calculate the cooking time allowing 5 minutes per 450g (1lb).

3 Bring the stock to a rolling boil, add the crab, cover, and boil for the calculated cooking time. Lift out the crab carefully with a slotted spoon. Strain and reserve the stock. When the crab is cool enough to handle, remove the white crabmeat and place in a bowl to cool completely (reserve the dark meat for another recipe).

4 For the sauce, heat the oil in a saucepan and fry the ginger, garlic, red onion, and chilli paste over medium-low heat for about 8 minutes until the oil separates. Add the ketchup, chilli sauce, and measured crab stock, stirring to mix evenly. Cook for a further 4 minutes. Remove from the heat and add the egg, stirring to blend. Set aside until ready to use.

5 To make the tortellini, place all the ingredients, except the wonton skins, in a bowl and mix until thoroughly combined.

6 Place 1 tsp of the filling in the middle of a wanton or tsui gao skin. Wet one edge with a little water and fold in half to form a crescent, making sure no air is trapped inside.

7 Pinch the 2 corners of the crescent and join them together to form a nugget-shaped tortellini. Repeat with the remaining wrappers and filling. Cover with a damp cloth to keep them moist until ready to cook.

8 Heat a pan of vegetable oil for deep frying over medium-high heat. Meanwhile, make the tempura batter. Place the rice flour in a bowl and gradually whisk in the ice cold water to make a thick batter. It should have the consistency of double cream.

9 Dip the samphire in the batter, shake off any excess, and deep fry a few at a time until crisp and pale golden. Drain on kitchen paper. Keep warm.

10 Bring a large pan of salted water to the boil. Add the tortellini to the pan and boil for 1 minute, until they rise to the surface. Remove from the pan with a slotted spoon and drain thoroughly.

11 Gently reheat the sauce but do not allow it to boil.

12 To serve, spoon the sauce in 4 shallow serving bowls and arrange the tortellini in the centre. Garnish with the tempura samphire, salmon roe, halved cherry tomatoes, and some herbs.

Simplify for **EVERY**DAY

• Use fresh or frozen white crabmeat and add the wine and vinegar to half fresh fish stock and half water, instead of cooking your own. • Use fine asparagus instead of samphire for the tempura.

FRESH CRAB WITH FEUILLE DE BRICK BISCUITS
Phil Vickery MBE England rubgy player and 2011 Celebrity champion

PREPARATION TIME
40 minutes

COOKING TIME
40 minutes, plus cooling

SERVES 4

"I want the crab
to do the talking
at the end of the
day and I want it
to look pretty on
the plate."

FOR THE CRAB
2 WHITE ONIONS, chopped
2 CARROTS, chopped
2 CELERY sticks, chopped
2 GARLIC cloves, halved
2 sprigs of THYME
2 BAY LEAVES
2 large CRABS
2 RED CHILLIES, finely chopped
100g (3½oz) SPRING ONIONS,
  finely chopped
2 RED ONIONS, finely chopped
2 tbsp finely chopped CORIANDER
2 tbsp finely chopped BASIL
1 tbsp finely snipped CHIVES
1 GARLIC clove, finely chopped
zest of 2 LEMONS
dash of FISH SAUCE
dash of SESAME OIL

FOR THE BISCUITS
4 sheets of FEUILLE DE
  BRICK PASTRY
25g (scant 1oz) BUTTER, melted

12 BASIL leaves
1 tbsp freshly ground RED or
  PINK PEPPERCORNS
1 tbsp WHITE SESAME SEEDS
1 tbsp BLACK SESAME SEEDS

FOR THE HERB DRESSING
100ml (3½fl oz) VEGETABLE OIL
1 bunch of BASIL
1 tbsp snipped CHIVES
1 GARLIC clove, chopped
SALT and freshly ground
  BLACK PEPPER

FOR THE CRABMEAT DRESSING
reserved BROWN CRABMEAT
VEGETABLE OIL
TABASCO SAUCE, to taste

TO SERVE
2 thin slices SMOKED PANCETTA
1 tbsp OLIVE OIL
handful each of MICRO
  CORIANDER, MICRO BASIL,
  MICRO RED CHARD, and
  RED SHISO

1 Put the vegetables, garlic, thyme, and bay leaves in a large pan of boiling water and simmer for 10 minutes. Bring to the boil, add the crabs, and cook for 20 minutes. Remove the crabs and cool for 10 minutes under the cold tap. Take the meat from the shells. Combine the white meat with the remaining ingredients.
2 For the biscuits, preheat the oven to 180°C (350°F/Gas 4). Cut the pastry into 24 squares, 6cm (2½in) each, and brush with butter. Lay half on a baking tray lined with baking parchment. Place a basil leaf on top of each, sprinkle with pepper, then a second square. Finally, sprinkle with the sesame seeds. Put a sheet of baking parchment on top, followed by a baking tray to press it down. Place in the oven for 6–8 minutes or until golden brown.
3 For the herb dressing, blitz the ingredients in a food processor until smooth. For the meat dressing, mix the crabmeat with vegetable oil to loosen and add Tabasco and seasoning to taste.
4 Fry the pancetta in the oil until crisp. Drain and crumble into small pieces. Using a 5cm (2in) chef's ring, place 3 mounds of the crab on each plate, spoon a line of crab dressing on top, and 3 lines of herb dressing on the plate. Rest a biscuit on each mound, and scatter micro leaves and pancetta around.

CRAB AND AVOCADO WITH YUZU DRESSING
Nick Pickard actor and 2011 Celebrity finalist

PREPARATION TIME
25 minutes

SERVES 4

FOR THE SALAD
225g (8oz) WHITE CRABMEAT
1 large RED CHILLI, deseeded,
  and finely chopped
2 small TOMATOES, skinned,
  deseeded, and finely diced
2 SHALLOTS, finely chopped
1 tbsp finely chopped
  FLAT-LEAF PARSLEY
2 tsp LEMON JUICE
2 tbsp EXTRA VIRGIN OLIVE OIL
1 AVOCADO, peeled, stoned,
  and finely diced

FOR THE DRESSING
2 tsp EXTRA VIRGIN
  OLIVE OIL
1¾ tsp YUZU or LIME JUICE
1 tbsp CLEAR HONEY
1 tsp WASABI POWDER
2 tbsp MIRIN
1¾ tsp RICE WINE VINEGAR
2 tbsp SOY SAUCE

TO GARNISH
small CORIANDER leaves

1 Combine all the ingredients for the salad, except the avocado, in a bowl.
2 Whisk all the dressing ingredients together.
3 Place a 12cm (5in) square chef's ring in the centre of a serving plate and spoon in a quarter of the avocado, then top with a quarter of the crab mixture. Lift off the ring and repeat with the other 3 plates.
4 Drizzle over a little dressing and garnish with a few small coriander leaves.

Simplify for EVERYDAY

• For quickness (and retro style), layer the ingredients in small glasses (verrines) instead of working with chef's rings.
• Alternatively, use 2 avocados, halve, fill with the crab meat tossed with a few chilli flakes, chopped spring onion, and tomato. Spoon the dressing over and serve.

LOBSTER BISQUE

Danny Goffey musician and 2011 Celebrity semi-finalist

PREPARATION TIME
10 minutes

COOKING TIME
45 minutes

SERVES 4

2 LOBSTER TAILS
1 tbsp OLIVE OIL
30g (1oz) cold UNSALTED BUTTER
2 GARLIC cloves, finely chopped
2 sprigs of ROSEMARY
2 sprigs of THYME
5 tbsp BRANDY
4 tbsp DRY WHITE WINE
juice of ½ LEMON
1 litre (1¾ pints) CHICKEN STOCK

300ml (10fl oz) DOUBLE CREAM
SALT and WHITE PEPPER

TO GARNISH
a pinch of SMOKED PAPRIKA
2 tbsp finely snipped CHIVES

1 Remove the lobster meat from the tails and set aside. Heat the olive oil and a third of the butter in a heavy-based pan and add the garlic, rosemary, thyme, and lobster shells. Cook for 5 minutes over high heat until the lobster shells turn deep red.
2 Remove the pan from the heat and use a rolling pin or a potato masher to crush the shells. Return to the heat and cook for a further 5 minutes.
3 Add 4 tbsp of the brandy, ignite, then cook for a further 2 minutes, shaking the pan gently, until the flames subside and the liquid has almost evaporated. Add the wine and lemon juice, and cook for a further 2 minutes.
4 Add the chicken stock, bring to the boil, then reduce the heat and simmer for 20 minutes.
5 Strain the bisque through a fine sieve into a clean pan, then add the cream and season to taste.
6 Just before serving, reheat gently and whisk in half of the remaining cold butter.
7 Dice the lobster meat and sauté in the remaining butter and remaining brandy for 2 minutes until the meat turns white. Season to taste.
8 Divide the lobster meat between 4 soup bowls, then ladle over the bisque. Garnish with a sprinkling of smoked paprika and the finely snipped chives.

To kill a lobster humanely, put it in the freezer for 2 hours. Once it is motionless, push a sharp knife into the centre of the cross on its head to kill it instantly, or place it in a pan of cold salted water and bring it slowly to the boil.

SHELLFISH TORTELLINI WITH SCALLOPS
Aggie MacKenzie journalist and 2011 Celebrity semi-finalist

PREPARATION TIME
35 minutes, plus chilling

COOKING TIME
25 minutes

SERVES 4

"I love scallops, so I'm going to try and make this a really elegant little number."

FOR THE PASTA DOUGH
280g (10oz) TYPE '00' PASTA FLOUR
250g (9oz) EGG YOLK (5–6 yolks)

FOR THE FILLING
10g (¼oz) SCALLOP MEAT
200g (7oz) cooked WHITE CRABMEAT
4 raw shelled KING PRAWNS, deveined
2 EGG WHITES
3 tbsp DOUBLE CREAM
pinch of CAYENNE PEPPER
1 tsp LEMON JUICE
pinch of SALT

FOR THE SAUCE
4 tsp WHITE WINE VINEGAR
4 tbsp DRY WHITE WINE
2 small SHALLOTS, very finely chopped
75g (2½oz) UNSALTED BUTTER, cubed
4 large TOMATOES ON THE VINE, skinned, deseeded, and finely chopped

TO SERVE
12 SCALLOPS WITH CORALS
1 tbsp OLIVE OIL
1 tsp UNSALTED BUTTER
a few drops of LEMON JUICE
2 tsp finely snipped CHIVES
4 tsp AVRUGA CAVIAR

1 Place the flour in a food processor and add the egg yolk while the motor is running. When the mixture has the consistency of coarse breadcrumbs, transfer to a lightly floured surface and bring together by hand. Knead for 5 minutes until the dough is smooth and elastic. Wrap in cling film and chill for 20 minutes.

2 Pulse the shellfish in a food processor until chopped, then add the remaining filling ingredients and blend until smooth. Chill for 15 minutes. Meanwhile, roll out the dough as thinly as you can, then cut out twenty 8cm (3¼in) discs. Brush a disc with a little water and place 1 tsp of the filling on top. Fold the pasta over to form a semicircular parcel and press the edges together to seal, ensuring no air is trapped inside. Bring the pointed edges together and seal with a little water. Repeat with the remaining filling and discs. Put on a floured plate and rest in the fridge.

3 To make the sauce, combine the vinegar, wine, and shallots in a pan. Bring to the boil and simmer until reduced by about half, and the shallots are softened. On a very low heat, whisk in the butter, 1 cube at a time, until the sauce is emulsified. Add a little water if it looks a little thick. Add the tomatoes and keep warm.

4 Cook the tortellini in salted simmering water for 3–4 minutes, then drain. Season the scallops with salt and fry in olive oil for 2 minutes on each side in a very hot frying pan. Finish with a little butter and lemon juice. Drain on kitchen paper.

5 Finish the sauce with the chives and lemon juice. arrange the tortellini on the plates with the scallops, then spoon the sauce over. Garnish with the Avruga caviar.

PEA, FRAGRANT HERB, AND LEMON RISOTTO WITH PAN-ROASTED SCALLOPS

Nick Pickard actor and 2011 Celebrity finalist

PREPARATION TIME
30 minutes

COOKING TIME
1 hour 30 minutes

SERVES 4

FOR THE VEGETABLE STOCK
1 tbsp OLIVE OIL
1 ONION, roughly chopped
2 CARROTS, roughly chopped
2 CELERY sticks,
  roughly chopped
1 LEEK, roughly chopped
1 small SWEDE, roughly chopped
1 BOUQUET GARNI
1 tsp BLACK PEPPERCORNS

FOR THE RISOTTO
400g (14oz) fresh shelled PEAS,
  or thawed FROZEN PEAS
45g (1½oz) BUTTER
1 tbsp OLIVE OIL
1 SHALLOT, finely chopped
300g (10oz) RISOTTO RICE
120ml (4fl oz) WHITE WINE,
  preferably Chardonnay

1.5 litres (2¾ pints)
  reserved VEGETABLE STOCK
juice of 1 LEMON
3 tbsp finely chopped BASIL
3 tbsp finely chopped DILL
3 tbsp finely snipped CHIVES
50g (1¾oz) GRANA PADANO
  CHEESE, finely grated

FOR THE SCALLOPS
12 shelled SCALLOPS
SALT and freshly ground
  BLACK PEPPER
3 tbsp OLIVE OIL
15g (½oz) UNSALTED BUTTER
juice of 1 LEMON

Simplify for EVERYDAY

• Use ready prepared fresh vegetable stock instead of making your own. • If you want a quick pea risotto for a week night, use a packet of ready-to-cook saffron risotto, then add the puréed and whole peas at the end. • Serve with sautéed lardons instead of the scallops.

1 For the vegetable stock, heat the olive oil in a large pan. Stir in the vegetables. Cover and cook gently for 3–5 minutes until soft but not brown. Add the bouquet garni, peppercorns, and 2.5 litres (4¼ pints) water. Bring to the boil, reduce the heat, part-cover, and simmer gently for 1 hour. Strain well and reserve.
2 For the risotto, purée half of the peas and set aside. Heat 15g (½oz) of the butter and the olive oil over medium heat. Add the shallots and cook gently, stirring, for 2–3 minutes. Increase the heat, add the risotto rice, and stir until all the grains are coated.
3 Add the wine. Boil until nearly evaporated, stirring. Add the measured stock, a ladleful at a time, stirring continuously until absorbed before adding more. It will take 15–20 minutes in all.
4 When just cooked, stir in the pea purée along with the whole peas. Stir and cook for a further 2 minutes. Add the lemon juice, herbs, grated cheese, and the remaining butter in small flakes. Stir well. It should be very moist, rich, and creamy.
5 Season the scallops on both sides. Heat the oil in a large frying pan over very high heat until smoking. Add the scallops. Quickly fry for 2 minutes on each side. Remove the frying pan from the heat. Add the butter and the lemon juice. Turn the scallops in the liquid for 1 minute.
6 Divide the risotto between 4 plates. Top each with 3 scallops.

LASAGNE OF SCALLOPS, WILD MUSHROOMS, AND TRUFFLES WITH A BUTTERNUT SQUASH VELOUTÉ

Alice Taylor MasterChef 2011 contestant

PREPARATION TIME
30 minutes

COOKING TIME
40 minutes

SERVES 4

FOR THE PASTA
pinch of SAFFRON
2 tsp boiling WATER
175g (6oz) "00" PASTA FLOUR
75g (2½oz) SEMOLINA FLOUR,
  plus extra for dusting
2 EGGS
3 EGG YOLKS
1 tbsp OLIVE OIL
pinch of SALT

FOR THE VELOUTÉ
1 small BUTTERNUT SQUASH,
  peeled and cubed
2 tbsp VEGETABLE OIL
SALT and freshly ground
  BLACK PEPPER
knob of UNSALTED BUTTER
2 SHALLOTS, finely diced
500ml (16fl oz) CHICKEN STOCK
75ml (2½fl oz) DOUBLE CREAM

FOR THE FILLING
12 DRIED PORCINI, sliced
1 large PEMBROOKE or MARIS
  PIPER POTATO, peeled
  and quartered
knob of UNSALTED BUTTER
splash of WHOLE MILK
2 tsp WHITE TRUFFLE OIL
2 tbsp VEGETABLE OIL
200g (7oz) CHESTNUT
  MUSHROOMS, finely chopped
1–2 BLACK TRUFFLES,
  finely shaved
12 SCALLOPS, shelled and cleaned

FOR THE PARMESAN CRISPS
100g (3½oz) PARMESAN CHEESE,
  finely grated

FOR THE GARNISH
1 tbsp FLAT-LEAF PARSLEY,
  finely chopped

1 Preheat the oven to 180°C (350°F/Gas 4). In a small bowl, soak the saffron in the boiling water and leave to infuse. Place all the remaining ingredients for the pasta in a food processor and pulse until the mixture starts to come together. Add the saffron-infused water to the pasta dough and pulse again. Turn out onto a floured work surface and knead until you have a smooth ball of dough. Wrap tightly in cling film and place in the fridge to rest.

2 For the velouté, place the cubed squash in a roasting tin, drizzle with the oil, and season with salt and pepper. Roast for 20 minutes until soft. Meanwhile, melt the butter in a saucepan, add the shallots, and fry until soft. When the squash is ready, add it to the pan with the chicken stock and warm through. Place in a food processor and blend until smooth. Pass through a sieve into a clean pan, add the cream, and stir to combine.

3 While the squash is roasting, reconstitute the dried porcini for the filling by pouring some boiling water into a bowl and steeping them in it for 20 minutes. Drain, reserving the liquor.

4 Bring a pan of salted water to the boil, add the potato, and cook until soft. Drain, then mash with the butter, milk, truffle oil,

Take care not to overcook scallops – it is easily done, as they continue to cook when removed from the heat. The flesh should still be springy to the touch, not firm and stiff.

seasoning to taste, and enough reserved liquor from the porcini to loosen the potato mixture to a soft, pipeable consistency.

5 While the potato cooks, heat 1 tbsp vegetable oil in a frying pan, add the chestnut mushrooms, and cook until softened. Add the black truffle shavings, then combine with the mashed potato. Transfer to a piping bag just before serving.

6 Preheat the grill to high. Place small mounds of Parmesan cheese in a large, non-stick frying pan and heat gently until the cheese starts to melt. Put the pan under the grill for 1–2 minutes until the cheese has fully melted and is bubbling. Remove from the heat, allow to cool slightly, then transfer the cheese to kitchen paper to cool completely until crisp.

7 Bring a large pan of salted water to the boil. Roll out the pasta thinly and cut out 16 discs of pasta, about 7cm (2³⁄₄in) in diameter. Drop the pasta discs into the boiling water and cook for 2 minutes, then drain well.

8 Heat the remaining oil in a frying pan and fry the porcini until golden. Cut each scallop into 3 smaller discs, season, and fry for 30 seconds on each side until just golden.

TO SERVE

To assemble the lasagne, place a disc of pasta in the centre of each serving dish. Pipe a little of the mushroom and potato mix onto the pasta, top with 3 scallop slices, then a disc of pasta. Repeat 3 times. Lay the fried porcini on top of the final disc of pasta, then garnish with a little chopped parsley. Surround the lasagne with the velouté and garnish with a Parmesan crisp.

PAN-FRIED BABY SQUID WITH SUN-BLUSHED TOMATO AND ROCKET

Sharon Maughan actress and 2011 Celebrity semi-finalist

PREPARATION TIME
10 minutes

COOKING TIME
5 minutes

SERVES 4

450g (1lb) BABY SQUID, cleaned and tentacles discarded
SALT
2 tsp PIMENT D'ESPELETTE POWDER (or 1 tsp each of HOT and SWEET SMOKED PAPRIKA)
3 tbsp OLIVE OIL

18 SUNBLUSH TOMATOES
3 GARLIC cloves, finely chopped
1 tbsp chopped FLAT-LEAF PARSLEY
50g (1¾oz) ROCKET LEAVES
1 RED CHILLI, deseeded and finely chopped (optional)

1 Slice the squid into 5mm (¼in) thick rings and pat dry on kitchen paper. Season the squid with salt to taste, and add the piment d'Espelette.

2 Heat a frying pan until very hot. Add the olive oil and then the squid. Cook for no more then 1 minute, until the squid is golden in colour. Turn over and add the tomatoes, garlic, and parsley.

3 Cook for a further minute, then remove from the heat and serve immediately, garnished with rocket leaves.

4 For some extra heat, add some finely chopped red chilli just before serving.

SCALLOP CEVICHE
Nick Pickard actor and 2011 Celebrity finalist

PREPARATION TIME
25 minutes

SERVES 4

3 tbsp CLEAR tequila
6 LIMES
12 very fresh SCALLOPS,
   without roes
1 RED CHILLI, deseeded and
   finely chopped
1 RED ONION, finely chopped
1 ripe AVOCADO, finely chopped
10 RADISHES, finely chopped
100g (3½oz) CHERRY TOMATOES,
   finely chopped

2 tbsp finely chopped CORIANDER
2 tbsp finely chopped MINT

TO SERVE
EXTRA VIRGIN OLIVE OIL
MICRO CORIANDER, or a few torn
   CORIANDER leaves

1 Put the tequila and the juice of 4 of the limes in a bowl.
2 Slice the scallops to the thickness and size of a two pence piece and marinate in the tequila and lime juice for 5 minutes.
3 Combine the chilli, onion, avocado, radishes, tomatoes, coriander, and mint in a bowl.
4 Drain the scallop slices and mix with the rest of the chopped ingredients.
5 Slice the remaining limes, squeeze some of the juice into the mixture, and combine the slices with the mixture.
6 Divide the mixture equally between 4 serving glasses.
7 Drizzle with a little olive oil and garnish with coriander.

Simplify for **EVERY**DAY

• Fresh salmon, skinned and cut into thick strips makes a delicious, and cheaper, alternative to the scallops. • You can cheat and use bottled lime juice too, for speed.

PAN-FRIED FILLET OF GURNARD WITH OCTOPUS PEASE PUDDING AND MOLLUSC RAGOÛT

Tom Whitaker MasterChef 2011 finalist

PREPARATION TIME
1 hour, plus soaking

COOKING TIME
2 hours 50 minutes

SERVES 6

FOR THE PEASE PUDDING
1 medium OCTOPUS, cleaned
2 litres (3½ pints) RAPESEED OIL
300g (10oz) pre-soaked YELLOW
    SPLIT PEAS
1 litre (1¾ pints) HAM STOCK
2 BAY LEAVES
pinch of SAFFRON
1 tbsp finely chopped PARSLEY
juice of ½ LEMON
1 tsp CAPERS, roughly chopped
SALT and freshly ground
    BLACK PEPPER

FOR THE RAGOÛT
200g (7oz) WINKLES, washed
10 RAZOR CLAMS

1 tbsp OLIVE OIL
2 SHALLOTS, finely sliced
½ tsp GARLIC PASTE
1 tbsp WHITE WINE VINEGAR
SALT and freshly ground
    BLACK PEPPER

FOR THE GURNARD
6 fillets of GURNARD
SALT and freshly ground
    BLACK PEPPER
1 tbsp OLIVE OIL

1 First start to make the pease pudding. Clean the octopus by inverting the head and removing the insides. Place the octopus in a large pan and submerge completely in rapeseed oil. Simmer over very low heat for 2 hours until tender, then drain the octopus and wipe off any excess oil with kitchen paper.

2 Remove the legs from the octopus and griddle in a hot griddle pan until caramelized, turning frequently. Cut into 3mm (⅛in) thick slices, reserving the ends of the tentacles for use as a garnish, and set aside.

3 Add the pre-soaked split peas to a pan with the ham stock, bay leaves, and saffron. Bring to the boil, reduce the heat, and simmer for 1½ hours until tender. Allow to cool in the stock, then drain the peas, remove the bay leaves, and set aside.

4 To make the ragoût, add the winkles to a pan of simmering salted water and cook for 20 minutes. Drain the winkles and when they are cool enough to handle, remove the meat from the shells using a toothpick. Trim the 'foot' from the bottom of each winkle and remove and discard the food sac. Roughly chop the winkle meat and set aside.

5 Add the razor clams to another pan of slightly salted water for 10–15 seconds until they open, then drain them, reserving the cooking liquor. Thinly slice the tubular end of the clams and set aside. Place the leftover body parts of the clams in

a pan with 250ml (8fl oz) of the cooking liquor and heat through gently to infuse.

6   Heat the olive oil in a pan and gently sauté the shallots with the garlic paste until softened. Add the white wine vinegar and reduce until the liquid has almost completely evaporated. Season with salt and pepper.

7   Strain the infused calm liquor through a sieve and add 250ml (8fl oz) to the softened shallots and garlic. Bring to the boil and reduce until syrupy. Just before serving, add the chopped winkles and razor clams and heat through gently.

8   Assemble the pease pudding. Put the octopus slices, split peas, parsley, lemon juice, capers, and salt and pepper into a bowl and mix thoroughly.

9   To cook the gurnard, score the skin diagonally and season with salt and pepper. Heat the olive oil in a frying pan and fry the fish for 3 minutes, skin-side down. Turn the fillets over and remove the pan from the hob – the residual heat of the pan will finish cooking the fish.

10   To serve, spoon some peasepudding in the centre of each plate and sprinkle extra around. Place the fish on top and then finish with a spoonful of the ragoût and some octopus tentacles.

TOM'S PAN-FRIED GURNARD SIMPLIFIED FOR **EVERY**DAY... ▶ PAGE 74

SIZZLING SEA BASS

JOHN TORODE'S SPEEDY TAKE ON TOM'S FISH STARTER OFFERS A TWIST, WITH A BASE OF DELICIOUS LENTILS

PREP: 25–30 MINS • COOK: 6–8 MINS

PAN-FRIED SEA BASS AND PRAWNS

SERVES 4

100g (3½oz) raw peeled
  TIGER PRAWNS
3 tbsp OLIVE OIL
finely grated zest of ½ LIME
1 GARLIC clove, crushed
4 small SEA BASS FILLETS,
  skin on and any bones removed

1 Pat dry the prawns and mix together in a bowl with 2 tbsp oil, the lime zest, and the garlic. Preheat a frying pan then add the prawn mixture and pan fry for 1–2 minutes on each side or until pink and lightly golden and cooked through. Remove from the pan and keep warm.

2 Next, pat dry the sea bass fillets, add the remaining olive oil to the pan, and fry the sea bass fillets, for 3–4 minutes. Turn and cook for the same amount of time on the other side.

3 When the fish has a very crisp and golden skin and is cooked through, remove from the pan. If you need to cook the fish in batches, keep warm while you fry the second batch.

4 Serve the cooked sea bass on the braised lentils and prawns.

Pan fry the sea bass for 3–4 minutes on a medium to high heat.

Turn the sea bass over, and cook for a further 3–4 minutes.

When golden and crisp, remove the sea bass from the pan.

"The freshness of the fish and prawns against the earthiness of the lentils is an absolute delight to the palate."

...SERVE WITH

LENTILS

75g (3oz) PUY LENTILS
200ml (7fl oz) FISH STOCK
small pinch of SAFFRON
1 BAY LEAF, torn
½ SHALLOT, finely chopped

1 Place the lentils, stock, saffron, bay leaf, and shallot in a saucepan and bring to the boil.
2 Reduce the heat, cover, and simmer for 15–20 minutes or until just tender, checking every now and then to make sure you don't need to add any extra stock towards the end of cooking.

DRESSING

1 tbsp OLIVE OIL
1 tsp LEMON JUICE
1 tsp WHITE WINE VINEGAR
1 tsp CLEAR HONEY
¼ tsp DIJON MUSTARD
1 tbsp freshly
   chopped PARSLEY
1 tsp small CAPERS,
   roughly chopped
SALT and FRESHLY
   ground black pepper

1 Combine the dressing ingredients in a screwtop jar, shake until well mixed. Drizzle over the fish and lentils.

RAINBOW TROUT WITH HORSERADISH CREAM, CUCUMBER RIBBONS, AND SODA BREAD

Kirsty Wark journalist and presenter and 2011 Celebrity finalist

PREPARATION TIME
25 minutes

COOKING TIME
29 minutes

SERVES 4

FOR THE SODA BREAD
150g (5½oz) WHOLEMEAL FLOUR
½ tsp SALT
¼ tsp BICARBONATE OF SODA
150ml (5fl oz) BUTTERMILK

FOR THE HORSERADISH
1 tbsp grated fresh HORSERADISH
150ml (5fl oz) SOURED CREAM
freshly ground BLACK PEPPER

FOR THE CUCUMBER
1 small CUCUMBER
1 tbsp chopped DILL
juice of ½ LEMON

FOR THE TROUT
8 small RAINBOW TROUT FILLETS
2 tbsp OLIVE OIL

1 Preheat the oven to 200°C (400°F/Gas 6). Make the soda bread. Put the flour, salt, and bicarbonate of soda into a large mixing bowl and stir to combine. Make a well in the centre and pour in the buttermilk, mixing quickly with a large fork to form a soft dough.

2 Turn the dough onto a lightly floured surface and knead briefly, then shape into a round and place on a lightly greased baking tray. Cut a cross in the middle to a depth of 1cm (½in), then bake in the oven for 25 minutes until risen, golden, and the loaf sounds hollow when tapped on the base. Remove from the oven and transfer to a wire rack to cool.

3 Meanwhile, make the horseradish cream. Combine the grated horseradish with the soured cream, season to taste, then set aside until needed.

4 Use a potato peeler to pare the cucumber in long ribbons into a bowl. Toss with the chopped dill and lemon juice.

5 Season the trout fillets and fry in the olive oil for 2 minutes on each side. Arrange the cucumber ribbons in the middle of the plate and place the trout on top. Serve with the horseradish cream and a slice of the soda bread.

HALIBUT ON SMOKED HADDOCK AND MUSSEL STEW WITH ASPARAGUS AND WHITE WINE CREAM SAUCE

Kennedy Leitch MasterChef 2011 contestant

PREPARATION TIME
15 minutes

COOKING TIME
30 minutes

SERVES 4

"It's light. It sounds like it might not be, but it'll be light."

500g (1lb 2oz) MUSSELS, cleaned
125ml (4½fl oz) WHITE WINE
16 BABY ASPARAGUS SPEARS
300ml (10fl oz) DOUBLE CREAM
400g (14oz) undyed SMOKED HADDOCK FILLETS, skinned and cut into bite-sized chunks
4 HALIBUT FILLETS, 150–200g (5½–7oz) each

SALT and freshly ground BLACK PEPPER
small handful of CHIVES, finely snipped

TO GARNISH
3 BABY LEEKS, or 1 large LEEK
500ml (16fl oz) VEGETABLE OIL

1 For the stew place the cleaned mussels in a large, dry pan and cover with a lid. Cook over high heat for 4–5 minutes, shaking the pan occasionally, until the mussels are open.

2 Drain the mussels in a colander set over a bowl to save the liquid. Reserve 100ml (3½fl oz) of the liquid and place in a saucepan with the wine. Place over medium heat and simmer until the liquid has reduced by two-thirds to 150ml (5fl oz). Meanwhile, remove the mussels from their shells, reserve the meat and discard the shells.

3 Next, make the garnish. Finely slice the white part of the leeks, discarding the green part. Pour the vegetable oil into a saucepan and heat over medium heat. Test the oil by dropping a small piece of bread into it: if the bread floats and quickly starts to turn golden, the oil is ready. Deep fry the leeks until crisp, then drain on kitchen paper.

4 Bring a pan of salted water to the boil, add the asparagus and blanch for 2 minutes. Drain, refresh under cold running water, and set aside.

5 Add the cream to the wine reduction, bring to the boil, and simmer for 1 minute. Add the haddock to the cream sauce and simmer for a further 2 minutes until the haddock is cooked.

6 Heat a large frying pan over medium-high heat. Rub a little oil onto the skin of each piece of halibut and season well. Fry the halibut skin-side down until the skin is golden and crisp. Turn the fillets over, then remove the pan from the heat – the residual heat of the pan will finish cooking the fish.

7 Add the mussels and the asparagus to the sauce, heat through gently, then add the snipped chives to the cream sauce to finish.

8 Serve the mussel stew in the middle of the plates and place a halibut fillet on top of each. Garnish with the crispy leeks.

The largest of the flat fish and with dense, tasty white flesh, halibut has been over fished in the Atlantic. If possible, buy farmed or Pacific halibut.

SMOKED HADDOCK AND PANCETTA SOUFFLÉ
Kirsty Wark journalist and presenter and 2011 Celebrity finalist

PREPARATION TIME
25 minutes

COOKING TIME
1 hour

SERVES 6

"This is what I love to cook. I want to combine great flavours and fine ingredients with a bit of flair."

softened UNSALTED BUTTER, for greasing
75g (2½oz) fine WHITE BREADCRUMBS
75g (2½oz) PARMESAN CHEESE, very finely grated
300ml (10fl oz) WHOLE MILK
2 sprigs of PARSLEY
1 BAY LEAF
SALT and freshly ground BLACK PEPPER
½ tsp grated NUTMEG

zest of ½ large LEMON
1 small WHITE ONION, finely chopped
225g (8oz) UNDYED SMOKED HADDOCK FILLET
50g (1¾oz) diced PANCETTA
2 tsp finely chopped CHERVIL
2 tsp finely chopped DILL
knob of UNSALTED BUTTER
40g (1¼oz) PLAIN FLOUR, sifted
40g (1¼oz) BUTTER
4 large EGGS, separated

1 Preheat the oven to 190°C (375°F/Gas 5). Pour hot water into a roasting tin to the depth of about 2cm (¾in). Place the tin on the top shelf of the oven.

2 Butter the inside of six 175ml (6fl oz) ramekins. Combine the breadcrumbs and Parmesan in a bowl and use the mixture to coat the inside of the ramekins. Place in the fridge and until needed.

3 Put the milk, parsley, bay leaf, pepper, nutmeg, lemon zest, and onion in a wide pan. Bring gently to a simmer and then lay the haddock in the milk. Cover with a cartouche or a lid, and poach gently for 5–10 minutes, depending on the thickness of the fish.

4 Meanwhile, sauté the pancetta in butter for 5 minutes until golden, then drain on kitchen paper.

5 When the fish is ready, it will break apart easily. Lift it out of the pan and set aside to cool. Strain the milk through a sieve, discarding the parsley and bay leaf, but retaining the onion and lemon zest. Pour the milk into a measuring jug – you will need 300ml (10fl oz) to make the sauce (add more milk if necessary).

6 Remove any skin or small bones from the fish and flake the flesh with a fork. Tip the onion and lemon zest into a bowl with the fish, pancetta, and chopped herbs, and mix together.

7 Melt the butter in a pan and stir in the flour to make a paste. Gradually whisk in the milk, then cook gently for 10 minutes until thickened. Remove from the heat and whisk in the egg yolks. Add the haddock mixture, stir to combine, and season to taste.

8 In a separate bowl, whisk the egg whites to soft peaks. Stir a spoonful of the egg whites into the fish mixture to loosen it, then fold in the remainder. Divide the mixture between the ramekins and smooth the top with a palette knife. Place into the prepared roasting tin and cook for 15–20 minutes until the soufflés have risen and are golden brown on top. Serve immediately.

PAN-FRIED FILLET OF PIKE WITH CRAYFISH, WILTED SORREL, AND WATERCRESS SAUCE

Tom Whitaker MasterChef 2011 finalist

PREPARATION TIME
20 minutes

COOKING TIME
30 minutes

SERVES 4

"That's the way I've tried to put things together: things that work very well in the same environment often work very well on the same plate."

FOR THE SAUCE
3 BAY LEAVES
10 PEPPERCORNS
12 FRESHWATER CRAYFISH, chilled for 2 hours in the freezer
250ml (8fl oz) DOUBLE CREAM
300g (10oz) WATERCRESS, hard stalks removed
1 tsp ENGLISH MUSTARD POWDER

FOR THE PIKE
2 tbsp RAPESEED OIL
4 PIKE FILLETS, 100g (3½oz) each, pin-boned and with skin on

TO SERVE
250g (9oz) SORREL leaves, thoroughly washed

1 Bring a pan of water just big enough to hold the crayfish to the boil with the bay leaves and peppercorns. Add the chilled crayfish and boil for 5 minutes. Lift out of the pan with a slotted spoon. When cool enough to handle, remove the heads and claws and peel the tails, reserving the meat. Return the heads, claws, and tail shells to the pan and simmer for 30 minutes to reduce the liquid. Strain the liquid into a clean pan and add the cream. Bring to the boil and reduce by a third.

2 Add the watercress and mustard powder to the sauce, return to the boil, and simmer for 2 minutes. Remove the bay leaves, place the sauce in a jug blender, and blitz until smooth, then pour into a pan and keep warm until needed.

3 For the pike, preheat the oven to 200°C (400°F/Gas 6). Heat the oil in a frying pan over medium to high heat. Once it is hot, add the pike fillets skin-side down and cook them for 3–5 minutes until the skin is golden. Flip the fish and brown lightly again. Remove the fish to a roasting tray and place in the oven for 6–8 minutes, or until just cooked through.

4 To serve, divide the sorrel leaves between 4 bowls. Top with the hot pike fillets and 3 crayfish tails. Spoon the hot sauce over and serve immediately.

Simplify for EVERYDAY

• Use raw, whole tiger prawns instead of the crayfish (which are sold live, so are comatosed by freezing before cooking).
• Simply cook the prawns in the stock until pink (2–3 minutes), then continue as in the recipe.
• Use trout instead of pike, and spinach for sorrel.

SUSHI PLATTER WITH TOFU-WRAPPED SUSHI, SHIITAKE MUSHROOM AND VEGETABLE ROLLED SUSHI, AND GINGER-TOFU AND WASABI SUSHI

Jackie Kearney MasterChef 2011 final 4

PREPARATION TIME
2 hours

COOKING TIME
30 minutes

SERVES 25

FOR THE SEASONED RICE
630g (1lb 6oz) SUSHI RICE
6 tbsp SAKE, plus extra
    for cooking rice
1½ tsp SALT
15g (½oz) SUGAR
3 tbsp RICE VINEGAR

FOR THE ROLLED SUSHI
6 large DRIED SHIITAKE
    MUSHROOMS
8 sheets of NORI SEAWEED
3 cups of cooked SUSHI RICE
    (as prepared)
2 small CARROTS, cut into julienne
1 medium KOHLRABI, cut
    into julienne
1 CUCUMBER, deseeded

FOR THE GINGER-TOFU SUSHI
5cm (2in) fresh GINGER
2 tbsp VEGETABLE OIL
SALT, for seasoning
1 packet of firm TOFU, frozen
    the day before and left to
    thaw before use
1 sheet of NORI SEAWEED

2 cups of cooked SUSHI RICE
    (as prepared)
150ml tube of WASABI PASTE

FOR THE TOFU-WRAPPED SUSHI
500ml (16fl oz) VEGETARIAN
    DASHI, made from powder – add
    500ml (16fl oz) water according
    to instructions
120ml (4fl oz) SAKE
6 tbsp MIRIN
150g (5½oz) CASTER SUGAR
1 tsp SALT
14 sheets of dried
    BEAN-CURD SKIN
2 cups of cooked SUSHI RICE
    (as prepared)

TO SERVE
200g (7oz) GINGER PICKLE,
    light pink
200g (7oz) RADISH PICKLE,
    deep pink
LIGHT SOY SAUCE

1 Rinse the rice, then put it in a pan with the water, a generous splash of sake, and 1 tsp salt. Bring the water to the boil, turn the heat down to a simmer, and then cook, covered, for 10 minutes. Leave to rest for 20 minutes before seasoning it.
2 For the sushi-rice seasoning, mix together the sake, sugar, rice vinegar, and ½ tsp salt until the sugar is fully dissolved. Pour over the rested rice and mix well. Set aside until needed. There will be enough cooked sushi rice to make about 100 pieces of sushi.
3 For the rolled filling, soak the shiitake mushrooms in hot water for 15 minutes, then drain and lay on kitchen roll to dry. Cut the mushrooms into very fine strips. Lay out the sheets of nori seaweed on cling film, then add the cooked sushi rice along the centre, leaving a few centimetres of space at each end. Press the rice down to make it flatter and wider, gently shaping

a slight channel down the middle. Place strips of the vegetables through the middle to a depth of at least 1cm (½in).

4 Using the cling film, roll up the rice around the filling and ensure the nori seaweed is firmly wrapped, taking care not to tear it. Using a very sharp serrated knife, slice the ends to neaten them and then slice each length into about 6 pieces. Repeat with the remaining sheets of the nori seaweed, making about 50 pieces of vegetable-stuffed sushi.

5 To prepare the ginger-tofu sushi, blend the ginger with the oil to make a ginger paste, and season with salt. Slice the defrosted tofu into fingers about 1cm (½in) thick – one block of tofu should make about 25 pieces. Marinate in the ginger paste for 1 hour in the fridge.

6 Cut the nori seaweed into strips, 5mm (¼in) wide and about 15cm (6in) long. Shape the cooked sushi rice in the palm of your hand to make an oblong shape, about 5–6cm (2–2½in) long and 2–3cm (¾–1¼in) across. Using the wasabi paste as a glue, place a small blob on top of the shaped rice, then put a piece of marinated tofu on top. Wrap a strip of nori seaweed around the tofu and rice – the seaweed will stick to itself as it starts to soften. Repeat to make 25 pieces.

7 To prepare the tofu-wrapped sushi, put the dashi, sake, mirin, sugar, and salt in a large pan and place over medium heat. Once the dashi mixture is warm, lay the bean-curd skins in it, bring to the boil, and simmer for 20–30 minutes until all the liquid has been absorbed, taking care that the bean-curd skins do not stick to the pan. They can then be unfolded and opened out flat.

8 Using sharp scissors, cut the bean-curd skins into 10 x 5cm (4 x 2in) pieces (each one will make about 4). Place each piece on a flat surface, add a small ball of cooked sushi rice, and roll the bean-curd skin from one corner, making a small cone-shaped wrap around the sushi rice.

9 Lay out a selection of each of the sushi types on large platters and serve with the pickled ginger, pickled radish, and light soy sauce.

Rich, warm, and sweet, fresh ginger is a rhizome that is usually peeled, then grated, shredded, or sliced before use. Also available dried, ground, pickled, and in syrup.

SMUSHI SET – A SELECTION OF DANISH-JAPANESE INSPIRED CANAPÉS

Tim Anderson MasterChef 2011 champion

PREPARATION TIME
1 hour

COOKING TIME
30 minutes

SERVES 8

"The term was coined at the Royal Café in Copenhagen and it's bringing together concepts of Danish smørrebrød with sushi and sashimi, so it's a sort of Danish-Japanese fusion cuisine."

Tartare

8 small BANANA SHALLOTS
450ml (15fl oz) DANISH
    WALNUT BEER or other
    dark, strong lager
500ml (16fl oz) SAKE
100g (3½oz) RYE GRAINS
1 NASHI, peeled and cored

4 MACKEREL FILLETS, skinned
10–12 CHIVES
1 tbsp CARAWAY SEEDS
SALT and WHITE PEPPER
juice of 1 LEMON
3 tbsp CRÈME FRAÎCHE

1   Halve the shallots lengthways. Carefully peel off the outer layer of each, and reserve.
2   Put the beer and sake in a pan and bring to the boil. Add the rye grains, reduce the heat, and cook for about 45 minutes. Set the shallots in a sieve over the pan to steam above the simmering liquid for 5 minutes, or until tender. Rinse the shallots in cold water to cool them.
3   Roughly chop the nashi and put in a food processor with the mackerel, chives, caraway seeds, salt, and pepper. Blitz until the mixture is just minced. Mix with the rye grains, lemon juice, and crème fraîche, then spoon into the shallot boats.

Yellowtail sashimi

750g (1lb 10oz) very fresh
    YELLOWTAIL FILLET, skinned
100ml (3½fl oz) SHOYU SAUCE
juice of 1 LIME

3 tbsp DANISH WALNUT BEER
2 tbsp WALNUT OIL
5 leaves of BATAVIA LETTUCE, torn

1   Slice the yellowtail fillet into small pieces.
2   Mix the shoyu, lime juice, pilsner, and oil, and use to dress the lettuce. Arrange the yellowtail on top of the lettuce.

Monkfish liver

1 SHALLOT
1–2 MONKFISH LIVERS, at least
    500g (1lb 2oz), deveined
1 small WHITE BAGUETTE
RAPESEED OIL, for frying

BUTTER, for frying
50ml (1¾fl oz) YUZU-KOSHO PASTE
2 sprigs of TARRAGON

1   Slice the shallot into fine slivers.
2   Cut the monkfish liver into small chunks and thinly slice the baguette.
3   Heat the oil and butter in a frying pan and shallow fry the baguette slices. Remove from the pan, then add the liver to the pan and sear on both sides.
4   Spread a little yuzu-kosho on each piece of baguette, then set the liver on top. Garnish with a slice of shallot and a few leaves of tarragon.

Umeboshi remoulade

3 UMEBOSHI
3 tbsp pure BEETROOT JUICE
15g (½oz) CASTER SUGAR
3 EGG YOLKS

1 tbsp WASABI POWDER
juice of ½ LEMON
100ml (3½fl oz) RAPESEED OIL

1   Put all the ingredients except the oil in a blender and turn it on. While blending, slowly drizzle in the oil until the mixture is completely emulsified.

Salmon maki

2 JAPANESE CUCUMBERS
300g (10oz) lightly
   smoked SALMON
juice of 1 LEMON
200g (7oz) spreadable
   GOAT'S CHEESE

4–5 sprigs of DILL
2–3 sprigs of TARRAGON
50g (1¾oz) SAMPHIRE

1   Peel the cucumbers and cut into ten 3cm (1¼in) chunks. Remove the seeds from each chunk with an apple corer so that only a thin-walled cucumber tube remains.
2   Blend the salmon, lemon, and cheese in a food processor, then press through a drum sieve to form a fine mousse.
3   Carefully spoon the mousse into each cucumber tube, and garnish with the dill, tarragon, and samphire.

TO PLATE
Spoon a streak of the umeboshi remoulade through the centre of the plate. Arrange the tartare, sashimi, liver, and maki around it.

The intensity of flavour of smoked salmon depends upon the length of time it is smoked and the material used to produce the smoke, for example apple wood, oak, or peat.

SORREL SOUP WITH SALMON AND DILL AND OATCAKES

Kirsty Wark journalist and presenter and 2011 Celebrity finalist

PREPARATION TIME
25 minutes

COOKING TIME
50 minutes

SERVES 4

GREGG WALLACE

"It's thought-provoking, it's interesting, it's something different. It's good. It's really good."

FOR THE VEGETABLE STOCK
2 CELERY sticks, roughly chopped
2 CARROTS, roughly chopped
1 ONION, roughly chopped
1 LEEK, roughly chopped
1 BAY LEAF
100g (3½oz) FROZEN PEAS
2 sprigs of THYME
SALT and freshly ground
   BLACK PEPPER

FOR THE OATCAKES
100g (3½oz) MEDIUM OATMEAL
100g (3½oz) FINE-GROUND
   OATMEAL
pinch of BICARBONATE OF SODA
2 tsp melted LARD
PLAIN FLOUR, for dusting

FOR THE SOUP
45g (1½oz) UNSALTED BUTTER
1 ONION, chopped
1 small POTATO, peeled and diced
1 tsp VITAMIN C POWDER
350g (12oz) SORREL, stalks
   removed and leaves chopped
1 small, round LETTUCE, leaves
   separated and chopped
20g (¾oz) CHERVIL, chopped
900ml (1½ pints)
   VEGETABLE STOCK
4–6 tbsp DOUBLE CREAM
300g (10oz) fresh SALMON
   FILLET, skinned and diced
2 tbsp chopped DILL

1 For the stock, put all the vegetables and herbs in a heavy pan, cover with 900ml (1½ pints) water and add seasoning. Bring to the boil and simmer for 30 minutes, then strain. Set aside until needed.

2 To make the oatcakes, preheat the oven to 160°C (325°F/Gas 3). Mix the dry ingredients together, add the lard and 3 tablespoons of water, and draw together to form a dough.

3 Dust the work surface with flour and roll out the dough to a thickness of 5mm (¼in). Cut out rounds with a 6cm (2½in) biscuit cutter and transfer to a non-stick baking tray. Bake for 25 minutes until crisp, then leave to cool.

4 Meanwhile, make the soup. Melt the butter in a pan, then add the onion and potato and soften for 5 minutes – do not allow them to brown.

5 Add the vitamin C powder, sorrel, lettuce, and chervil and cook for 1–2 minutes until the leaves have wilted. Add the vegetable stock, then remove from the heat and purée in batches in a blender. Return to the pan, add the cream and seasoning to taste, and reheat. Transfer to a jug.

6 Combine the salmon and dill in a bowl, then divide between 4 soup bowls. Pour the soup around the salmon – the residual heat is sufficient to cook it. Serve with the oatcakes.

FISHCAKES WITH TARTARE SAUCE
Tim Lovejoy television presenter and 2011 Celebrity semi-finalist

PREPARATION TIME
10 minutes

COOKING TIME
35 minutes

SERVES 4

FOR THE TARTARE SAUCE
4 tbsp MAYONNAISE
2 tsp CAPERS
1 tsp ENGLISH MUSTARD
1 tsp CREAMED HORSERADISH
1 tbsp chopped DILL

FOR THE FISHCAKES
400g (14oz) SMOKED HADDOCK
    FILLET, cut into 3 pieces
2 tbsp OLIVE OIL

4 LARGE POTATOES, cut in chunks
1 tbsp snipped CHIVES
SALT and freshly ground
    BLACK PEPPER
100g (3½oz) PLAIN FLOUR
2 EGGS, beaten
200g (7oz) WHITE BREADCRUMBS
VEGETABLE OIL, for shallow-frying

1 Mix the tartare sauce ingredients together, then set aside.
2 Rinse and dry the haddock on kitchen paper. Heat the olive oil in a frying pan and gently fry the fish for 3 minutes on each side until cooked. Remove from the pan. When cool, flake the fish into a bowl, discarding the skin.
3 Boil the potatoes in a large pan of salted water until soft. Drain thoroughly, then mash.
4 Add the mashed potatoes to the fish with the chives. Season to taste with salt and pepper.
5 Divide the mixture into eight and shape into patties. Dust each fishcake with the flour and shake off the excess. Coat in the beaten egg, then the breadcrumbs.
6 Heat the vegetable oil in a large frying pan, then gently fry the fishcakes for 2–3 minutes on each side until golden. Drain on kitchen paper. Serve hot with the tartare sauce.

Simplify for **EVERY**DAY

• You can use flaked canned salmon or tuna to make quick fishcakes in the same way as this. • Bought good-quality tartare sauce, laced with a little chopped or dried dill, makes a quick alternative too.

MACKEREL TARTARE
Phil Vickery MBE England rugby player and 2011 Celebrity champion

PREPARATION TIME
15 minutes

COOKING TIME
5 minutes

SERVES 4

4 fresh MACKEREL FILLETS, all
  bones removed
6 CHIVES, finely snipped
1 SPRING ONION, finely chopped
¾ RED CHILLI, deseeded and
  finely chopped
¾ RED ONION, finely chopped
2–3 GARLIC cloves, crushed
2 LEMONS
SALT and freshly ground
  BLACK PEPPER

8 BAGUETTE slices, sliced on
  the angle as thinly as possible
2 tbsp OLIVE OIL
1 tsp HARISSA paste
3 tbsp VEGETABLE OIL
1 AVOCADO, peeled, stoned,
  halved, and thinly sliced
1 small pack MICRO PEA SHOOTS
1 small pack MICRO PURPLE BASIL
1 small pack MICRO CHIVES

1 Preheat the oven to 190°C (375°F/Gas 5). Skin the mackerel and chop into 5mm (¼in) cubes.

2 Place the mackerel in a bowl and add the chives, spring onion, chilli, onion, garlic, the zest of 1½ lemons and the juice of 1. Season to taste and place in the fridge until needed.

3 Place the slices of bread on a flat baking tray – they must not overlap, so use 2 trays if necessary. Drizzle the bread with olive oil and place in the oven. Bake for 3–5 minutes until golden and crisp. Remove to a cooling rack.

4 Mix the harissa paste with the vegetable oil.

5 To serve, paint a streak of the harissa oil across each plate before laying a chef's ring down. Spoon in a good amount of the tartare and push down. Remove the ring. Top the tartare with the avocado and garnish with an assortment of the micro herbs. Lay 2 slices of crisp, golden baguette, to the side of each plate.

GREGG WALLACE
"It's really light, it's really refreshing."

MUSHROOM AND TRUFFLE RISOTTO WITH BASIL OIL AND PARMESAN CRISPS
James Perry MasterChef 2011 final 5

PREPARATION TIME
15 minutes

COOKING TIME
1 hour 25 minutes

SERVES 4

JOHN TORODE

"Really nicely presented dish, I love the tang of the basil around the outside of it."

FOR THE STOCK
100g (3½oz) CHESTNUT MUSHROOMS, coarsely chopped
1 small LEEK, white part only, cut into chunks
1 small CARROT, coarsely chopped
1 small CELERY stick, coarsely chopped
2 GARLIC cloves, coarsely chopped
4 tbsp WHITE WINE
1 BAY LEAF
1 small ONION, quartered

FOR THE RISOTTO
2 tbsp OLIVE OIL
50g (1¾oz) BUTTER
1 large BANANA SHALLOT, finely chopped
225g (8oz) ARBORIO RICE
5 tbsp DRY WHITE WINE

100g (3½oz) CHANTERELLE MUSHROOMS
1 BLACK SUMMER TRUFFLE, from a jar, finely sliced
1 tbsp finely chopped PARSLEY, plus 4 leaves
SALT and freshly ground BLACK PEPPER

FOR THE PARMESAN CRISPS
4 tbsp finely grated PARMESAN CHEESE

FOR THE BASIL OIL
25g (scant 1oz) BASIL
75ml (2½fl oz) EXTRA VIRGIN OLIVE OIL
pinch of SALT

1 Place all of the stock ingredients in a large pot, with 1 litre (3¾ pints) water and bring to the boil. Reduce the heat and simmer for 45 minutes. Strain and keep warm.

2 In a large pan, heat the olive oil and half the butter, add the shallot, and sweat gently until softened. Add the rice, ensuring you coat every grain in oil before adding the wine. When the wine is almost completely reduced, start to add the stock, one ladle at a time, stirring continuously.

3 Preheat the oven to 180°C (350°F/Gas 4). While the risotto is cooking, make the Parmesan crisps. Line a baking tray with non-stick baking parchment and place 1 tbsp of grated Parmesan on top. Gently spread out to form a rough circle of about 6–7cm (2½–2¾in) in diameter. Repeat with the remaining Parmesan to make 4 circles. Bake for 5 minutes, or until the cheese is bubbling, then remove from the oven and leave to cool.

4 Sauté the chanterelles in the remaining butter and season them. Ten minutes before the risotto finishes cooking, add the truffle, parsley, and chanterelles, and check the seasoning.

5 Bring a pan of water to the boil, add the basil, and blanche for 6 seconds, then refresh in iced water. Dry off and place in a food processor with the olive oil and a pinch of salt, and blitz. Strain into a squeezy bottle. Serve the risotto on a plate. Top with a Parmesan crisp and parsley leaf. Drizzle the basil oil around.

BEETROOT TASTING PLATE
Annie Assheton MasterChef 2011 final 6

PREPARATION TIME
40 minutes, plus chilling

COOKING TIME
1 hour 30 minutes

SERVES 4

Beetroot tarte tatin

2 raw BABY BEETROOT,
  4cm (1½in) in diameter
60g (2oz) PLAIN FLOUR
60g (2oz) WHOLEMEAL FLOUR
SALT and freshly ground
  BLACK PEPPER
60g (2oz) UNSALTED BUTTER,
  plus extra for greasing

25g (scant 1oz) CHEDDAR
  CHEESE, grated
4 sprigs of THYME
1 EGG YOLK
2 tbsp BALSAMIC VINEGAR
30g (1oz) SUGAR

1 Twist the tops off the beetroot and put the beetroot in a large saucepan. Cover with boiling water and simmer until tender, for about 30 minutes.
2 While the beetroot are cooking, make the pastry. Put the flour, a pinch of salt, 30g (1oz) butter, cubed, the cheese, and the leaves from 2 sprigs of thyme into a food processor, and pulse until combined. Add the egg yolk and process again until the mixture comes together, adding a dash of cold water if necessary. Wrap the mixture in cling film and rest in the fridge for 20 minutes.
3 When the beetroot are cooked and have cooled enough to handle, slip off the skins and slice in half horizontally.
4 Put the balsamic vinegar, remaining butter, sugar, and salt and pepper into a large frying pan and heat gently until the sugar has dissolved. Add the halved beetroot and the remaining thyme sprigs and turn up the heat so that the mixture simmers and starts to caramelize. After a few minutes, turn the beetroot over and cook again until they start to colour.
5 Preheat the oven to 200°C (400°F/Gas 6). Grease a muffin tin with a little butter. Put a piece of beetroot into each recess of the tin, adding 1 tsp of the balsamic caramel to each one. Roll out the pastry on a lightly floured surface and stamp out rounds just bigger than the holes of the tin. Sit a round of pastry on each piece of beetroot, tucking it in so that the beetroot is partly encased. Put into the oven for 10–15 minutes until the pastry is golden. Leave to rest for 5 minutes and then turn out onto a board.

Simplify for EVERYDAY

• Use ready-cooked natural baby beetroot for all the dishes (not ones preserved in vinegar).
• For the soup, use ready-made vegetable stock (either fresh or concentrate). • Buy good-quality ready-made hot horseradish cream, instead of making your own, and stir in ½ tsp dried dill.

Beetroot and apple soup

FOR THE VEGETABLE STOCK
1 ONION, chopped
2 CARROTS, chopped
2 CELERY sticks, chopped
1 GARLIC bulb, halved horizontally
1 bulb of FENNEL, chopped
5 PEPPERCORNS
SALT
1 BAY LEAF
sprig of ROSEMARY
sprig of THYME

FOR THE SOUP
1 tbsp OLIVE OIL
knob of BUTTER
1 large ONION, chopped
1 GARLIC clove, chopped

375g (13oz) large BEETROOT,
   peeled and cut into small cubes
2 EATING APPLES, peeled, cored,
   and chopped
1 large TOMATO
400ml (14fl oz) VEGETABLE STOCK
1 tbsp CRÈME FRAÎCHE
SALT and freshly ground
   BLACK PEPPER

1 First, make the vegetable stock by putting all the ingredients into a pan and covering with 1 litre (1¾ pints) cold water. Bring to the boil and then simmer for at least 10 minutes. Leave to cool a little, then drain through a colander into a measuring jug, pressing all the moisture out of the cooked vegetables, using the back of a spoon.
2 For the soup, heat the oil and butter in a large saucepan until foaming, then add the onion and garlic and cook gently for 5 minutes, or until soft but not coloured. Add the beetroot, apples, whole tomato, and stock, bring to the boil, and simmer for 30 minutes, or until the beetroot is tender. Remove the tomato, then blitz with a hand-held blender and pass through a sieve. Put back into the pan and stir in the crème fraîche. Season to taste with salt and pepper.

Beetroot and walnut hummus

125g (4½oz) raw BABY BEETROOT
25g (scant 1oz) WALNUTS
1½ tsp CUMIN SEEDS
1 tbsp DRY WHITE BREADCRUMBS
1½ tsp TAHINI
1 GARLIC clove
juice of ½ LEMON

SALT and freshly ground
   BLACK PEPPER
1 tbsp WALNUT OIL
1½ tsp SUNFLOWER OIL
1½ tsp SHERRY VINEGAR
2 LITTLE GEM LETTUCES,
   leaves separated

1 Preheat the oven to 200°C (400°F/Gas 6). Twist off the beetroot
tops and put the beetroot into a saucepan. Cover with boiling
water and simmer until tender, for about 30 minutes, depending on
their size. When cooked, drain, and when cool enough to handle,
slip off their skins. Cut into cubes and leave to cool.
2 Put the walnuts on a flat baking tray and toast for 5 minutes
in the oven, then leave to cool. Toast the cumin seeds for a few
minutes in a dry frying pan, until beginning to colour. Grind the
seeds thoroughly with a pestle and mortar. Put the breadcrumbs,
cooked beetroot, ground cumin, walnuts, tahini, garlic, and
lemon juice in a food processor and blitz until smooth. Season
with salt and pepper and adjust to taste with more lemon juice,
spices, or tahini.
3 Make a dressing with the oils, vinegar, and seasoning. Select 4
perfect small leaves from the Little Gem lettuces, slicing the back
if necessary to make them sit nicely on the plate.

Horseradish cream

75g (2½oz) fresh
   HORSERADISH ROOT
150ml (5fl oz) SOURED CREAM
10g (¼oz) SUGAR

squeeze of LEMON JUICE
2 tsp chopped DILL
SALT and freshly ground
   BLACK PEPPER

1 Peel and finely grate the horseradish and combine with the
soured cream. Leave to infuse for 5 minutes before passing
through a sieve, pressing down well to extract all the flavour
from the horseradish. Stir in the sugar, lemon juice, and dill,
and season to taste with the salt and pepper. Put into a
piping bag, fitted with a plain nozzle, and chill until needed.

TO SERVE
Pour the soup into shot glasses and make quenelles of the
hummus with 2 teaspoons. Brush some dressing onto the
lettuce leaves, and sit a quenelle of hummus on each one. Place
a tart, shot glass, and hummus leaf on each plate. Pipe a blob
of horseradish cream in between the hummus leaf and tart.

SCOTCH QUAIL'S EGG WITH PICCALILLI
Tim Lovejoy television presenter and 2011 Celebrity semi-finalist

PREPARATION TIME
25 minutes

COOKING TIME
40 minutes

SERVES 4

"The hardest
thing is my lack
of knowledge
and skills – I'm
having to sort
of try and do it
through guessing
and instinct."

FOR THE SCOTCH QUAIL'S EGG
8 QUAIL'S EGGS
200g (7oz) SAUSAGEMEAT
1 tbsp chopped PARSLEY
1 tbsp chopped THYME LEAVES
6 SPRING ONIONS,
  finely chopped
SALT and freshly ground
  BLACK PEPPER
200g (7oz) PLAIN FLOUR
2 EGGS, beaten
150g (5½oz) dry WHITE
  BREADCRUMBS
VEGETABLE OIL, for
  deep frying

FOR THE PICCALILLI
½ head of CAULIFLOWER
150g (5½oz) GREEN BEANS
½ CUCUMBER
100g (3½oz) PICKLED
  SILVERSKIN ONIONS
100g (3½oz) small GHERKINS
600ml (1 pint) MALT VINEGAR
1 tbsp ENGLISH MUSTARD
  POWDER
3 tbsp PLAIN FLOUR
thumb-sized piece of FRESH
  GINGER, grated
1 tbsp ground TURMERIC

1   Boil the quail's eggs for 1 minute, then drain and run under cold water until completely cool. Peel the eggs and set aside.
2   In a bowl, mix the sausagemeat with the parsley, thyme, and spring onions and season with salt and pepper. Divide the sausagemeat mixture into 8 equal-sized balls and flatten them out into ovals. Place a quail's egg on each oval and wrap the sausagemeat around each egg.
3   Put the flour, beaten egg, and breadcrumbs in three separate dishes. Dip each sausagemeat-coated egg in the flour, then shake off any excess. Next, dip in the beaten egg, rolling to coat completely and then cover completely in the breadcrumbs.
4   Heat the vegetable oil in a deep pan and fry the Scotch eggs for 4–5 minutes, until golden brown.
5   To make the piccalilli, cut the vegetables into small shapes, all about the same size.
6   Place the vinegar in a pan, bring to the boil, and simmer for 10–15 minutes to reduce it. Mix together the mustard, flour, ginger, and turmeric. Whisk into the vinegar and stir on low heat for 2–3 minutes until thick.
7   Add the vegetables to the thickened sauce, then remove from the heat and allow to cool completely.
8   To serve, put two Scotch eggs on each plate, one halved to display the inside. Spoon the piccalilli alongside.

ROASTED PEPPER AND TOMATO SOUP
WITH WARM ROSEMARY SCONES

Justin Ryan property developer and 2011 Celebrity contestant

PREPARATION TIME
20 minutes

COOKING TIME
50 minutes

SERVES 4

FOR THE SCONES
225g (8oz) SELF-RAISING FLOUR
½ tsp SALT
1 tsp BAKING POWDER
2 tsp chopped ROSEMARY
50g (1¾oz) BUTTER
150ml (5fl oz) MILK
1 EGG, beaten, to glaze

FOR THE SOUP
1 ONION, quartered
4 GARLIC cloves
2 RED PEPPERS, deseeded
  and quartered

2 YELLOW PEPPERS, deseeded
  and quartered
3 tbsp OLIVE OIL
grated zest and juice
  of 1 ORANGE
400g can CHOPPED TOMATOES
SALT and freshly ground
  BLACK PEPPER
150ml (5fl oz) DOUBLE CREAM
1½ tbsp snipped CHIVES

1 For the scones, preheat the oven to 230°C (450°F/Gas 8) and grease a baking tray.

2 Sift the flour, salt, and baking powder in a bowl. Add the rosemary and then rub in the butter until the mixture is the consistency of breadcrumbs. Finally, add the milk to form a dough.

3 Knead the dough briefly on a floured surface until it is smooth. Roll it out to a thickness of 1.5cm (½in) and cut out discs about 7.5cm (3in) diameter. Brush with the beaten egg, place on the baking tray, and bake for 8–10 minutes until risen and golden. Transfer to a wire rack, and serve whilst still warm.

4 Meanwhile, make the soup. Preheat the oven to 200°C (400°F/Gas 6). Place the onion, garlic, and red and yellow peppers in a roasting tin. Drizzle all over with the olive oil and roast for 30 minutes until the vegetables are charred.

5 Remove from the oven and blitz in a blender with the orange zest and juice, tomatoes, and 600ml (1 pint) water. Press through a sieve into a saucepan. Season with salt and pepper and heat thoroughly.

6 Ladle the soup into bowls and add a large drizzle of the cream and some snipped chives. Serve with the warm rosemary scones.

When buying peppers, look for ones that are glossy and heavy, with a stalk that looks moist and as if it has been freshly cut. Avoid any with soft patches of flesh.

DUO OF SAVOY-WRAPPED YELLOW AND RED PEPPER BAKE WITH AUBERGINES À LA PARMIGIANA AND RATATOUILLE

Sara Danesin Medio MasterChef 2011 finalist

PREPARATION TIME
35 minutes

COOKING TIME
1 hour 35 minutes

SERVES 6

FOR THE PEPPER BAKE
1 RED PEPPER, deseeded and finely diced
1 YELLOW PEPPER, deseeded and finely diced
1 BANANA SHALLOT, finely chopped
1 tbsp OLIVE OIL
SALT and freshly ground BLACK PEPPER
1 sprig of THYME, leaves only
2 EGGS
60g (2oz) PARMESAN CHEESE, finely grated
150ml (5fl oz) DOUBLE CREAM
9 large SAVOY CABBAGE, leaves, thick stalks removed
BUTTER, for greasing

FOR THE RATATOUILLE
1 ITALIAN AUBERGINE, diced into 1cm (½in) cubes
1 GARLIC clove, crushed
1 tbsp OLIVE OIL
75g (2½oz) TAGGIASCHE OLIVES, pitted
small bunch of BASIL leaves, chopped

FOR THE AUBERGINES
3 ITALIAN AUBERGINES
SALT
VEGETABLE OIL, for deep frying
1 ONION, finely chopped
1 tbsp OLIVE OIL
1kg (2¼lb) SAN MARZANO or PLUM TOMATOES, skinned, deseeded, and diced
small bunch of BASIL, leaves chopped
2 BUFFALO MOZZARELLA CHEESES, sliced
100g (3½oz) PARMESAN CHEESE shavings

FOR THE PESTO
85g (3oz) BASIL leaves, plus extra for garnish
1 GARLIC clove
4 tbsp PINE NUTS
8 tbsp EXTRA VIRGIN OLIVE OIL
4 tbsp grated PARMESAN CHEESE, plus extra for garnish
pinch of SALT

TO SERVE
200g (7oz) TOMBERRRIES
small handfuls of MICRO CRESS
small handfuls of PEA SHOOTS

1 Preheat the oven to 180°C (350°F/Gas 4). Make the pepper bake. Sauté the peppers and shallot in the olive oil for around 30 minutes until soft, occasionally adding a splash of water if the mixture becomes too dry. Season to taste and add the thyme leaves, then leave to cool. Once the mixture has cooled, blitz until smooth in a food processor and pass through a fine sieve.
2 Whisk together the eggs, Parmesan cheese, and cream, then add the pepper purée and mix well.
3 Blanch the cabbage leaves for 2 minutes in boiling water, then refresh in iced water. Pat dry on a clean tea towel.

4 Lightly butter 6 dariole moulds and line with the cabbage leaves so they hang over the edges. Fill each lined mould with the pepper mixture until two-thirds full, then wrap the overhanging cabbage leaves over the top to make loose parcels. Loosely cover the top of each parcel with foil, then place in a roasting tin. Add hot water to the tin so that it comes halfway up the sides of the dariole moulds. Bake in the oven for 25–30 minutes until the parcels are firm and bouncy to the touch. Rest in a warm place until serving.

5 For the ratatouille, sauté the aubergines in a pan with the garlic in a little olive oil until golden. Add the olives and basil and season to taste. Set aside until serving.

6 For the aubergines, slice into 5mm (¼in) thick slices, then sprinkle with salt and leave to rest for 10 minutes. Pat dry and deep fry in batches at 180°C (350°F/Gas 4) until golden, then drain on kitchen paper. Gently fry the onion in a little olive oil until soft, then add the tomatoes. Cook for 20–25 minutes until reduced and thickened, then add the chopped basil.

7 Place six 6cm (2½in) diameter, deep cooking rings onto a non-stick baking tray. Layer the aubergine slices, mozzarella cheese, tomato sauce, and Parmesan cheese inside the rings until full, seasoning to taste as you go. Bake for 30 minutes until the cheese is bubbling and golden. Leave to rest for a few minutes before serving.

8 For the pesto, place all the pesto ingredients with a pinch of salt into a small food processor and blitz until smooth.

9 To serve, skewer the tomberries on 6 small skewers. Turn out the Savoy bakes onto 6 warm serving plates. Put an Aubergine à la Parmigiana alongside each. Add a spoonful of ratatouille and top with a tomberry skewer. Garnish the plates with a little micro cress and pea shoots, and serve straight away.

SARA'S DUO OF PEPPERS SIMPLIFIED FOR **EVERY**DAY... ▶ PAGE 102

RATATOUILLE BAKE

THIS RATATOUILLE-STYLE VEGETABLE BAKE IS A SIMPLE VARIATION OF SARA'S PEPPERS, AND IS SERVED WITH A TASTY PESTO DRESSING **PREP: 35–40 MINS • COOK: 40–45 MINS**

THE BAKE

SERVES 4

I small RED and YELLOW PEPPER, each cored, deseeded, and diced into 2cm (¾in) cubes
½ small AUBERGINE, diced into 2cm (¾in) cubes
1 small RED ONION, diced
3 tbsp OLIVE OIL
60g (2oz) pitted BLACK OLIVES, roughly chopped
60g (2oz) sun-blush TOMATOES, chopped
SALT and freshly ground BLACK PEPPER
25g (scant 1oz) PARMESAN cheese, freshly grated
1 ball BUFFALO MOZZARELLA, drained and diced
32 large BASIL leaves

1 Preheat the oven to 200°C (400°/Gas 6). Mix the peppers and aubergine in a roasting tin, pour the oil over and roast for 15 minutes. Add the onion and cook for a further 20 minutes.
2 Transfer the vegetables to a bowl then stir in the remaining ingredients except the basil.
3 Oil 4 large ramekins and line with the basil leaves. Spoon in the ratatouille mix, keeping the leaves in place around the sides, then press down slightly to compact. Place on a baking tray and cook in the oven for a further 10 minutes. Leave the bakes to cool slightly.

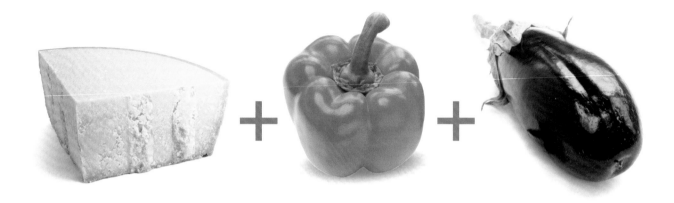

...SERVE WITH

PESTO DRESSING

25g (scant 1oz) fresh BASIL leaves
2 tbsp PINE NUTS
1 tbsp freshly grated PARMESAN CHEESE
1 GARLIC clove
4 tbsp OLIVE OIL
SALT and freshly ground BLACK PEPPER

1 To make the pesto, combine the basil, pine nuts, Parmesan, and garlic in a small food processor or spice grinder and process until finely chopped. Add the oil and seasoning to taste and process again until well mixed.
2 Turn the bakes out onto warmed serving plates and serve straight away with a spoonful of the pesto alongside.

TRIO OF DUMPLINGS
Jackie Kearney MasterChef 2011 final 4

PREPARATION TIME
4 hours

COOKING TIME
2 hours 15 minutes

SERVES 4

"I'm trying to represent some of the things that I have learned as well as being true to the street food that I love."

POT STICKER DUMPLING FILLING
20g (¾oz) FRESH GINGER, shredded
1 SPRING ONION, shredded
1 tbsp GROUNDNUT OIL
50g (1¾oz) SHIITAKE MUSHROOMS, finely chopped
50g (1¾oz) ENOKI MUSHROOMS, finely chopped
50g (1¾oz) OYSTER MUSHROOMS, finely chopped
1–2 tsp LIGHT SOY SAUCE, or to taste
1½ tsp SHAOXING RICE WINE
¾ tsp SALT
½ tsp SUGAR
2 pinches of WHITE PEPPER
1½ tsp SESAME OIL
50g (1¾oz) SMOKED TOFU, crumbled

POT STICKER DUMPLING DOUGH
125g (4½oz) DUMPLING FLOUR
5 tbsp boiling WATER
POTATO FLOUR, for dusting

GLASSY DUMPLING DOUGH
125g (4½oz) DUMPLING FLOUR
4 tbsp ice-cold WATER
POTATO FLOUR, for dusting

HOISIN GLAZE
6 tbsp DARK SOY SAUCE
2–3 tbsp BLACK BEAN PASTE
1–2 tbsp CLEAR HONEY
2 tsp SHAOXING RICE WINE VINEGAR
8 tsp GARLIC POWDER
2 tsp SESAME SEED OIL
1 tbsp hot CHILLI PASTE

LIME AND GINGER-GLAZED BLACK BEANS
2 tbsp TAMARI
100g (3½oz) CASTER SUGAR
juice of 1 LIME
150g (5½oz) GINGER-PRESERVED BLACK BEANS

MISO DAUPHINOISE FILLING
4 large MARIS PIPER POTATOES, peeled and sliced
8 tbsp WHITE MISO PASTE
200ml (7fl oz) DOUBLE CREAM
8 sheets VIETNAMESE RICE PAPER

GLASSY STEAMED DUMPLING FILLING
200g (7oz) PORK RIBS
5 tbsp SHAOXING RICE WINE
50g (1¾oz) CHOY SUM
100g (3½oz) PORK MINCE
1 tbsp GROUNDNUT OIL
1 tbsp SESAME OIL
4 SCALLOP CORALS
SALT and WHITE PEPPER

DUMPLING STOCK
1 LEEK, roughly chopped
1 WHITE ONION, roughly chopped
2 CELERY sticks, roughly chopped
2 CARROTS, roughly chopped
1 FENNEL bulb, roughly chopped
6 GARLIC cloves
1 tbsp BLACK PEPPERCORNS
8 JUNIPER BERRIES, lightly crushed
2 STAR ANISE
1 tbsp CORIANDER SEEDS
2 BAY LEAVES
small sprig of THYME
small sprig of PARSLEY
4 tbsp DRY WHITE WINE
juice of ½ LEMON

FRITTERS
25g (scant 1oz) RICE FLOUR
75g (2½oz) CORNFLOUR
1 tsp BAKING POWDER
100ml (3½fl oz) SPARKLING WATER

FRITTERS (CONTINUED)
freshly ground BLACK PEPPER
50g (1¾oz) BEANSPROUTS
25g (scant 1oz) PRESERVED
   BLACK BEANS
100g (3½oz) NAPA CABBAGE, finely
   shredded
25g (scant 1oz) CHINESE
   BLACK MOSS
bunch of CORIANDER, finely chopped

1 tbsp SZECHUAN PEPPERCORNS,
   crushed
VEGETABLE OIL, for deep frying

GARNISH
reserved inner leaves and flowers
   from CHOY SUM
small handful of PEA SHOOTS

1 Preheat the oven to 180°C (350°F/Gas 4). Put the pork ribs in a heavy saucepan or casserole with the Shaoxing wine. Cover with a lid and braise over a low heat for 2 hours.
2 For the pot sticker dumpling filling, crush the ginger and spring onion with a cleaver blade and leave to soak in 3 tbsp water.
3 To prepare the doughs for the pot sticker and glassy dumplings, mix together the flour and water for each in 2 separate bowls. Season both with a little salt. Remove the doughs from the bowls and knead each for 10 minutes. Leave to rest for 30 minutes.
4 Whisk together the ingredients for the hoisin glaze and heat gently. Add water or honey as needed to make a thick syrupy glaze and adjust proportions to taste. Leave to cool until needed.
5 For the lime and ginger-glazed black beans, put the tamari, sugar, and lime juice in a pan and bring to the boil. Reduce by half until sticky. Add the black beans and coat with glaze. Leave to cool until needed.
6 To prepare the miso dauphinoise, line a small, deep baking tray with baking parchment and layer the potato on top. Mix together the miso paste and cream and pour over the potatoes. Press down and leave for 10 minutes before pressing down again. Cover with foil and bake in the oven for 45 minutes. Remove the foil and cook until golden brown. Leave to cool, then refrigerate until needed.
7 Put all the stock ingredients except the wine and lemon juice into a pan. Bring to the boil and simmer for 15 minutes. Add the wine and lemon juice, then strain through a fine sieve and cool.
8 Lightly sauté the mushrooms for the pot sticker dumpling filling in the oil. Drain on kitchen paper, transfer to a bowl, and then add the ginger and onion water, soy sauce, rice wine, salt, sugar, white pepper, sesame oil, and tofu. Mix well and set aside.
9 For the glassy dumpling filling, reserve the inner leaves and flowers from the choy sum and blanch the outer leaves in boiling water for 20 seconds. Drain, squeeze out excess water, and chop finely. Shred the pork rib meat. Mix with the choy sum leaves, pork mince, groundnut oil, sesame oil, and salt and white pepper.
10 For the pot sticker dumpling, dust the work surface with potato flour. Knead the dough and roll out into a sausage shape about 2cm (¾in) thick. Break off 15g (½oz) pieces, flatten in the

palm of your hand and roll out to circles of 10cm (4in) diameter. With a damp tea towel, cover the dough you are not working with. Put a teaspoon of stuffing in the centre of one circle, fold in half, and pinch the sides together. Repeat to make 4 dumplings.

11 For the glassy dumplings, dust the work surface with potato flour. Roll out the dough into circles as above. Pile up the circles, dusting between them with potato flour. Using a wooden spoon handle, press around the edge of each circle to make the edges thinner, which will create a more frilly top. Take a teaspoonful of pork mixture, place in the centre, and bring up the edges of the pastry to enclose the stuffing, leaving an open top so that you can still see the filling. Repeat to make 4 dumplings.

12 For the miso dauphinoise, cut out four 10cm (4in) rounds of miso potato. Soften the rice papers by dipping them in very hot water for 10 seconds. Place a round of potato between 2 sheets of rice paper, then press down to seal. Use a 10cm (4in) cutter to trim the size of the dumpling. Repeat to make 4 dumplings.

13 To cook the miso potato dumplings, pour some stock into a baking tray and add the dumplings. Add more stock until it comes halfway up the side of the dumplings. Bake at 180°C (350°F/Gas 4) for 12 minutes, then remove and drain on kitchen paper.

14 To cook the glassy steamed dumplings, place a bamboo steamer, lined with a small piece of lightly oiled greaseproof paper, over a pan of simmering water. Add the dumplings and steam for 3 minutes. Remove the lid, sprinkle with a little water to wash away any excess potato flour, then steam for a further 3 minutes. Meanwhile, pan fry the scallop corals in a little groundnut oil until firm, then slice into fine strips. Lay the strips of coral on top of the steamed dumplings just before serving.

15 To cook the pot stickers, heat a little groundnut oil in a frying pan, add the dumplings and fry for 2 minutes. Add 2 tbsp water and immediately cover the dumplings with a lid. Steam for 4–5 minutes. Remove the lid and continue to fry for a further 2 minutes, then remove from the pan and drain on kitchen paper.

16 For the fritters, mix the rice flour, cornflour and baking powder in a large bowl. Whisk in the water to make a batter of the consistency of double cream. Season with salt and pepper. Add the beansprouts, black beans, cabbage, black moss, coriander, and Szechuan peppercorns, and mix until combined. Heat the oil to 180°C (350°F) and carefully add dessertspoons of fritter mixture. Deep fry in batches for 2–3 minutes until golden and crisp. Remove from the oil and drain on kitchen paper.

17 To serve, place 2 fritters on each plate. Drizzle a zigzag of the hoisin glaze across the plate and place one of each of the dumplings in a line through the centre of the zigzag. Place several glazed black beans around the plate. Garnish with pea shoots and reserved leaves and flowers from the choy sum.

SPICED VEGETARIAN HAGGIS PARCEL WITH SCOTTISH POTATO SCONE, WHISKY CREAM SAUCE, NEEP 'N' TATTIE CRISPS, AND WEE DRAM PEARLS

Alice Taylor MasterChef 2011 contestant

PREPARATION TIME
20 minutes

COOKING TIME
1 hour 15 minutes

SERVES 4

"Even as a meat-eater I really like this dish. It's lots of pulses and beans and nuts."

FOR THE STOCK
1 small LEEK, roughly chopped
1 ONION, chopped
4 CELERY sticks, roughly chopped
1 CARROT, roughly chopped
2 BAY LEAVES
6 BLACK PEPPERCORNS

FOR THE POTATO SCONES
250g (9oz) FLOURY POTATOES, peeled and cut into chunks
SALT and freshly ground BLACK PEPPER
50g (1¾oz) SELF-RAISING FLOUR
1 tbsp OLIVE OIL

FOR THE HAGGIS PARCEL
1 small VEGETARIAN HAGGIS
SALT and freshly ground BLACK PEPPER
small pinch of DRIED PARSLEY
small pinch of GROUND NUTMEG
small pinch of CAYENNE PEPPER
4 large leaves from a SAVOY CABBAGE

FOR THE SAUCE
120ml (4fl oz) WHISKY
375ml (13fl oz) VEGETABLE STOCK
1 tsp GRAINY MUSTARD
175ml (6fl oz) DOUBLE CREAM
small knob of BUTTER
SALT and freshly ground BLACK PEPPER

FOR THE WEE DRAM PEARLS
150ml (5½fl oz) WHISKY
pinch of SODIUM ALGINATE
1 tsp CALCIUM LACTATE

FOR THE CRISPS
VEGETABLE OIL, for deep frying
1 large FLOURY POTATO, peeled into wide ribbons
1 small SWEDE, peeled into wide ribbons

TO GARNISH
sprigs of CHERVIL

1 First make the stock by putting the vegetables, bay leaves, and black peppercorns in a large pan and covering with water. Bring to the boil, then reduce the heat and simmer for about 30 minutes. Strain and set aside.

2 For the scones, boil the potatoes for 15–20 minutes until soft, then mash until smooth. Season with the salt and pepper, gradually add the flour, and knead until the mixture is soft and no longer sticky. Turn the mixture out onto a lightly floured surface and knead gently until smooth. Roll out the dough to a thickness of around 5mm (¼in), then cut out 7cm (2¾in) rounds using a pastry cutter. Preheat a griddle pan over medium heat. Rub each scone with a little olive oil, then griddle for 2 minutes on each side. Keep warm until serving.

3 Empty the haggis into a bowl and season with salt, pepper, dried parsley, ground nutmeg, and cayenne pepper to taste. Blanch the cabbage leaves in boiling water for 2 minutes and then refresh in iced water. Drain and firmly cover with a clean tea towel to remove any excess moisture. Take each leaf and fill with a small sausage-shaped piece of haggis, then roll up tightly. Roll each parcel in cling film and set aside to be steamed later.

4 To make the sauce, heat the whisky in a saucepan for 2 minutes until the alcohol has burnt off. Add the stock and mustard, then simmer for 20 minutes until reduced. Add the cream and butter and season with salt and pepper. Reheat gently before serving.

5 For the wee dram pearls, heat the whisky in a small saucepan and reduce to 100ml (3½fl oz). Leave to cool completely. Add the sodium alginate to the reduced whisky, then blitz with a hand-held blender or in a liquidizer. Whisk the calcium lactate into 200ml (7fl oz) water in a bowl, until completely dissolved.

6 Fill a plastic syringe with the whisky mixture and carefully drop single droplets into the calcium lactate mixture. Lift out the pearls with a small slotted spoon and transfer to a bowl of plain water. Just before serving, remove from the water with a small slotted spoon to use as a garnish.

7 For the crisps, heat the oil for deep frying to 180°C (350°F). Pat the potato and swede dry on kitchen paper. Deep fry them until crisp and golden and drain on kitchen paper. Season with salt while still warm.

8 Place the haggis parcels in a steamer and steam for 8 minutes. Unwrap them, then cut diagonally in half.

9 Place a potato scone in the centre of each plate with a haggis parcel on top. Serve with the crisps and sauce and garnish with the pearls and a sprig of chervil.

MAINS

SANG CHOY BAO CHICKEN WRAPS

Colin McAllister property developer and 2011 Celebrity contestant

PREPARATION TIME
20 minutes
COOKING TIME
5 minutes

SERVES 4

"It's an Asian
street meal, a
chicken stir fry
that should be a
nice little bite-size
bit of perfection."

250g (9oz) boneless,
  skinless CHICKEN BREAST
  or THIGHS, roughly chopped
1 tsp CORNFLOUR
1 tsp SOY SAUCE
1 tbsp VEGETABLE OIL
1 ONION, finely chopped
50g (1¾oz) CHINESE SAUSAGE,
  cut into 5mm (¼in) pieces
2 GARLIC cloves, finely chopped
1 tbsp SUGAR

pinch of SALT
1 EGG, lightly beaten
4 tbsp finely snipped YELLOW or
  GREEN CHIVES, plus whole ones
  to garnish
1 tbsp finely chopped CORIANDER
1 tbsp chopped PICKLED GINGER
HOISIN SAUCE, for dipping
6 ICEBERG LETTUCE leaves,
  torn in half

1 Place the chicken, cornflour, and soy sauce in a food processor and pulse until the chicken is roughly minced. Leave to stand for 10 minutes.

2 Heat a wok or large frying pan over high heat until hot. Add the oil and swirl to coat the sides.

3 Add the onion, Chinese sausage, and garlic, and cook, stirring, for about 30 seconds until fragrant.

4 Add the chicken to the wok and stir-fry until it is no longer pink but still moist – about 3 minutes.

5 Scatter in the sugar and salt, drizzle the egg over the chicken, and cook, stirring, for about 2 minutes until both the egg and chicken are cooked through.

6 Stir in the chives, coriander, and pickled ginger and cook for a further 30 seconds, then remove the wok from the heat.

7 To serve, spoon in some of the chicken onto each halved lettuce leaf. Arranage three on each plate, and garnish with whole chives. To finish, place tiny dishes of hoisin sauce alongside. Roll the lettuce around the chicken, dip in the sauce, and eat straight away, whilst the chicken is still warm.

SUMAC AND THYME-ROASTED CHICKEN WITH SAFFRON JUS, PIMENTÓN-ROASTED POTATOES, AND GARLIC BEANS

Matthew Driver MasterChef 2011 contestant

PREPARATION TIME
10 minutes, plus marinating
COOKING TIME
40 minutes

SERVES 4

JOHN TORODE

"I really like the moistness of your chicken, and the crust with all that lemony sumac on top – it's really very, very powerful."

FOR THE CHICKEN
4 CHICKEN SUPREMES, skin on
1 tbsp SUMAC, plus extra
   to garnish
leaves from 2 sprigs of
   THYME, chopped
2 GARLIC cloves, crushed
2 tbsp OLIVE OIL
SALT and freshly ground
   BLACK PEPPER

FOR THE POTATOES
4 MARIS PIPER POTATOES, peeled
   and cut into small cubes
1 tbsp SMOKED PAPRIKA
2 tbsp OLIVE OIL

FOR THE JUS
500ml (16fl oz) fresh
   CHICKEN STOCK
pinch of SAFFRON
125g (4½oz) very cold UNSALTED
   BUTTER, cubed

TO SERVE
350g (12oz) FRENCH
   BEANS, trimmed
1 tbsp OLIVE OIL
1 tbsp finely chopped
   FLAT-LEAF PARSLEY
½ tsp finely chopped GARLIC

1 Preheat the oven to 200°C (400°F/Gas 6). Trim and score the chicken and place in a bowl with the sumac, thyme, garlic, olive oil, and salt and pepper. Ensure the chicken is coated in the mixture, then leave to marinate for at least 30 minutes.
2 Pat the potato cubes dry on kitchen paper and season with smoked paprika (pimentón), salt, and pepper. Add the olive oil to a roasting tin, then add the potato cubes and place in the oven for 20–25 minutes until crisp and golden brown.
3 Set a frying pan on a high heat. Rub the marinated chicken with a little extra oil and sear skin-side down for 5 minutes until the skin begins to crisp. Remove from the pan, dip in a little more sumac mixture, and place in a roasting tin. Roast in the oven, skin-side up, for 15 minutes. Transfer to a warm plate to rest.
4 While the chicken is roasting, place the chicken stock and saffron in a small saucepan, bring to the boil, and reduce by three-quarters until syrupy. Gradually whisk in the cold cubed butter until thickened. Season to taste and keep warm.
5 Bring a large pan of salted water to the boil, add the beans, and cook for 3 minutes until just tender. Drain and toss with the olive oil, parsley, garlic, and some seasoning.
6 To serve, carve each piece of chicken into half, sprinkle with a little sumac, and serve with the potatoes, beans, and saffron jus.

SPICY CHICKEN WITH PLANTAIN

Darren Campbell MBE Olympic champion and
2011 Celebrity contestant

PREPARATION TIME
20 minutes

COOKING TIME
45 minutes

SERVES 4

"West Indian cooking's about cooking from the soul. So yeah, I'll go out there and cook the best dish that I can cook today."

FOR THE CHICKEN
4 CHICKEN BREASTS, with skin
juice of 1 LEMON
2 tbsp OLIVE OIL
1 tbsp SCHWARTZ SEASON-ALL
2 tbsp SCHWARTZ NO ADDED
SALT CHICKEN SPECIAL
BLEND SEASONING
1 tbsp CURRY POWDER
2 ONIONS, chopped
3 GARLIC cloves, crushed
1 tbsp chopped THYME leaves
1 RED CHILLI, deseeded and finely
chopped
1 GREEN CHILLI, deseeded and
finely chopped
1 RED PEPPER, deseeded
and chopped

1 YELLOW PEPPER, deseeded
and chopped
1 GREEN PEPPER, deseeded
and chopped
3 tbsp TOMATO PURÉE
a small handful of
CORIANDER, chopped

FOR THE PLANTAIN
1 large ripe PLANTAIN
1 tbsp OLIVE OIL

FOR THE RICE
200g (7oz) BASMATI RICE
2 CLOVES
1 BAY LEAF
1 tsp OLIVE OIL

1 Wash the chicken breasts in lemon juice. Add the olive oil, seasoning, and curry powder to a frying pan and fry over medium heat. Allow the flavours to gently fuse together. Add the onions, garlic, thyme, chilli peppers, and peppers and fry for a few minutes until soft.

2 Increase the heat to high, add the chicken and fry until browned. Turn the heat down and add water to halfway up the chicken breasts. Cover and simmer for 20 minutes, then add the tomato purée. Cook for a further 10 minutes until the chicken is cooked through. Remove the chicken from the sauce and leave to rest. Finish the sauce with the coriander. Reheat to serve.

3 Cut the tips off both ends of the plantain. Make 4 lengthways slices through the skin from one end to the other. Peel the skin from the flesh sideways, cut the peeled plantain in thirds crossways, and then cut each half lengthways. Heat the oil in a pan over medium heat, add the plantain, and cook until golden.

4 Wash the rice until the water runs clear. Add the rice and 300ml (10fl oz) water to a pan with the cloves, bay leaf, and olive oil. Bring to the boil, then cover, and reduce the heat to the lowest setting. Cook for 10 minutes, then remove from the heat, leaving the lid on, for a further 10 minutes, then remove the cloves and bay leaf and fluff up the rice with a fork.

5 To serve, mound the rice on 4 warmed plates. Top with 3 plantain slices. Diagonally slice the chicken, and place on top. To finish, spoon the sauce over, and serve immediately.

DUCK BREAST BALLOTINE WRAPPED IN PANCETTA WITH A SHOT OF BEETROOT PURÉE

James Perry MasterChef 2011 final 5

PREPARATION TIME
45 minutes

COOKING TIME
20 minutes

SERVES 4

FOR THE BALLOTINE
2 large DUCK BREASTS, skinned
12 thin slices of PANCETTA
4 tbsp OLIVE OIL
60g (2oz) BUTTER
SALT and freshly ground
   BLACK PEPPER

FOR THE STUFFING
6 tbsp chopped
   FLAT-LEAF PARSLEY
2 GARLIC cloves, finely diced
2 SHALLOTS, finely diced

1 DUCK THIGH (and the reserved
   DUCK BREAST TRIMMINGS)

FOR THE BEETROOT PURÉE
250g (9oz) BEETROOT, freshly
   cooked and peeled whilst warm
1 tbsp melted BUTTER
1 tbsp DOUBLE CREAM

TO GARNISH
2 ORANGES, peeled and sliced
2 handfuls FRISÉE LETTUCE

The meat on duck breasts is dense and rich, so when beaten out and stuffed, a large one is enough for two people. Store well-wrapped in the fridge for up to 3 days.

Simplify for **EVERY**DAY

• For a quick stuffing, reconstitute about 4 tbsp dried sage and onion stuffing mix. Add some chopped fresh parsley and a crushed garlic clove. Season.
• For instant beetroot shots, whisk shop-bought beetroot juice with some cream and seasoning.

1 For the ballotine, trim off the thin tail end of the duck breasts and reserve for the stuffing.
2 Put the breasts one at a time in a plastic sandwich bag and beat out, using a meat mallet or rolling pin, ensuring they are as square as possible. Ideally, they should be 5mm (¼in) thick.
3 Put greaseproof paper between each breast and set aside.
4 For the stuffing, place the parsley in a food processor with the garlic and shallots. Pulse until everything is very finely diced.
5 Remove the bones from the duck thighs and chop the thigh meat and the reserved duck breast trimmings. Add to the food processor and blitz again. Transfer to a bowl and season.
6 On a large piece of cling film, lay 6 rashers of pancetta, all facing the same way and slightly overlapping. Place a duck breast on top, then a layer of half the stuffing. Roll up tightly, using the cling film to help. Twist and tie the ends tightly. Make a second ballotine.
7 Bring a large pan of water to the boil, add the ballotines, and poach for 15 minutes. Remove and leave to rest.
8 Chop the beetroot into small chunks and add to a food processor along with the melted butter and double cream. Purée until smooth. Pass through a fine conical sieve and season to taste. Pour into 4 shot glasses, and set aside.
9 Unwrap the ballotines. Heat the olive oil and butter in a frying pan and fry the ballotines until golden all over, seasoning to taste whilst cooking. Leave the ballotines to rest for 10 minutes, then carve each one into 4 slices. Fry again, briefly, if too soft.
10 Arrange orange slices along with frisée on 4 serving plates. Top with the ballotine slices and stand the shot glasses of beetroot to one side.

TEA-SMOKED DUCK BREAST WITH A CELERIAC ROSTI, WHITE BEAN PURÉE, PARSNIP CRISPS, AND A JUNIPER JUS

Peter Seville MasterChef 2011 contestant

PREPARATION TIME
35 minutes,
including smoking

COOKING TIME
1 hour 15 minutes

SERVES 4

"This competition's definitely brought out my competitive side and I think my father will be proud of that."

FOR THE DUCK
50g (1¾oz) LONG-GRAIN RICE
30g (1oz) LOOSE-LEAF
  JASMINE TEA
sprig of THYME
sprig of ROSEMARY
4 DUCK BREASTS, skin on

FOR THE JUS
1 CARROT, chopped
1 CELERY stick, chopped
1 ONION, chopped
2 tbsp OLIVE OIL
1 BAY LEAF
sprig of THYME
2 tsp JUNIPER BERRIES,
  lightly crushed
120ml (4fl oz) PORT
250ml (8fl oz) RED WINE
250ml (8fl oz) CHICKEN STOCK

FOR THE ROSTI
1 small CELERIAC, grated
1 tbsp melted BUTTER, plus
  extra for greasing
grated NUTMEG
SALT and WHITE PEPPER
1 EGG, beaten

FOR THE WHITE BEAN PURÉE
1 small head of GARLIC
400g can CANNELLINI BEANS,
  drained
300ml (10fl oz) CHICKEN STOCK

FOR THE PARSNIP CRISPS
1 litre (1¾ pints) GROUNDNUT
  OIL or VEGETABLE OIL for
  deep frying
1 PARSNIP

1 Place the rice, jasmine tea, thyme, and rosemary on a foil-lined baking tray. Place a wire rack over the top and completely seal the tray using foil. Place the tray over gentle heat until the materials are generating plenty of smoke. Remove from the heat. Trim the duck breasts and score the skin. Loosen the foil a little, quickly slide the duck onto the wire rack, and reseal. Leave the duck in the sealed tray to cold-smoke for 30 minutes, or longer, according to taste.

2 To make the jus, gently fry the carrot, celery, and onion in olive oil with the bay leaf, sprig of thyme, and the juniper berries, stirring, until lightly browned. Add the port and red wine and reduce to a syrup. Add the chicken stock and reduce by half. Strain the sauce and return to the pan. Continue to reduce the sauce until it has a thick, glossy appearance. Adjust the seasoning to taste.

3 Preheat the oven to 220°C (425°F/Gas 7). Put the celeriac in a clean tea towel and squeeze out the moisture. Transfer to a bowl.

4 Stir in the melted butter, and season with nutmeg, salt, and pepper. Add enough beaten egg to bind the mixture.

5 Place spoonfuls of the mixture onto well-buttered baking trays, using a food ring to help create a neat shape. Bake for 20–30 minutes, or until cooked through and crisp on the outside.

6 Wrap the head of garlic in foil and roast in the oven for about 20 minutes until soft.

7 Meanwhile, put the drained cannellini beans in a saucepan with the chicken stock and simmer for 5 minutes. Drain, reserving the liquid. Blitz in a small food processor or with a hand-held blender, adding enough reserved liquid to produce a thick but spoonable consistency. Remove the roasted garlic from the foil and squeeze the garlic into the bean purée. Blitz again and season to taste.

8 Turn the oven down to 180°C (350°F/Gas 4). Season the smoked duck breasts. Heat a large frying pan and add the duck breasts, skin-side down (no need to add oil to the pan). Cook until the skin is crisp (about 5 minutes). Transfer to a baking tray, then cook in the oven for 8 minutes. Allow to rest in a warm place for 8 minutes.

9 Meanwhile, heat the groundnut oil or vegetable oil in a large pan. Peel the parsnips, then use the peeler to cut into ribbons. Deep fry the parsnip ribbons in batches in the oil until crisp. Drain on kitchen paper and season with salt.

10 Whilst the duck is resting, reheat the bean purée and the juniper jus, and place the rosti back into the oven to warm through completely.

11 To serve, place the rosti on plates. Slice the duck breasts and place on top. Place spoonfuls of the bean purée around and drizzle the juniper jus around the plate and over the duck. Top with the parsnip crisps and serve straight away.

DISH UP DUCK

JOHN TORODE USES THE ESSENCE OF PETER'S TEA-SMOKED DUCK FOR THIS EASY-COOK MEAL

PREP: 30 MINS • COOK: 45–55 MINS

DUCK AND SAUCE

SERVES 4

4 DUCK BREASTS, skin on
  or 2 DUCK CROWNS
SALT and freshly ground
  BLACK PEPPER
150ml (5fl oz) RED WINE
60ml (2fl oz) CHICKEN STOCK
4 tbsp REDCURRANT JELLY
3 tbsp PORT
knob of BUTTER

1 Preheat the oven to 200ºC (400ºF/Gas 6). Season the duck liberally. Cook, skin sides down, in a sauté pan for 4–5 minutes or until golden, turn over and brown the udersides. Drain off the fat (good for roast potatoes).

2 Roast the duck, skin sides down, on a baking tray for 10–15 minutes for the breasts, and 20–30 minutes for the crowns, depending on preference. Set aside and keep warm.
3 Quickly deglaze the frying pan with the red wine. Add the stock and reduce slightly. Lower the heat, stir in the redcurrant jelly and port, then boil rapidly, stirring, until thickened. Whisk in the butter and reheat before you serve.
4 Cut the breasts off the crown, if using, slice the duck, and plate (see right).

"Duck crowns are often a good buy and so succulent. Use the carcasses for duck soup – flavour with soy sauce, and sherry or sake."

SIMPLE STEPS TO CARVING DUCK CROWNS

To remove the breasts, cut downwards, following the breastbone line. As you hit the bone, cut along it.

Lift off the breast then cut it in thick slices. Repeat with the other side.

...SERVE WITH

PANCETTA BEANS

115g (4oz) diced PANCETTA
1 GARLIC clove, crushed
1 tbsp chopped ROSEMARY
400g can CANNELLINI BEANS,
   drained and rinsed
2 tbsp OLIVE OIL
SALT and freshly ground BLACK PEPPER
1 tsp RED WINE VINEGAR

1 Dry-fry the pancetta, stirring, for 3–4 minutes until crisp. Add the remaining ingredients except the vinegar and cook, stirring, for 4–5 minutes.
2 Stir in the wine vinegar (the beans should have softened slightly). Taste, season, and keep warm.

SMOKY MASH

1 POTATO, peeled and diced
700g (1lb 9oz) CELERIAC,
   peeled and diced
generous pinch of SMOKED SEA SALT
   and freshly ground BLACK PEPPER
4 tbsp CRÈME FRAÎCHE

1 Boil the potato and celeriac until very soft.
2 Drain thoroughly then mash together with the remaining ingredients. Keep warm.
3 Spoon the mash neatly on plates. Arrange the duck slices on top. Spoon the sauce over. Place the pancetta beans to one side and serve.

WOOD PIGEON AND PANCETTA RISOTTO DRESSED WITH BLACK TRUFFLE AND PARMESAN SHAVINGS

Sara Danesin Medio MasterChef 2011 finalist

PREPARATION TIME
25 minutes

COOKING TIME
1 hour 25 minutes

SERVES 4

FOR THE WOOD PIGEON
6 reserved WOOD PIGEON BREASTS
SALT and freshly ground
  BLACK PEPPER
30g (1oz) BUTTER
1 tsp chopped THYME

FOR THE STOCK
3 oven-ready WOOD
  PIGEON CARCASSES
pinch of FENNEL SEEDS
2 tsp DIJON MUSTARD
3 JUNIPER BERRIES, crushed
2 GARLIC cloves, crushed
1 BAY LEAF
2 sprigs of THYME
1 CELERY stick, roughly chopped
1 CARROT, roughly chopped
2 SHALLOTS, chopped
2 tbsp OLIVE OIL

150ml (5fl oz) RED WINE
500ml (16fl oz) GAME STOCK
500ml (16fl oz) CHICKEN STOCK

FOR THE RISOTTO
50g (1¾oz) diced PANCETTA
20g (¾oz) BUTTER
1 SHALLOT, finely chopped
250g (9oz) ARBORIO RICE
2 tbsp RED WINE
100g (3½oz) PARMESAN CHEESE,
  finely grated

FOR THE SAUCE
2 tbsp RED WINE
150ml (5fl oz) reserved STOCK
30g (1oz) cold BUTTER, diced

TO GARNISH
1 small BLACK TRUFFLE, shaved
CYPRUS SALT

Pancetta is a dry-salted,
air-dried pork belly product, often
sold in packs of slices or diced.
If you buy it freshly cut you can
store it loosely wrapped in the
fridge for a week.

Simplify for EVERYDAY

• For the risotto, use ready-
prepared pigeon breasts and just
use bought fresh game (or beef)
• Use chicken stock, simmered
with the crushed juniper, garlic,
herbs, and wine.

1 Preheat the oven to 180°C (350°F/Gas 4). Remove the breasts from the birds, season, and set aside.
2 Make the stock. In a roasting tin, season the carcasses with the fennel seeds, mustard, juniper berries, garlic, bay leaf, and thyme. Roast in the oven for 30 minutes. In a separate pan, brown the celery, carrot, and shallots in the oil. Add the roasted carcasses and wine. Boil for 3 minutes. Add the stock and simmer 45 minutes. Strain. Keep hot. Reserve the roasting tin.
3 Meanwhile, sear the breasts in 15g (½oz) of the butter for 2–3 minutes on each side. Leave in a warm place to rest.
4 Make the risotto. Dry fry the pancetta in a saucepan, stirring, until crisp. Add the butter and shallots. Sauté until soft. Add the rice and cook, stirring, for 3 minutes. Add the wine and boil until evaporated. Add a ladleful of the hot stock. Simmer, stirring, until absorbed. Repeat a ladleful at a time until the rice is 'al dente' and creamy. It will take about 15–20 minutes. Add the Parmesan.
5 For the sauce, deglaze the roasting tin with the wine. Add the stock, reduce, and season. Whisk in the diced butter to thicken.
6 Refry the pigeon in a clean pan in the remaining butter and the thyme for 2–3 minutes. Slice each breast in two. Serve the risotto in deep plates, topped with the pigeon slices and sauce. Garnish the plates with black truffle shavings and Cyprus salt.

STUFFED BREAST AND BRAISED LEG OF PARTRIDGE WITH CELERIAC PURÉE, SAVOY CABBAGE, AND SPICED BREADCRUMBS

Annie Assheton MasterChef 2011 final 6

PREPARATION TIME
45 minutes

COOKING TIME
2 hours

SERVES 4

JOHN TORODE

"I think it's really elegant, I think it's really sophisticated."

FOR THE PARTRIDGE
4 PARTRIDGES, plus their
   hearts and livers
1 litre (1¾ pints) GAME STOCK
2 BAY LEAVES
4 sprigs of THYME
2 tbsp OLIVE OIL
140g (5oz) UNSALTED BUTTER,
   chilled and cut into cubes
2 GARLIC cloves, crushed
4 SHALLOTS, roughly chopped
2 CARROTS, roughly chopped
2 CELERY sticks, roughly chopped
5 PEPPERCORNS
700ml (1¼ pints) MADEIRA
1 tbsp BRAMBLE JELLY
1 tbsp OLIVE OIL
35g (1¼oz) BUTTER
4 tsp SHERRY VINEGAR

FOR THE STUFFING
40g (1¼oz) cooked, peeled
   CHESTNUTS, finely chopped
40g (1¼oz) ready-to-eat
   PRUNES, finely chopped
½ APPLE, preferably Cox's, cored,
   peeled, and grated
½ tsp THYME leaves
SALT and freshly ground
   BLACK PEPPER

pinch of freshly grated NUTMEG
35g (1¼oz) UNSALTED BUTTER
4–6 large slices PARMA HAM

FOR THE SHALLOTS
200g (7oz) SHALLOTS
35g (1¼oz) UNSALTED
   BUTTER, cubed

FOR THE BREADCRUMBS
35g (1¼oz) UNSALTED BUTTER
50g (1¾oz) stale WHITE
   BREADCRUMBS
pinch of GROUND CLOVES
½ tsp GROUND ALLSPICE
small handful of FLAT-LEAF
   PARSLEY, finely chopped
zest of 1 LEMON

FOR THE CELERIAC PURÉE
300g (10oz) CELERIAC, cut into
   2cm (¾in) pieces
35g (1¼oz) UNSALTED BUTTER
1 sprig of THYME
150ml (5fl oz) DOUBLE CREAM
pinch of GROUND NUTMEG

FOR THE CABBAGE
450g (1lb) SAVOY CABBAGE,
   finely shredded
35g (1¼oz) BUTTER

1 Remove the partridge legs and breasts. Skin the breasts and flatten them with your hand, then cover and set aside. Wash and trim the hearts and livers and set aside. Place the carcasses in a pan and cover with stock. Add 1 bay leaf and a sprig of thyme, bring to the boil, then simmer uncovered for 45 minutes.
2 Meanwhile, trim and scrape the ends of the legs so the bones are clean. Heat the oil and 60g (2oz) of the butter in a pan and fry the legs for 1–2 minutes until browned. Add the remaining bay leaf, 2 sprigs of thyme, garlic, shallots, carrot, celery, and

peppercorns. Cover the legs with Madeira, bring to the boil, then cover and simmer very gently for 40–45 minutes or until tender.

3 Meanwhile, mix the chestnuts, prunes, apple, thyme, salt and pepper, and nutmeg in a bowl. Heat the butter in a pan and add the livers and hearts. Season and cook for 30 seconds on each side, basting with the butter. Remove from the pan, chop, then fold into the chestnut mix. Divide into quarters and set aside to cool.

4 Place a slice of ham on a piece of cling film. Sandwich a portion of stuffing between 2 breasts, place at one end of the ham, and roll up tightly. Wrap with the cling film, twisting the ends. Repeat with the remaining breasts and chill for at least 30 minutes.

5 Place the shallots and butter in a pan. Cover tightly and cook on low heat for 15–20 minutes until the shallots are very tender.

6 To make the crumbs, heat the butter in a pan until it froths. Add the crumbs and stir until the butter is absorbed. Stir in the spices and cook, stirring, for 2 minutes or until the crumbs turn golden. Stir in the parsley and zest, put in a bowl, and set aside.

7 Place the celeriac, butter, and thyme in a pan. Cover and cook on medium heat for 6–8 minutes. Stir in the cream, cover, and cook for 15 minutes until the celeriac is soft. Blend with a hand-held blender until smooth. Season with nutmeg, salt, and pepper.

8 When the partridge legs are tender, remove from the Madeira and cover. Strain the liquid and game stock into separate clean pans. Bring both to the boil and simmer until reduced by two-thirds. Combine them and simmer until thickened. Lower the heat and whisk in the bramble jelly, then 50g (1¾oz) of the chilled butter cubes. Keep warm until needed, stirring occasionally.

9 Preheat the oven to 200°C (400°F/Gas 6). Heat an ovenproof frying pan and add the oil. Unwrap the breasts, season, and cook for about 4 minutes or until brown all over. Halfway through, add 30g (1oz) butter and the remaining thyme and baste the breasts until cooked through. Transfer to the oven for 5 minutes, then cover loosely in foil and leave to rest for 5 minutes.

10 Blanch the cabbage for 1–2 minutes in boiling salted water until just tender. Drain, then return to the heat with the butter. Stir until well coated with the butter, then season to taste.

11 To finish the legs, melt the remaining butter in a pan and add the legs and shallots. Cook for 2 minutes until browned, then turn and add the vinegar and 1 tbsp Madeira sauce. Bring to a simmer, then baste the legs and shallots with the sauce until glazed.

12 To serve, use a 3cm (1¼in) cooking ring to make a stack of breadcrumbs on each plate. Spoon the purée on the plates. Slice the ends off the partridge breast parcels and cut in half. Arrange on top of the celeriac. Use a 6cm (2½in) cooking ring to make a neat shape of the cabbage and top with the partridge legs. Spoon the shallots onto the plates to one side. Serve the remaining sauce in small warmed jugs set on the plate.

RACK OF LAMB WITH A HERB CRUST SERVED WITH POTATO DAUPHINOISE, JERUSALEM ARTICHOKE FLAN, AND AROMATIC LAMB JUS

Sara Danesin Medio MasterChef 2011 finalist

PREPARATION TIME
1 hour

COOKING TIME
2 hours

SERVES 4

FOR THE LAMB JUS
1kg (2¼lb) LAMB BONES
2 CARROTS, roughly chopped
2 CELERY sticks,
   roughly chopped
1 sprig of THYME
2 sprigs of ROSEMARY
375ml (13fl oz) young DRY
   WHITE WINE, such as
   GEWURTZTRAMINER
   or RIESLING

FOR THE DAUPHINOISE
150ml (5fl oz) WHOLE MILK
150ml (5fl oz) DOUBLE CREAM
25g (scant 1oz)
   UNSALTED BUTTER
1 sprig of THYME
1 GARLIC clove, lightly crushed
6 BLACK PEPPERCORNS
1 BAY LEAF
450g (1lb) FLOURY POTATOES
SALT, to taste

FOR THE FLAN
250g (9oz) JERUSALEM
   ARTICHOKES

½ small ONION, finely chopped
OLIVE OIL, for frying
175ml (6fl oz) DOUBLE CREAM
1 EGG
2 EGG YOLKS
50g (1¾oz) PARMESAN CHEESE,
   finely grated
1 tsp finely chopped MARJORAM
BUTTER for greasing

FOR THE LAMB
2 x 6-bone RACKS OF LAMB,
   French-trimmed
1 tbsp DIJON MUSTARD
2 tbsp finely chopped ROSEMARY
2 tbsp finely chopped THYME
SALT and freshly ground
   BLACK PEPPER

TO GARNISH
small sprigs of THYME

This cut of rack of lamb for roasting is sold chined (with the backbone removed), so that it is easily cut into portions. In a "French trimmed" rack, the ends of the bones are scraped clean.

1 Preheat the oven to 200°C (400°F/Gas 6). First prepare the lamb jus. Put the lamb bones with the roughly diced vegetables, thyme, and 1 sprig of rosemary in a roasting tin and cook in the oven for 20 minutes.

2 Place the bones in a large stock pot and add the wine. Add enough water to cover. Simmer for 2 hours, frequently skimming.

3 Strain the stock into a small pan. Bring to the boil, and boil to reduce to about 5 tbsp, and the sauce coats the back of a spoon. Remove from the heat. Add a fresh sprig of rosemary. Cover and leave to infuse. Remove the sprig when ready to serve.

4 Meanwhile, make the Dauphinoise potatoes. Add the milk, cream, butter, thyme, garlic, peppercorns, and the bay leaf to a pan. Bring to the boil, then remove from the heat. Cover and leave to infuse for at least an hour, then strain into a large bowl.

5 Peel the potatoes and thinly slice with a mandolin. Do not put the sliced potatoes in water, otherwise they will lose all their starch. Make sure you use them straight away to prevent them from discolouring.

6 Add the sliced potatoes to the cream mixture and season to taste with salt. Layer the slices of potato in a small, deep, roasting tin, about 25 x 20cm (10 x 8in) and 5cm (2in) deep. Pour the remainder of the cream mixture over, cover with foil, and place in the oven for 40 minutes.

7 Turn the oven down to 180°C (350°F/Gas 4), remove the foil, and cook for a further 25 minutes, or until a nice brown crust has formed on the surface and the potatoes are soft. Make sure the potatoes are not too wet, if so, allow more time in the oven at a lower temperature.

8 Make the Jerusalem artichoke flans. Turn the oven down to 160°C (325°F/Gas 3). Peel and boil the artichokes in a large pan of salted water until tender. Drain well.

9 Fry the onion in a little olive oil until completely soft, then add the cooked artichokes and cook over medium heat for 5–7 minutes.

10 Transfer the mixture to a food processor and blitz until smooth. Add the cream, eggs, egg yolks, Parmesan, and marjoram, then blitz again until smooth.

11 Grease four 100ml (3½fl oz) dariole moulds with a little butter, then divide the mixture between the moulds. Place in a small roasting tin, then add hot water to come halfway up the side of the moulds. Bake for 25–30 minutes until set, then remove from the oven and keep warm.

12 Turn the oven up to 200°C (400°F/Gas 6). Season the racks of lamb well.

13 Brush the fat sides with the Dijon mustard and coat with the finely chopped rosemary and thyme.

14 Heat a little oil in a frying pan until very hot, then sear the meat until brown all over. Transfer to a roasting tin and roast in the oven for 12–15 minutes.

15 Remove and keep warm. Allow at least 30 minutes for the meat to rest, to prevent bleeding on the plate. When ready to serve, slice the racks allowing 3 chops per person, served interlocked.

TO SERVE

Place 3 lamb chops in the centre of each plate. Cut square portions of the Dauphinoise potatoes and place on the plates. Unmould the artichoke flan next to the other ingredients. Reheat the lamb jus and spoon a little over the meat. Garnish each plate with a sprig of thyme.

Simplify for **EVERY**DAY

• Instead of making stock from scratch, add the wine to 200ml (7fl oz) fresh commercial lamb stock and reduce, then add the rosemary to infuse.

CANNON OF LAMB, BABY TURNIPS AND FENNEL, TURNIP GREENS, AND A QUINCE SAUCE

Tom Whitaker MasterChef 2011 finalist

PREPARATION TIME
20 minutes

COOKING TIME
50 minutes

SERVES 4

FOR THE LAMB
2 tbsp SUNFLOWER OIL
4 x 250g (9oz) CANNONS OF LAMB
2 tbsp BLACK MUSTARD
   SEEDS, crushed
SALT and freshly ground
   BLACK PEPPER
knob of BUTTER

FOR THE VEGETABLES
2 tbsp SUNFLOWER OIL
200g (7oz) BACON LARDONS
8 BABY FENNEL bulbs, halved
   vertically (or 2 large ones,
   cut into eighths)
8 BABY TURNIPS, halved vertically

2 BANANA SHALLOTS, thinly sliced
1 GARLIC clove, thinly sliced
splash of DRY WHITE WINE
250ml (8fl oz) CHICKEN STOCK

FOR THE QUINCE SAUCE
200ml (7fl oz) TAWNY PORT
2 tbsp RED WINE VINEGAR
1 tbsp QUINCE JAM OR JELLY
2 QUINCES, peeled, cored, and
   diced into 1cm (½in) chunks

TO SERVE
SUNFLOWER OIL, for shallow frying
handful of BABY TURNIP GREENS
   or SPINACH

1 Cook the lamb. Preheat the oven to 200°C (400°F/Gas 6). Heat the oil in a frying pan over high heat. Season the lamb with the crushed mustard seeds and salt and pepper. When the oil is hot, add the cannons of lamb. Brown on all sides. Reduce the heat and add the butter. Spoon the melted butter over the cannons.
2 Transfer the browned meat and juices to a shallow roasting tin and roast in the oven for 8–13 minutes, depending on how you like your lamb cooked. Remove from the oven, cover with foil, and leave in a warm place until ready to eat.
3 For the vegetables, heat the oil in a frying pan over medium to high heat. Add the lardons and fry until the fat runs, and they have turned golden and slightly crisp.
4 Add the fennel, turnips, shallots, and garlic. Sauté for 3–4 minutes until the shallots have softened slightly. Increase the heat and add the white wine. Reduce by half before adding the chicken stock. Reduce the heat and simmer until the vegetables are tender and the liquid is a coating consistency.
5 Make the sauce. Place the port, vinegar, and jam into a saucepan. Reduce by half before adding the chunks of quince. Boil until syrupy, and the quince chunks are tender.
6 Heat the oil in a shallow pan. When hot, add the turnip greens or spinach leaves. Shallow fry for 45 seconds, then transfer with a slotted spoon to kitchen paper to drain excess oil.
7 Place a small mound of fennel and turnips on a plate. Top with the sliced cannon of lamb, before dressing with the sauce, and the fried turnip greens or spinach leaves.

NECK OF LAMB WITH MERGUEZ SAUSAGE ON A BED OF ROASTED VEGETABLES AND COUSCOUS

Phil Vickery MBE England rugby player and 2011 Celebrity champion

PREPARATION TIME
20 minutes

COOKING TIME
45 minutes

SERVES 4

½ RED PEPPER
½ YELLOW PEPPER
½ COURGETTE
½ AUBERGINE
1 RED ONION, peeled
2 tsp HARISSA PASTE
3 sprigs of THYME, leaves only
2 tbsp VEGETABLE OIL
4 MERGUEZ SAUSAGES
600g (1lb 5oz) NECK OF LAMB
   FILLET, trimmed, fat and
   trimmings reserved
SALT and freshly ground
   BLACK PEPPER
25g (scant 1oz) SALTED BUTTER

4 sprigs of ROSEMARY, leaves of
   3 removed and finely chopped
400ml (14fl oz) CHICKEN STOCK
1 SPRING ONION, finely chopped
1 GARLIC clove, finely chopped
5 sprigs of MINT, leaves removed
   and finely chopped
juice and zest of 1 LEMON
200g (7oz) COUSCOUS
2–3 WILD GARLIC LEAVES,
   finely chopped
75g (2½oz) PITTED BLACK
   OLIVES, sliced
MICRO GREEK BASIL
MICRO PINK-STEMMED RADISH

1 Preheat the oven to 180°C (350°F/Gas 4). Chop the vegetables into finger-width batons, ensuring that they are the same size so that they cook evenly. Place them in a baking tray with the harissa and thyme, drizzle with vegetable oil, and stir to combine. Roast in the oven for 10 minutes, then lay the sausages on top and cook for a further 20 minutes.

2 Heat an ovenproof frying pan and add the lamb trimmings and fat. Cook gently for 3–4 minutes to render the fat, then turn the heat up high. Season the lamb, add to the pan, and sear for 2 minutes on each side. Add the butter and baste the lamb for a further 2 minutes. Add the rosemary sprig to the pan, transfer it to the oven, and roast for 15 minutes. Remove the lamb from the oven, cover with foil, and leave to rest for at least 10 minutes.

3 Put the stock in a pan and bring to the boil with the spring onion, garlic, rosemary leaves, two-thirds of the mint, the lemon juice and zest, and a little salt and pepper. Simmer for 5 minutes.

4 Place the couscous in a bowl and cover with the stock. Cover the bowl and leave for 5 minutes. Add the garlic leaves and black olives, fluffing up the couscous with a fork to separate the grains. Check the seasoning and add some chopped mint to taste.

5 Remove the vegetables from the oven and quarter the sausages.

6 Press the couscous down onto the plates in a chef's ring. Add a layer of vegetables. Slice the lamb and place on top of the vegetables, then place the sausages on top of the lamb. Pour on the resting juices from the lamb and some juices from the vegetables and sausages, and finish with the micro herbs.

This spicy North African sausage is made from lamb, beef, or both, in a lamb casing. The red colour comes from the chilli that contributes to its characteristic flavour.

LAMB FILLET WITH FONDANT POTATOES, BABY CARROTS, AND ASPARAGUS WRAPPED IN PARMA HAM

Phil Vickery MBE England rugby player and 2011 Celebrity champion

PREPARATION TIME
10 minutes

COOKING TIME
30 minutes

SERVES 4

JOHN TORODE

"Your lamb is perfectly cooked, your potatoes are beautiful, I think it's wonderfully, classically done, I love the presentation."

FOR THE POTATOES
600ml (1 pint) CHICKEN STOCK
2 sprigs of THYME
1 BAY LEAF
salt and freshly ground
   BLACK PEPPER
12 small maris PIPER POTATOES,
   trimmed to even shape

FOR THE LAMB
2 LAMB LOIN FILLETS
4 CARROTS, roughly chopped
2 tbsp DUCK FAT at
   room temperature
15g (½oz) BUTTER

FOR THE GARNISH
12 ASPARAGUS SPEARS
12 BABY CARROTS, scrubbed
few sprigs of mint, finely chopped
12 slices of parma ham
30g (1oz) BUTTER

FOR THE SAUCE
15g (½oz) BUTTER
1 tbsp DUCK FAT
½ onion, finely chopped
3 tbsp MADEIRA
400ml (14fl oz) CHICKEN STOCK
2 sprigs of thyme
2 BAY LEAVES

1 Preheat the oven to 180°C (350°F/Gas 4). For the potatoes, heat the chicken stock in a pan with herbs. Place the potatoes in a roasting tin. Pour over the hot stock, season, and roast for 10–15 minutes, basting often, until soft. Remove and set aside.
2 Season the lamb well. Place the roughly chopped carrots in a small roasting tin with 1 tbsp of the duck fat. Stir well. Roast in the oven while preparing the garnish. Trim 2cm (¾in) off the ends of the asparagus. Blanch with the baby carrots for 2 minutes, then refresh in iced water.
3 Sprinkle some mint on a slice of the Parma ham, roll up a spear of asparagus in the ham. Secure with a cocktail stick. Repeat with the other spears and ham. Set aside.
4 Heat the 15g (½oz) butter and the remaining 1 tbsp duck fat in a frying pan over medium heat and sear the lamb for a minute until brown all over. Transfer to the chopped carrots and roast for 7–10 minutes, according to taste. Wrap in foil, keep warm.
5 For the sauce, soften the onion in 15g (½oz) butter, add the Madeira, reduce by half. Add the stock, the lamb juices and roasting carrots, and herbs. Reduce by half. Strain through a sieve and check the seasoning. Reheat before serving.
6 Fry the asparagus until the ham is crisp. Remove the sticks.
7 Toss the baby carrots in 15g (½oz) hot butter in a pan. Repeat with the remaining butter and the potatoes. Season to taste.
8 Slice each lamb loin in 8 slices. Arrange on serving plates, surround with the vegetables and a drizzle of the sauce.

THYME-ROASTED FILLET OF BEEF WITH ROAST POTATOES, CARAMELIZED SHALLOTS, AND YORKSHIRE PUDDING

Fiona Luck MasterChef 2011 contestant

PREPARATION TIME
45 minutes

COOKING TIME
1 hour 15 minutes

SERVES 4

"They liked it.
And it really came
from the heart."

FOR THE HORSERADISH SAUCE
2 tbsp finely grated HORSERADISH
2 tbsp CRÈME FRAÎCHE
1 tsp DIJON MUSTARD
pinch of SUGAR
1 tbsp WHITE WINE VINEGAR
5 tbsp DOUBLE CREAM
SALT and freshly ground
   BLACK PEPPER

FOR THE POTATOES
3 large MARFONA or MARIS PIPER
   POTATOES, peeled and quartered
2 tbsp GOOSE FAT, at room
   temperature
SALT and freshly ground
   BLACK PEPPER
2 sprigs of THYME

FOR THE SHALLOTS
25g (scant 1oz)
   UNSALTED BUTTER
1 tbsp CASTER SUGAR
8 small round SHALLOTS, whole
splash of RED WINE VINEGAR
3 tbsp RED WINE
3 tbsp BEEF STOCK

FOR THE JUS
200ml (7fl oz) robust RED WINE
200ml (7fl oz) BEEF STOCK
1 SHALLOT, halved
sprig of THYME
1 BAY LEAF
1 STAR ANISE
5 BLACK PEPPERCORNS
2 tsp REDCURRANT JELLY
20g (¾oz) cold UNSALTED
   BUTTER, cubed

FOR THE PURÉE
3 large CARROTS, diced
1 SWEDE, diced
25g (scant 1oz)
   UNSALTED BUTTER
200ml (7fl oz) CHICKEN STOCK
splash of DOUBLE CREAM

FOR THE PUDDINGS
2 large EGGS
150g (5½oz) PLAIN FLOUR
pinch of SALT
3 tbsp WHOLE MILK
2 tsp RAPESEED OIL

FOR THE BEEF
800g (1¾lb) dry-aged ABERDEEN
   ANGUS BEEF FILLET, trimmed
   of any sinew and fat
½ tbsp RAPESEED OIL
2 sprigs of ROSEMARY
2 sprigs of THYME
SALT and freshly ground
   BLACK PEPPER
splash of BEEF STOCK
30g (1oz) BUTTER

FOR THE GREENS
250g (9oz) SWISS CHARD, stems
   removed, leaves finely shredded
250g (9oz) SPRING GREENS, stems
   removed, leaves finely shredded
200ml (7fl oz) CHICKEN STOCK
25g (scant 1oz)
   UNSALTED BUTTER

TO GARNISH
2 PARSNIPS, peeled
RAPESEED OIL, for deep frying

1 Preheat the oven to 200°C (400°F/Gas 6). For the horseradish sauce, mix all the ingredients except the double cream in a bowl until smooth. Whip the cream to soft peaks, fold into the sauce mixture, and season to taste. Cover and chill until needed.
2 Parboil the potatoes in salted water for 10 minutes, then drain,

shaking the colander to fluff the edges. Put the goose fat into a roasting tray and place in the oven. When piping hot, add the potatoes, coating evenly with the fat, then season and sprinkle with thyme. Cook for about 40 minutes, turning and basting regularly until evenly golden and crisp.

3 For the shallots, melt the butter and sugar in a small pan. Add the shallots and brown evenly over medium heat. Add the vinegar, wine, and stock. Simmer gently for about 20 minutes until the shallots are cooked and the liquid is reduced and syrupy.

4 To make the jus, put all the ingredients except for the redcurrant jelly and butter into a saucepan. Bring to the boil and simmer for around 20 minutes until reduced by two-thirds. Strain into a clean pan, add the redcurrant jelly and heat gently, stirring, for 2–3 minutes until the jelly dissolves. Remove from the heat. Just before serving, reheat and whisk in the butter.

5 Put the purée ingredients except the cream, in a saucepan. Bring to the boil, reduce the heat and simmer until very tender, and most of the liquid has evaporated. Blitz in a food processor with the cream until smooth. Season well. Reheat before serving.

6 For the Yorkshire puddings, Mix the eggs, flour, and a pinch of salt in a bowl. Add the milk, stirring constantly, until you have a smooth batter. Take a small petit four tray or muffin tray and pour a very small amount of oil into each mould. Heat the tray in the oven until piping hot, then pour the mixture into the moulds. Bake for about 20 minutes until risen, crisp, and golden.

7 Rub the beef fillet with rapeseed oil. On a chopping board, finely chop the rosemary and thyme with some salt and pepper. Roll the beef in the herbs until evenly coated. Heat an ovenproof frying pan until very hot. Place the beef fillet in the pan and quickly sear all over, turning frequently to avoid overcooking one edge, but at the same time allowing the beef to develop a slightly caramelized crust. Remove from the heat and pour in a splash of beef stock to cool the pan. When it is almost evaporated, add the butter and baste generously. Place the beef in the oven with the potatoes for about 15 minutes for rare. Remove and rest for at least 10 minutes under kitchen foil.

8 Place the chard and spring greens in a small pan with the chicken stock and butter. Steam lightly for about 8 minutes until most of the liquid has evaporated and the greens are cooked, but with a slight crunch. Season to taste.

9 Using a peeler, peel long, even shards of the parsnip. Heat about 4cm (1½in) of oil in a small pan and when hot (test with a single piece of parsnip first), fry lightly until golden. Drain on kitchen paper.

10 Carve the beef into thick slices and serve with the accompaniments and a garnish of parsnip shards.

Thymus vulgaris comes from the Mediterranean but will grow happily in a British garden. It is often sold in pots in supermarkets, giving it a much longer life in the kitchen than cut thyme.

FILLET OF BEEF WITH ONION PURÉE, MUSHROOM SAUCE, AND FONDANT POTATOES

Nick Pickard actor and 2011 Celebrity finalist

PREPARATION TIME
20 minutes

COOKING TIME
1 hour 15 minutes

SERVES 4

"It was one of the hardest things I've ever done. I mean I've done opening nights in the West End and it's worse than that!"

Simplify for **EVERY**DAY

• For speed, don't trim the potatoes, just peel and halve, then cook in the butter and stock with the thyme and garlic until tender. • Use sliced chestnut mushrooms in the sauce, frozen chopped onion, and chopped garlic from a jar for the purée. • For a less expensive meal, use frying steaks instead of fillet, sautéed to your liking.

FOR THE FONDANT POTATOES
4 large BAKING POTATOES
200g (7oz) BUTTER, cut in
  5–6 slices
3 sprigs of THYME
4 GARLIC cloves, chopped

FOR THE SAUCE
500ml (16fl oz) BEEF STOCK
100ml (3½fl oz) WHIPPING CREAM
150g (5½oz) CHANTERELLE
  MUSHROOMS
25g (scant 1oz)
  UNSALTED BUTTER

FOR THE BEEF
800g (1¾lb) CENTRE-CUT
  BEEF FILLET
OLIVE OIL, to coat beef fillet
SALT and freshly ground
  BLACK PEPPER

FOR THE ONION PURÉE
20g (¾oz) UNSALTED BUTTER
2 tsp OLIVE OIL
1 large ONION, chopped
3 GARLIC cloves, chopped
1 tsp chopped THYME

1 Preheat the oven to 180°C (350°F/Gas 4). Peel the potatoes and slice in half down the middle. Trim the rounded side then cut out a ring of potato from each half using a 6cm (2½in) round cutter so that you have a cylinder of potato.

2 Lay the butter slices in the bottom of an ovenproof sauté pan. Put the potatoes on top and add water to almost cover the potatoes. Bring to the boil, turn the heat down, and simmer gently for 30 minutes until the potatoes are just tender.

3 Turn the potatoes, add the thyme and garlic, and cook for another 20 minutes. Drain the potatoes and keep warm.

4 For the sauce, pour the stock into a pan, boil to reduce by two-thirds, then whisk in the cream. Fry the mushrooms in butter for 5 minutes until golden brown, then add to the stock and cream. Season to taste. Reheat gently before serving.

5 Rub the beef all over with the olive oil and season generously. Heat a large ovenproof frying pan until smoking, then add the beef and sear for 2 minutes on each side until golden brown. Transfer to the oven and roast for 15–20 minutes until cooked to your liking, then remove from the oven and rest for 15 minutes.

6 Meanwhile, make the onion purée. Heat the butter and oil in a pan. Add the onion, garlic, and thyme. Cook gently for 15 minutes until completely soft but not brown. Cool slightly. Purée in a blender until smooth. Return to the pan and season. Reheat gently before serving.

7 To serve, spread a little onion purée on each plate, Carve the beef into 4 thick slices and place on top of the purée. Serve with the fondant potatoes and the mushroom sauce.

MALAYSIAN BEEF AND POTATO CURRY WITH CHAPATI AND CUCUMBER RAITA
Linda Lusardi actress and 2011 Celebrity semi-finalist

PREPARATION TIME
45 minutes

COOKING TIME
1 hour 30 minutes

SERVES 4

"My children love this curry, so when I said I've got one dish to show off with, everyone said, 'your curry'."

FOR THE CHAPATIS
250g (9oz) CHAPATI or WHOLEMEAL FLOUR, plus extra for rolling
1 tbsp VEGETABLE OIL

FOR THE CURRY AND RICE
5 SHALLOTS, chopped
2 GARLIC cloves, crushed
5cm (2in) piece FRESH GINGER, grated
2 tbsp GROUNDNUT OIL
1 tbsp HOT CURRY POWDER
1 tbsp CHILLI POWDER
1 tsp GROUND CINNAMON
1 tsp GROUND CUMIN
1 tsp GROUND CORIANDER
4 CURRY LEAVES
1 STAR ANISE
4 CLOVES

800g (1¾lb) SIRLOIN STEAK, cut into 2.5cm (1in) cubes
2 large POTATOES, cut into 2.5cm (1in) cubes
2 large RED CHILLIES, deseeded and finely chopped
½ tsp SALT
400ml (14fl oz) COCONUT MILK
2 tbsp LIME JUICE
1 tsp LIGHT BROWN SUGAR
200g (7oz) BASMATI RICE

FOR THE CUCUMBER RAITA
½ CUCUMBER, deseeded and finely diced
200g (7oz) PLAIN GREEK YOGURT
½ tsp SUGAR
1 tbsp CORIANDER, chopped

TO GARNISH
2 RED CHILLIES, sliced

1 Make the chapatis, mix the flour with ¼ tsp salt in a large bowl. Make a well in the centre, add the oil. Gradually add 200ml (7fl oz) boiling water to form a dough. Knead on a lightly floured surface for 10 minutes until smooth and elastic. Cover with a damp cloth and leave to rest for 45 minutes.

2 Divide the chapati dough into 8 pieces, then roll into small balls. Dust the work surface with more flour and roll out each ball to a thin disc, around 12cm (5in) in diameter.

3 Heat a non-stick frying pan over medium heat. Cook a chapati for 2 minutes on each side. Wrap and keep warm while you repeat with the remaining chapatis.

4 Meanwhile, make the curry and rice. Fry the shallots, garlic, and ginger in the oil for 5 minutes until soft. Add all the spices and fry, stirring for 1 minute. Stir in the beef, until coated, then the potatoes, chillies, salt, and coconut milk. Bring to the boil, cover, reduce the heat, and simmer for 40 minutes, stirring occasionally. Stir in the lime juice and brown sugar, and cook uncovered for 2 minutes more.

5 Cook the rice according to packet directions. Drain. Keep hot.

6 Mix the raita ingredients together. Season to taste.

7 Serve the curry with the rice, raita, and chapatis, and garnished with the sliced red chillies.

PAN-FRIED BEEF WITH ROCKET, SPINACH, AND A MOREL CREAM SAUCE

Ricky Groves actor and 2011 Celebrity contestant

PREPARATION TIME
10 minutes

COOKING TIME
20 minutes

SERVES 4

"Hopefully, if I just get my head down, we're in with a pretty good chance of just producing some good food."

FOR THE BEEF
8 BEEF MEDALLIONS, each 75g (2½oz)
OLIVE OIL, to coat beef medallions
SALT and freshly ground BLACK PEPPER

FOR THE SAUCE
2 tbsp OLIVE OIL
2 SHALLOTS, finely chopped
2 GARLIC cloves, crushed
150g (5½oz) MOREL MUSHROOMS
100ml (3½fl oz) MADEIRA
300ml (10fl oz) DOUBLE CREAM
30g (1oz) UNSALTED BUTTER

FOR THE CROÛTONS
8 thin slices of WHITE BREAD
OLIVE OIL, for frying

FOR THE SPINACH
OLIVE OIL, for frying
300g (10oz) BABY LEAF SPINACH
100g (3½oz) ROCKET
1 GARLIC clove, crushed
handful of BASIL leaves, chopped

1 Heat a large frying pan until smoking. Rub the beef medallions with a little olive oil and season with salt and pepper. Fry the medallions for 1 minute on each side and transfer to a warm plate.
2 Make the sauce. Heat the olive oil in the same pan, over medium heat. Add the shallots and garlic. Cook, stirring, for 3–4 minutes until soft. Add the mushrooms and cook for a further 2 minutes. Increase the heat. Deglaze the pan with the Madeira. Boil until the liquid has reduced by half.
3 Add the cream. Cook for a further 3–4 minutes until the sauce has thickened, then whisk in the butter. Set aside until needed.
4 Cut croûtons from the bread to roughly the same size as the medallions. Fry in olive oil until crisp. Drain on kitchen paper.
5 Heat a little olive oil in a large frying pan, then add the spinach, rocket, garlic, and basil. Fry quickly until the spinach and rocket have wilted, then season to taste and remove from the heat.
6 Add the beef medallions to the sauce and reheat gently for 2–4 minutes.
7 To serve, place the medallions on the croûtons on 4 plates. Pour over the sauce and place the spinach and rocket on the side.

In spring, young and tender rocket leaves have an earthy, peppery flavour that is slightly bitter; as the summer wears on, rocket becomes increasingly hot to the taste.

COCKNEY PIE AND MASH WITH LIQUOR
Nick Pickard actor and 2011 Celebrity finalist

PREPARATION TIME
20 minutes, plus chilling

COOKING TIME
1 hour

SERVES 4

"It means a lot
to me, it's
something close
to my heart."

FOR THE PASTRY
250g (9oz) PLAIN FLOUR
pinch of SALT
115g (4oz) BUTTER, cubed
1 EGG, lightly beaten

FOR THE FILLING
1 tbsp OLIVE OIL
1 ONION, finely chopped
500g (1lb 2oz) minced BEEF
1 GARLIC clove, crushed
6 MUSHROOMS, finely diced
1 sprig of THYME
1 BAY LEAF
1 BEEF STOCK CUBE
1 tbsp PLAIN FLOUR
150ml (5fl oz) RED WINE
300ml (10fl oz) BEEF STOCK

SALT and freshly ground
   BLACK PEPPER

FOR THE MASHED POTATOES
3 large POTATOES, peeled
   and cut in chunks
50g (1¾oz) UNSALTED BUTTER
3 tbsp SINGLE CREAM

FOR THE LIQUOR
25g (scant 1oz) UNSALTED
   BUTTER
25g (scant 1oz) PLAIN FLOUR
300ml (10fl oz) CHICKEN STOCK
25g (scant 1oz) PARSLEY,
   finely chopped
1 tbsp WHITE WINE VINEGAR

1 For the pastry, place the flour and salt in a food processor, add the butter, and pulse to the consistency of breadcrumbs. Add 3–4 tbsp of cold water and pulse again until the mixture starts to form a ball. Turn out onto a floured work surface and knead gently for 1 minute until smooth. Wrap in cling film and refrigerate for 30 minutes.

2 For the filling, heat the oil in a large frying pan, add the onion, and sweat for 5 minutes until soft. Increase the heat, add the beef, and fry for 5 minutes until browned.

3 Add the garlic, mushrooms, thyme, bay leaf, beef stock cube, flour, red wine, and beef stock. Cover and simmer for 20 minutes, stirring occasionally. Season to taste, then leave to cool.

4 Preheat the oven to 200°C (400°F/Gas 6). Generously butter 4 individual pie dishes or a 23cm (9in) pie dish. Roll out the pastry to the thickness of 5mm (¼in) and line the pie dishes with it, completely covering the base and sides. Spoon in the pie filling, then place a pastry lids on top, pushing down the edges to seal. Brush generously with beaten egg and bake in the oven for 35 minutes or until golden brown.

5 Meanwhile, boil the potatoes in a large pan of salted water until tender, then drain thoroughly. Mash with the butter and cream, and season to taste.

6 For the liquor, melt the butter in a pan, add the flour, and stir to combine. Slowly add the chicken stock, stirring continuously, and bring to the boil. Simmer for 5 minutes until thickened, then remove from the heat. Add the parsley and vinegar and season.

INTERNATIONAL GOURMET SCOUSE
Margi Clarke actress and 2011 Celebrity contestant

PREPARATION TIME
20 minutes

COOKING TIME
1 hour 30 minutes

SERVES 4

"Scouse is one of the most nutritious meals you could ever get to eat.
The Beatles were raised on it, the whole of Liverpool's been raised on it."

750g (1lb 10oz) LAMB SHOULDER, boned and cubed
SALT and freshly ground BLACK PEPPER
2 tbsp OLIVE OIL
30g (1oz) UNSALTED BUTTER
2 large ONIONS, diced
1 LEEK, diced
1 CELERY stick, diced
2 tbsp PEARL BARLEY
4 POTATOES, diced
4 large CARROTS, diced

2 tbsp LIGHT SOY SAUCE
1 tsp DRIED THYME
2 tsp MALT VINEGAR
2 tsp MINT SAUCE
1 tsp ENGLISH MUSTARD
1 canned ANCHOVY, finely chopped
900ml (1½ pints) LAMB STOCK
3 tbsp FROZEN GARDEN PEAS

1 Check the lamb and trim any remaining fat. Season the lamb well with salt and pepper.

2 Heat 1 tbsp of the oil and half the butter in a large, flameproof casserole and fry the lamb in batches until golden brown, stirring and turning all the time and reheating the casserole between batches. Remove each batch with a slotted spoon and set aside until required.

3 Heat the remaining oil and butter in the casserole, Add the onions, leek, and celery, and fry, stirring for 4–5 minutes until softened but not browned. Add the barley and fry for a further 1 minute until glistening.

4 Return the lamb to the pan along with the potatoes and carrots and stir well. Add the soy sauce, thyme, vinegar, mint sauce, mustard, chopped anchovy, and the lamb stock. Bring to the boil, then cover, reduce the heat and simmer gently for 1½ hours until the lamb is meltingly tender.

5 Ten minutes before the end of cooking, add the peas and season to taste. Serve in large soup bowls.

BALLOTINE OF RABBIT STUFFED WITH ALBA TRUFFLES AND PORCINI, SERVED WITH FONTINA FONDUE AND CANEDERLI

Sara Danesin Medio MasterChef 2011 finalist

PREPARATION TIME
50 minutes, plus soaking

COOKING TIME
1–2 hours

SERVES 4

FOR THE BALLOTINE
1 heaped tbsp DRIED PORCINI
4 soft SAVOY CABBAGE leaves
3 tbsp OLIVE OIL
1 SHALLOT, finely chopped
1 CELERY stick, finely chopped
1 CARROT, finely chopped
40g (1¼oz) SMOKED PANCETTA,
   finely diced
1 BAY LEAF
sprig of THYME
200ml (7fl oz) DRY WHITE WINE
SALT and freshly ground
   BLACK PEPPER
1 SADDLE OF RABBIT (with the
   liver and kidneys), boned by
   your butcher
20g (¾oz) BUTTER
1 small BLACK TRUFFLE, shredded
the RABBIT KIDNEYS, trimmed
   and halved
half the RABBIT LIVER,
   finely chopped

FOR THE FONDUE
200ml (7fl oz) WHOLE MILK
40g (1¼oz) BUTTER
30g (1oz) FLOUR
SALT and freshly ground
   BLACK PEPPER

a little freshly grated NUTMEG
200g (7oz) FONTINA or GRUYÈRE
   CHEESE, diced
400ml (14fl oz) SINGLE CREAM
3 EGG YOLKS
4 tsp COGNAC

FOR THE CANEDERLI
150g (5½oz) DRY BREAD
200ml (7fl oz) MILK
¼ ONION, finely chopped
½ SHALLOT, finely chopped
2 tbsp OLIVE OIL
1 slice of SMOKED PANCETTA,
   finely diced
1 ITALIAN SAUSAGE
¼ EGG, beaten
2 tsp finely grated
   PARMESAN CHEESE
SALT and freshly ground
   BLACK PEPPER
a little freshly grated NUTMEG
1 tbsp finely chopped PARSLEY
FLOUR for dusting
500ml (16fl oz) BEEF STOCK
500ml (16fl oz) CHICKEN STOCK

TO SERVE
a few WHITE TRUFFLE shavings
2 tsp THYME leaves

White truffles are actually beige on the outside and darker inside, with white veins. Avoid those that look shrunken or dry as they will have lost the intensity of their aroma; they should be firm, with an earthy, fruity scent.

1 Preheat the oven to 180°C (350°F/Gas 4). For the ballotine, place the porcini in a bowl, cover with warm water, and leave for 25 minutes. Drain. Blanch the cabbage in boiling water for 2 minutes. Drain, then finely shred.

2 In a flameproof casserole, heat the olive oil and sauté the shallot, celery, carrot, and pancetta until the vegetables have softened. Add the bay leaf, thyme, previously rehydrated porcini, wine, and shredded cabbage. Cook the mixture for 25–30 minutes until the liquid has evaporated and the cabbage is well amalgamated with the other ingredients. Add a little water during cooking if too dry. Discard the herbs. Season to taste.

4 Place the boned rabbit on a piece of buttered foil. Season generously and stuff with the cabbage mixture, the black truffle, the halved kidneys, and the chopped half of the rabbit liver.

5 Wrap the rabbit tightly in foil to make a neat sausage-shape. Cook at high heat in a dry frying pan until the foil is well coloured. Transfer to the oven for 15–18 minutes. Remove and leave to rest for 5 minutes. When ready to serve, unwrap, pour off any watery juices, and cut in slices.

6 Meanwhile, make the fondue. Heat the milk in a small pan until just boiling. Melt the butter in a non-stick pan, stir in the flour. Add the boiling milk, stirring continuously until smooth. Season and add a little grated nutmeg and the diced cheese.

7 Stir until the cheese melts, then cook gently for 15–20 minutes. Stir to prevent sticking. Remove from the heat. Add the cream and egg yolk. Blend with a hand-held blender, return to the heat. Add the cognac and keep warm.

8 For the canederli, cut the bread into small cubes and soak in the milk for 10–20 minutes. Squeeze out excess liquid, transfer to a bowl. Meanwhile, sauté the onion and shallot in a little olive oil, until soft. Add the pancetta and sauté until brown.

9 Remove the sausage skin and mix the meat with the bread. Add the egg, Parmesan, and pancetta mixture. Season with the salt, pepper, nutmeg, and parsley. Mix well. Shape into 12 small dumplings. Dust with flour. Bring the beef and chicken stocks to a simmer in a large pan. Add the canederli and simmer for 10–15 minutes, until they are cooked through and float to the surface. Drain on kitchen paper.

10 To serve, spoon some fondue on 4 serving plates. Place a slice or two of rabbit ballotine on top and add a few shavings of white truffle. Place 3 canederli around the plate, sprinkle with some thyme leaves, and serve at once.

Simplify for **EVERY**DAY

• Buy ready-diced pancetta and use a ready-prepared packet of cheese fondue. • You could use split pork fillet instead of the rabbit. • Use 1 pig's kidney instead of the rabbit offal.

SADDLE OF HARE WITH THYME-SCENTED POLENTA AND AUTUMN MUSHROOM MEDLEY

Sara Danesin Medio MasterChef 2011 finalist

PREPARATION TIME
1 hour 15 minutes,
plus chilling

COOKING TIME
1 hour 20 minutes

SERVES 4–6

"Ecstatic.
I'm absolutely
ecstatic. It's
the wow factor
that I was
hoping for."

FOR THE JUS
2 HARES, skinned
4 tbsp OLIVE OIL
1 CARROT, diced
1 CELERY stick, diced
1 SHALLOT, diced
1 TOMATO, roughly chopped
2 BAY LEAVES
small sprig of ROSEMARY
3 JUNIPER BERRIES,
    lightly crushed
100ml (3½fl oz) RED WINE
400ml (14fl oz) CHICKEN STOCK
SALT and freshly ground
    BLACK PEPPER
1 heaped tsp BITTER CHOCOLATE
    (70% cocoa), grated
20g (¾oz) UNSALTED BUTTER

FOR THE POLENTA
500ml (16fl oz) SALTED WATER
200g (7oz) POLENTA
4½ tbsp WHOLE MILK
40g (1¼oz) UNSALTED BUTTER
1 tbsp finely chopped
    THYME leaves
2 tbsp OLIVE OIL, for frying
30g (1oz) UNSALTED BUTTER,
    for frying

FOR THE BLACKBERRY JAM
150g (5½oz) BLACKBERRIES
60g (2oz) CASTER SUGAR
3 tbsp LIQUID GLUCOSE

FOR THE PARSNIP SILK
2 large PARSNIPS, peeled
    and diced
30g (1oz) UNSALTED BUTTER
250ml (8fl oz) WHOLE MILK
3 tbsp SINGLE CREAM
SALT and WHITE PEPPER

FOR THE CHESTNUT PURÉE
100g (3½oz) cooked and
    peeled CHESTNUTS
100ml (3½fl oz) WHOLE MILK
3 tbsp SINGLE CREAM
SALT and WHITE PEPPER

FOR THE HARE
reserved FILLETS from the
    SADDLES OF HARE, trimmed
    of any sinew
SALT and freshly ground
    BLACK PEPPER
1 tbsp GROUNDNUT OIL
knob of UNSALTED BUTTER

FOR THE MUSHROOM MEDLEY
1 tbsp OLIVE OIL
20g (¾oz) UNSALTED BUTTER
1 GARLIC clove, finely sliced
150g (5½oz) GIROLLE
    MUSHROOMS
150g (5½oz) CHIODINI
    MUSHROOMS
SALT and freshly ground
    BLACK PEPPER

TO GARNISH
THYME leaves

1 To make the jus, remove the shoulders and legs from the hares. Carefully cut the fillets from the saddles and set them aside. Remove the meat from 2 of the legs and set aside. The remaining meat from the hares can be used for another recipe later.

2 Heat the olive oil in a large casserole and gently sauté the carrot, celery, shallot, tomato, and herbs until the onion is softened and golden.

3 Add the hare carcasses and the meat from 2 of the legs and brown over a high heat. Add the wine, simmer for 5 minutes until reduced slightly, then add the stock. Bring to the boil and then simmer until the liquid has reduced by two-thirds. Strain through a sieve into a clean pan, then simmer gently for 10 minutes until further reduced. Season with the salt and pepper. Just before serving, reheat the jus gently then whisk in the chocolate and butter until smooth and glossy.

4 For the polenta, line a non-stick tin measuring about 30 x 20cm (12 x 8in) with cling film. Bring the water to the boil in a large pan. Remove from the heat and add the polenta. Whisk until smooth and then add the milk. Return to the heat and cook for 25–30 minutes, whisking regularly, until soft – you may need to add a little extra water or milk during cooking if the polenta looks as if it is drying out.

5 Whisk in the butter and thyme, then pour into the lined tin. Smooth the polenta into an even layer no deeper than 1cm (½in) deep, then transfer to the fridge and chill for 30 minutes or until set firm.

6 A few minutes before serving, turn the polenta out onto a chopping board and peel off the cling film. Trim the edges, cut into 8 triangles, then fry in the olive oil and butter for 2 minutes on each side until golden and crisp. Drain on kitchen paper.

7 For the blackberry jam, put the blackberries, sugar, and glucose in a small heavy pan and cook over high heat. When the berries are soft and the mixture is syrupy, transfer to a food processor and blitz until smooth. Pass through a fine sieve into a small bowl and cover with cling film until needed.

8 For the parsnip silk, put the parsnips, butter, milk, and cream into a pan and simmer until the parsnips are soft. Drain the parsnips, reserving the cooking liquid, then blitz in a food processor until smooth. Add a little of the cooking liquid, then blitz again – the mixture should be thick enough to make it into quenelles. Season with salt and white pepper and keep warm until serving.

9 For the chestnut purée, put the chestnuts, milk, and cream into a pan and simmer for 10 minutes until the chestnuts are very soft. Drain the chestnuts, reserving the cooking liquid, then blitz in a food processor until smooth. Add a little of the cooking liquid, then blitz again – the purée should be thick enough to pipe onto the serving plate. Season with salt and white pepper and keep warm. Transfer to a piping bag fitted with a 5mm (¼in) star-shaped nozzle just before serving.

10 For the hare, season the fillets with salt and black pepper. Heat a little groundnut oil in a heavy frying pan until very hot, then add the fillets. Cook for 2–3 minutes, turning regularly to ensure they are evenly coloured. Add a knob of butter and when it is foaming, baste the fillets in butter for a minute or so until golden. Remove from the pan and leave to rest on a warm plate for 10 minutes before carving.

11 To make the mushroom medley, heat the olive oil and butter in a frying pan with the garlic and sauté the mushrooms until tender. Season with salt and pepper and keep warm.

TO SERVE

To serve, spoon some blackberry jam on the plates and place 3 polenta triangles beside it. With 2 spoons, form the parsnip silk into quenelles and place on the plates. Cut the hare fillets obliquely into slices 1cm (½in) thick, discarding the end pieces. Place the hare on top of the jam and pour the jus over the meat. Arrange the mushrooms in a neat pile, and pipe star shapes of chestnut purée all around. Garnish with thyme leaves to add colour, and serve.

GREGG WALLACE

"When I got that jam on the end of that hare, I was like, 'Woah!' I didn't expect that. Lovely."

RABBIT NOSE TO TAIL – RABBIT BALLOTINE, MINCE AND OFFAL SAUSAGE, OFFAL TOASTS, PARSNIP PURÉE, RADISHES, AND MUSTARD CREAM SAUCE

Tom Whitaker MasterChef 2011 finalist

PREPARATION TIME
2 hours, plus chilling

COOKING TIME
1 hour

SERVES 4–6

FOR THE MUSTARD SAUCE
2 tbsp ENGLISH MUSTARD
2 tsp WHITE WINE VINEGAR
100ml (3½fl oz) DOUBLE CREAM
SALT and freshly ground
  BLACK PEPPER

FOR THE SAUSAGES
2 tsp FENNEL SEEDS,
  finely crushed
RAPESEED OIL, for frying
1 BANANA SHALLOT, finely diced
75g (2½oz) RABBIT OFFAL (heart,
  kidney, liver), trimmed, and very
  finely chopped
400g (14oz) RABBIT MINCE, from
  legs and hindquarters
50g (1¾oz) PANKO
  BREADCRUMBS
1 tbsp YELLOW MUSTARD SEEDS
1 tbsp chopped FLAT-LEAF
  PARSLEY
1 tbsp snipped CHIVES
1 tsp TRUFFLE OIL
1 tsp CAYENNE PEPPER
2 sheets of CAUL FAT, each
  approx. 20 x 15cm (8 x 6in)

FOR THE BALLOTINES
200g (7oz) SHELLED, UNSALTED
  PISTACHIO NUTS
1 tsp MUSTARD POWDER
2 tbsp finely chopped
  FENNEL leaves
30g (1oz) UNSALTED BUTTER
100g (3½oz) GIROLLE
  MUSHROOMS, cleaned and sliced
100g (3½oz) CHANTERELLE
  MUSHROOMS, cleaned and sliced
approx. 30g (1oz) PANKO
  BREADCRUMBS

8 SADDLE FILLETS of FARMED
  RABBIT, approx. 900g (2lb)
  in total
10 large slices of PROSCIUTTO
2 sheets of CAUL FAT, each
  approx. 20 x 20cm (8 x 8in)
RAPESEED OIL, for frying

FOR THE PARSNIP PURÉE
650g (1lb 7oz) PARSNIPS, cut
  into 2cm (¾in) chunks
350ml (12fl oz) DOUBLE CREAM
1 litre (1¾ pints) WHOLE MILK
200g (7oz) UNSALTED
  BUTTER, cubed
1 LEMON, quartered
2 BAY LEAVES, lightly crushed

FOR THE OFFAL TOASTS
50g (1¾oz) RABBIT OFFAL (heart,
  kidney, liver), trimmed
  and chopped
85g (3oz) DUCK LIVER, trimmed
  and chopped
4 sprigs of THYME, leaves only
pinch of MUSTARD POWDER
4 slices WHITE BREAD,
  crusts removed
100g (3½oz) CLARIFIED BUTTER
  or GHEE for frying

FOR THE RADISHES
50g (1¾oz) DUCK FAT
1 litre (1¾ pints) RABBIT or
  GAME STOCK
2 bunches of RED BABY RADISHES
  with leaves

1 For the mustard sauce, whisk all the ingredients together in a small bowl until smooth. Season to taste with salt and pepper, then cover and set aside until ready to serve.

2 To make the sausages, dry-toast the fennel seeds in a large frying pan. Add the rapeseed oil and then fry the shallot for 2–3 minutes until slightly softened. Transfer the mixture to a large bowl and combine with the rabbit offal and mince, panko breadcrumbs, mustard seeds, herbs, truffle oil, and cayenne pepper. Mix thoroughly and add more crumbs if the mixture is too wet. Season with salt and pepper.

3 Place 2 large pieces of cling film on a flat surface and lay a piece of caul fat over each. Divide the sausage mixture evenly and place on the caul fat, leaving a 2cm (¾in) border. Fold to encase the mince mixture, then roll tightly into a sausage shape. Twist the ends tightly and secure with a knot. Wrap in the cling film and place in the fridge until ready to cook.

4 For the ballotines, pulse the pistachio nuts in a food processor until roughly chopped. Add the mustard and fennel and pulse for 15 seconds until combined. Heat the butter in a hot pan and fry the mushrooms for 2–3 minutes, then add the nut mixture and cook for a further 1 minute. Transfer the mixture to a bowl – it should have the consistency of sausage meat. If the mixture seems a little loose, gradually add pinches of panko breadcrumbs to thicken. Set aside to cool slightly.

5 Place the rabbit fillets between 2 pieces of cling film and beat with a meat mallet or rolling pin until the meat is just under 1cm (½in) thick. Place 2 large pieces of cling film on a flat surface and lay out a piece of caul fat on each. Arrange 5 slices of prosciutto on each piece of caul fat, close together to ensure there are no gaps. Lay the flattened rabbit saddles over the prosciutto, slightly overlapping each one, and spread the nut stuffing over them. Roll up tightly, wrap in cling film, and twist the ends to make a neat shape. Chill for at least 30 minutes before cooking.

6 For the parsnip purée, simmer the parsnips in a saucepan with the cream, milk, butter, lemon, and bay leaves for 15–20 minutes until tender. Drain the parsnips and blend in a food processor until smooth, adding a little more cream if the mixture is too thick. Season to taste with salt and pepper, then set aside and keep warm.

7 To cook the ballotines and sausages, preheat the oven to 220°C (425°F/Gas 7). Remove the cling film from the ballotines and sausages and heat the rapeseed oil in 2 large ovenproof frying pans. Fry the ballotines and sausages in separate pans for 3 minutes until browned on all sides, then transfer the ballotines to the oven and cook for 12 minutes. Cook the sausages for a further 5 minutes on the hob, then transfer to the oven and cook for 3 minutes. Remove the pans from the oven and set aside in a warm place to rest.

8 For the offal toasts, combine the offal, liver, thyme, and mustard powder in a small food processor and blend until smooth. Season with salt and pepper. Spread the mixture firmly and evenly onto 2 pieces of the bread and top with the remaining slices. Fry the sandwiches, in batches, in clarified butter for 1 minute on each side, basting with more butter as they cook. Cut each sandwich into 4 soldiers.

9 Cut the leaves off the radishes and trim off the tops and bottoms. Heat the duck fat and game stock in a pan until boiling. Add the radishes and cook for 5 minutes until just tender, then add the leaves and immediately remove the pan from the heat. Strain through a fine sieve.

TO SERVE

Slice the ballotines and sausages into even pieces. Arrange attractively on slate or plates. Rest a toast soldier on the ballotine. Place a quenelle of parsnip purée on one side. Add small piles of radish leaves, topped with the radishes. Finish by piping the mustard sauce onto the plate. Serve the remaining mustard sauce in small sauce boats alongside.

JOHN TORODE

"Everything you have done is beautifully cooked, technically amazing, wonderfully seasoned."

KYUSHU-STYLE PORK RAMEN WITH TRUFFLED LOBSTER GYOZA AND AROMATIC OILS

Tim Anderson MasterChef 2011 champion

PREPARATION TIME
2 hours 30 minutes

COOKING TIME
10 hours

SERVES 4

FOR THE TONKOTSU STOCK
1.5kg (3lb 3oz) PORK THIGH
   BONES, broken
500g (1lb 2oz) PORK SPARE
   RIBS, broken
1 CARROT
½ ONION
1 LEEK
SALT, to taste

FOR THE DASHI
1 sheet KONBU SEAWEED
2 litres (3½ pints) SOFT
   MINERAL WATER
80g (2¾oz) KATSUOBUSHI FLAKES

FOR THE BROTH
200ml (7fl oz) DASHI
400ml (14fl oz) PREPARED
   TONKOTSU STOCK
4 tsp SOY SAUCE
4 tsp MIRIN
4 tsp SAKE
8 tsp WATER
2 tsp RICE VINEGAR
20g (¾oz) DRIED PORCINI
   MUSHROOMS

FOR THE PORK BELLY
RAPESEED OIL, for frying
250g (9oz) PORK BELLY,
   rind removed
200ml (7fl oz) PREPARED DASHI
200ml (7fl oz) PREPARED
   TONKOTSU STOCK
200ml (7fl oz) DRY SHERRY
200ml (7fl oz) ROOT BEER
100ml (3½fl oz) SOY SAUCE
100ml (3½fl oz) MAPLE SYRUP

FOR THE NOODLES
8 tsp PILSNER BEER
4 tbsp RAPESEED OIL

2 EGGS
1 EGG YOLK
150g (5½oz) "00" PASTA FLOUR
½ tsp SALT
500ml (16fl oz) PREPARED DASHI

FOR THE GYOZA WRAPPERS
125g (4½oz) "00" PASTA FLOUR
1 tbsp RICE FLOUR
5 tbsp boiling WATER

FOR THE GYOZA FILLING
1 raw LOBSTER TAIL, removed
   from the shell
10g (¼oz) fresh BLACK
   TRUFFLE, shaved
1 tsp finely snipped CHIVES
pinch of SALT
pinch of WHITE PEPPER

TO ASSEMBLE THE GYOZA
1 EGG WHITE
RAPESEED OIL, for frying
splash of SAKE

FOR THE RED AROMATIC OIL
25g (scant 1oz) RED MISO
25g (scant 1oz) TOMATO PURÉE
5 tsp RAPESEED OIL
2 tsp TRUFFLE OIL

FOR THE BLACK AROMATIC OIL
1 tsp RAPESEED OIL
4 GARLIC cloves, minced
1 tbsp CHINESE BLACK BEANS
2 tsp SOY SAUCE
1 tsp BLACK SESAME SEEDS
5 tsp SESAME OIL

FOR THE GREEN AROMATIC OIL
3 tbsp AVOCADO OIL
20 SHISO LEAVES
2 SPRING ONIONS, green parts
¼ tsp GREEN YUZU-KOSHO PASTE

FOR THE GARNISH
RAPESEED OIL, for deep-frying
reserved PORCINI MUSHROOMS,
   well-drained and dried on
   kitchen paper
20cm (8in) RHUBARB, cut into
   julienne strips 5cm (2in) long

4 SPRING ONIONS, white parts
   only, cut into julienne strips
   5cm (2in) long
16 ENOKI MUSHROOMS, cut into
   julienne strips 5cm (2in) long
500ml (16fl oz) PREPARED DASHI

1 For the tonkotsu pork stock, place all the bones in a large stockpot and cover with water. Bring to the boil and cook for 10 minutes. Drain the bones and briefly rinse them. Return the bones to the pot and add the vegetables and about 4 litres (7 pints) of fresh water. Boil rapidly for 8 hours, frequently skimming the scum and replenishing the liquid with fresh water to keep it from over-reducing. Strain through a large sieve or colander lined with a muslin cloth. Season to taste with salt and set aside.

2 For the dashi, place the konbu and water in a large pan and leave to soak for 10 minutes. Bring to the boil, then reduce the heat and simmer for 10 minutes. Add the katsuobushi and leave to infuse until all the flakes have sunk, then strain through a muslin cloth. There will be more dashi than you need for this recipe, but you can store the remainder in the fridge for several days or freeze it in convenient quantities for up to 6 months.

3 For the broth, combine all the ingredients and bring to the boil. When the porcini have softened, remove them and set aside. Strain the broth through a sieve lined with muslin cloth. Keep warm until serving.

4 For the pork belly, heat the rapeseed oil in a casserole and sear the pork until golden all over. Add all the other ingredients and bring to the boil. Simmer for 2 hours, turning the pork occasionally, until the liquid has reduced to a sticky glaze. Leave the pork to cool in the pan, then cut into 3cm (1¼in) cubes. Set aside until needed.

5 To make the noodles, beat the pilsner, 3 tbsp of the rapeseed oil, eggs, and egg yolk together in a jug. Combine them with the flour and salt in a food processor and blitz until the mixture comes together to form a dough. Turn out onto a lightly floured surface and knead until smooth.

6 Using a pasta machine, roll the dough out into a very thin sheet and cut into fine noodles using the capellini attachment. Dust the noodles with plenty of flour to prevent them from sticking together.

7 Bring the dashi to the boil in a large saucepan, add the noodles, and cook for 2–3 minutes. Drain, then rinse under cold water. Drain again, then transfer to a bowl and toss with the remaining 1 tbsp rapeseed oil. Set aside until needed.

8 To make the gyoza wrappers, mix all the ingredients together in a food processor and blitz until a rough dough is formed. Turn out onto a floured surface and knead until smooth. Roll out into a very thin sheet using a pasta machine and cut into twelve 8cm (3¼in) circles with a pastry cutter. Dust each disc of pastry with flour and cover with cling film to prevent the dough from drying out.

9 For the gyoza filling, roughly mince the lobster and combine with the truffle and chives. Season with salt and white pepper.

10 To assemble the gyoza, add 1 tsp of filling to the centre of each wrapper, then brush around the outside with a little egg white. Seal the edges with a series of pleats. Repeat with the remaining wrappers and filling.

11 Heat a little rapeseed oil in a frying pan and fry the gyoza on one side for 2–3 minutes until golden and crisp. Add a splash of sake to the pan and quickly cover with a lid. Remove the pan from the heat and leave to steam for 2–3 minutes, being careful not to shake the pan as this can damage the gyoza. (You may need to cook the gyoza in batches to prevent overcrowding the pan). Carefully remove the gyoza from the pan and set aside.

12 For the red aromatic oil, mix all the ingredients together into a thick, paint-like consistency.

13 For the black aromatic oil, heat the rapeseed oil in a pan until smoking. Add the garlic and cook until charred, then add the black beans, soy sauce, and sesame seeds and cook until the liquid is mostly evaporated. Add the sesame oil and heat briefly. Transfer to a pestle and mortar and grind to a smooth oil. Transfer to 4 small dishes.

14 For the green aromatic oil, blend all the ingredients in a blender until very smooth. Transfer to 4 small dishes.

15 For the garnish, heat the rapeseed oil to 190°C (375°F) and deep fry the reserved porcini mushrooms until crisp. Drain on kitchen paper.

TO SERVE

Smear some red oil across the bottom of 4 deep ramen bowls. Arrange the pork cubes in a line bisecting the red oil. Pile the noodles in front of the pork belly cubes and set the gyoza on top of the pork. Arrange the garnish on top of the noodles. Transfer the broth to decorative teapots. To serve, pour the broth into the bowl, then drizzle in the black and green oils.

GREGG WALLACE

"There is no denying the skill, the beauty, and the excitement of that dish. Your food is exciting."

HERB-STUFFED WEST COUNTRY PORK TENDERLOINS WITH SPICED RED CABBAGE, AND A ROASTED CHESTNUT SAUCE

Danny Goffey musician and 2011 Celebrity semi-finalist

PREPARATION TIME
40 minutes

COOKING TIME
50 minutes

SERVES 4

"The cabbage is inspired by going to my grandad's and staying there as a lad for the weekend. When he did a roast he did a really nice red cabbage and it reminds me of him."

FOR THE PORK TENDERLOINS
2 PORK TENDERLOINS
1 tbsp finely chopped ONION
85g (3oz) UNSALTED BUTTER, softened
75g (2½oz) fresh BREADCRUMBS
3 tbsp finely chopped PARSLEY
3 tbsp finely chopped ROSEMARY
PLAIN FLOUR, for dusting
SALT and freshly ground BLACK PEPPER
good pinch of GROUND MACE

FOR THE RED CABBAGE
30g (1oz) BUTTER
2 tsp OLIVE OIL
1 RED ONION, chopped
2 COX'S APPLES, peeled, cored, and finely chopped

2 GARLIC cloves, chopped
½ small RED CABBAGE, shredded
¼ tsp GROUND MIXED SPICE
1 STAR ANISE
1 piece CINNAMON STICK
SALT and freshly ground BLACK PEPPER
1 tbsp LIGHT SOFT BROWN SUGAR
1 tbsp RED WINE VINEGAR

FOR THE CHESTNUT SAUCE
200g (7oz) CHESTNUTS, a slit cut in flat side of shells
100g (3½oz) LARDONS
1 tbsp OLIVE OIL
3 tbsp RED WINE
150ml (5fl oz) CHICKEN STOCK
a few drops of TABASCO

1 Preheat the oven to 180°C (350°F/Gas 4). Halve the pork tenderloins widthways, then split lengthways, not right through.
2 Fry the onion gently in 15g (½oz) of the butter for 5 minutes until soft. Add the breadcrumbs and herbs. Season. Use to stuff the tenderloins, then dust them all over with flour.
3 Cut 4 rectangles of greaseproof paper 25 x 15cm (10 x 6in). Spread the remaining softened butter thickly over the centre of each paper and season with salt, pepper, and the mace.
4 Place one piece of pork on each buttered sheet of greaseproof paper. Roll the pork in the paper and twist the ends to seal, like Christmas crackers. Place on a baking tray and bake for 30 minutes. Remove and rest 10 minutes before serving.
5 For the red cabbage, heat the butter and oil in a pan, then soften the onions for 5 minutes. Add the remaining ingredients. Bring to the boil, reduce the heat and simmer gently for 30 minutes, stirring occasionally, until tender. Discard whole spices.
6 For the sauce, roast the chestnuts in a heavy frying pan, turning until blackened. Cool, then peel and roughly chop. Fry the lardons in the olive oil for 5 minutes until crisp. Add the red wine, chestnuts, stock, and Tabasco. Simmer for 10 minutes until the chestnuts are soft and breaking up. Blitz in a blender until smooth. Season and serve with the stuffed pork and cabbage.

ROASTED FILLET OF VENISON WITH A RED WINE AND PORT REDUCTION, ROASTED BEETROOT AND SHALLOTS, AND SWEET POTATO MASH

Tim Lovejoy television presenter and 2011 Celebrity semi-finalist

PREPARATION TIME
20 minutes

COOKING TIME
45 minutes

SERVES 4

FOR THE REDUCTION
200ml (7fl oz) MERLOT, or other
   full-bodied red wine
5 tbsp PORT
150ml (5fl oz) CHICKEN STOCK
1 GARLIC clove, roughly chopped
2 sprigs of THYME
1 tsp SUGAR
25g (scant 1oz) BUTTER

**FOR THE ROASTED
VEGETABLES**
4 BEETROOTS, peeled
2 tbsp OLIVE OIL
12 small round SHALLOTS,
   peeled but left whole

FOR THE VENISON
700g (1lb 9oz) LOIN OF VENISON
2 tbsp OLIVE OIL
SALT and freshly ground
   BLACK PEPPER

FOR THE MASH
2 large SWEET POTATOES, peeled
   and diced
1 large MARIS PIPER POTATO,
   peeled and diced
50g (1¾oz) UNSALTED BUTTER

1 Preheat the oven to 180°C (350°F/Gas 4). In a saucepan, reduce the wine, port, stock, garlic, thyme, and sugar for about 20 minutes, until syrupy. Strain through a fine sieve into a clean pan, to remove the garlic and thyme, then add the butter and whisk until smooth and glossy. Reheat gently before serving.
2 For the roasted vegetables, cut the beetroot in quarters, toss in the olive oil, and season with the salt and pepper. Place in a roasting tin and roast in the oven for 20 minutes or until almost tender. Add the shallots and roast for a further 10 minutes.
3 Heat a large frying pan until smoking. Brush the venison with the olive oil and season generously with salt and pepper. Seal the venison until golden brown, about 2 minutes each side.
4 Place on top of the shallots and beetroot in the oven and cook for 10–12 minutes. Remove from the oven and leave the venison to rest for 10 minutes.
5 Whilst the venison is cooking, bring a large pan of salted water to the boil and add the cubed sweet potato and the Maris Piper potato. Boil until soft, then drain thoroughly. Add the unsalted butter, season, and mash until smooth.
6 Carve the venison into 4 thick slices and arrange on plates with the beetroot, shallots, and mash. Spoon over a little reduction and serve straight away.

BRINGING UMAMI OUT OF CHAOS
Tim Anderson MasterChef 2011 champion

PREPARATION TIME
1 hour

COOKING TIME
3 hours

SERVES 4

FOR THE DASHI
20cm (8in) DRIED KONBU SEAWEED
10 DRIED SHIITAKE MUSHROOMS
1 litre (1¾ pints) SOFT MINERAL
   WATER (or softened tap water)
50g (1¾oz) KATSUOBUSHI FLAKES

FOR THE PORK BELLY
500g (1lb 2oz) PORK BELLY,
   rind removed
450ml (15fl oz) COLA
300ml (10fl oz) PREPARED DASHI
150ml (5fl oz) SHOYU
150ml (5fl oz) WORCESTERSHIRE
   SAUCE
5 tbsp RED WINE
5 tbsp MIRIN
2 STAR ANISE
1½ tsp MARMITE

FOR THE CELERY
1 CELERY stick,
   halved widthways
100g (3½oz) CASTER SUGAR
3 tbsp WATER
1 tsp YUZU JUICE

FOR THE FONDANT SQUASH
1 small RED KURI SQUASH,
   approx. 12cm (5in) in
   diameter, washed
2 tbsp OLIVE OIL
100g (3½oz) BUTTER

100ml (3½fl oz) DASHI
100ml (3½fl oz) RED WINE

FOR THE ROASTED TURNIPS
16 BABY TURNIPS
2 tbsp WALNUT OIL
SALT and WHITE PEPPER

FOR THE PEAS
250ml (8fl oz) PREPARED DASHI
2 tbsp shelled PEAS

FOR THE MISO MUSTARD
30g (1oz) WHITE MISO
30g (1oz) DIJON MUSTARD
3 tbsp DRY WHITE VERMOUTH
100ml (3½oz) PREPARED DASHI
1 EGG YOLK
2 tbsp WALNUT OIL
30g (1oz) PARMESAN CHEESE,
   grated

FOR THE DASHI PEARLS
100ml (3½oz) PREPARED DASHI
2 tsp SHOYU
2 tsp MIRIN
1 tsp YUZU JUICE
2.5g SODIUM ALGINATE
7.5g CALCIUM CHLORIDE POWDER
120ml (4fl oz) SOFT WATER

TO GARNISH
handful of SHISO CRESS
handful of SALAD CRESS

Simplify for EVERYDAY

• For dashi, substitute chicken
stock with a splash of shoyu (or
light soy sauce), and a pinch of
sugar. • Use lime juice instead of
yuzu. • Omit the pearls, use
twice as many peas, and add the
mirin and shoyu when cooking.
• Drain, thicken the stock with
cornflour and use a little to coat
the peas to a shiny glaze.

1 To make the dashi, steep the konbu and mushrooms in the
water for 15–20 minutes until soft. Heat the water very gently,
removing the mushrooms before it boils. Once it boils, reduce to
a simmer and cook the konbu for 10 minutes, then remove. Add
the katsuobushi flakes, strain the liquid once they sink, and
reserve to one side.
2 For the cola-roasted pork belly, preheat the oven to 160°C
(325°F/Gas 3). Place the pork in a roasting tin. Whisk together
the remaining ingredients and pour them over the pork. Roast

for 2 hours, basting frequently. Remove the pork from the oven and rest for 15 minutes. Care into 4 neat rectangular pieces.

3 Meanwhile, prepare the celery. Cut 4 strips of celery, no thicker than 3mm (⅛in) each, and trim into a neat, rectangular shape. Dissolve the sugar in the water and yuzu juice and bring to the boil. Allow the sugar to caramelize to a light amber colour, then add the celery and remove the pan from the heat. Leave the celery to cook in the syrup for 4 minutes, then drain and cool on greaseproof paper, brushing off the excess sugar syrup with a wet pastry brush.

4 For the pumpkin, slice the squash vertically into 4 rings, each around 2cm (¾in) thick, and scoop out the seeds. Melt the oil and butter in a frying pan and cook the squash rings on one side for about 4 minutes until nicely browned. Turn them over and add enough dashi and wine to come just below the top of the squash. Transfer to the oven and cook for about 30 minutes, until the squash is very soft and most of the liquid has evaporated.

5 Next, toss the turnips with the oil, salt, and pepper. Place in a roasting tray and roast in the oven for 45 minutes.

6 Meanwhile, to cook the peas, bring the dashi to the boil in saucepan and blanch the peas in it until they are just tender. When cool enough to handle, remove their outer skin.

7 To cook the miso mustard, whisk together the miso, mustard, vermouth, dashi, and egg yolk in a bain-marie or a bowl set over a pan of simmering water. Slowly drizzle in the oil, whisking constantly until emulsified. Whisk in the Parmesan cheese and keep warm.

8 To make the dashi pearls, ensure that the dashi is cool. Using a blender, mix together the dashi, shoyu, mirin, yuzu juice, and sodium alginate until completely homogenous. Allow the air bubbles to dissipate. Stir the calcium chloride into the soft water until completely dissolved. With a pipette, drop the dashi mixture into the calcium chloride bath and leave to set for 45 seconds, then remove with a small slotted spoon and rinse under cold water. Just before serving, combine with the peas.

TO SERVE

Set the squash in the middle of each plate and pour a small pool of its braising liquid in the centre. Place the pork on top and balance the celery on the pork. Arrange the turnips around the squash and spoon some mustard around the rim of the plates. Decorate with the peas and pearls, and finish by garnishing with the shiso and salad cress.

STUFFED SADDLE OF SUCKLING PIG WITH A CRISPY PIG'S EAR SALAD
Tom Whitaker MasterChef 2011 finalist

PREPARATION TIME
2 hours 30 minutes,
plus chilling

COOKING TIME
3 hours

SERVES 6

FOR THE BROTH
250ml (8fl oz) DRY WHITE WINE
2 litres (3½ pints) HAM STOCK
2 BAY LEAVES
3 PIG'S EARS
4 PIG'S TROTTERS
2 HAM HOCKS

FOR THE CRUBEENS
reserved TROTTER MEAT,
   shredded
reserved HAM HOCK
   MEAT, shredded
1 tbsp finely chopped THYME
1 tbsp finely chopped PARSLEY
1 tbsp ENGLISH MUSTARD
   POWDER
SALT and freshly ground
   BLACK PEPPER
200g (7oz) PLAIN FLOUR
2 EGGS, beaten
200g (7oz) PANKO BREADCRUMBS
VEGETABLE OIL, for deep frying

FOR THE STUFFING
200g (7oz) PIG'S LIVER,
   finely chopped
200g (7oz) BURY BLACK PUDDING,
   finely chopped
5 PICKLED WALNUTS, crushed
2 tbsp finely chopped THYME
2 tbsp finely chopped PARSLEY
25g (scant 1oz) ROLLED OATS
1 tsp MUSTARD SEEDS

FOR THE SUCKLING PIG
1 tbsp FENNEL SEEDS
1 boned SADDLE OF
   SUCKLING PIG
2 tbsp OLIVE OIL

FOR THE SALAD
200ml (7fl oz) MALT VINEGAR
3 tbsp SHERRY VINEGAR
50g (1¾oz) CASTER SUGAR
2 tsp FENNEL SEEDS
2 tsp CORIANDER SEEDS
1 BAY LEAF
3 CELERY sticks, finely sliced
3 SHALLOTS, finely sliced
reserved PIG'S EARS
100g (3½oz) PLAIN FLOUR
VEGETABLE OIL, for deep frying
leaves from 1 head of CELERY
1 head of CHICORY,
   leaves separated
20 SORREL LEAVES
2 tbsp chopped PARSLEY
juice of ½ LEMON
2 tbsp OLIVE OIL

FOR THE POMME PURÉE
6 KING EDWARD POTATOES,
   peeled and halved
500ml (16fl oz) WHOLE MILK
200ml (7fl oz) DOUBLE CREAM
2 BAY LEAVES
SALT and WHITE PEPPER
few drops of HICKORY ESSENCE

FOR THE SAUCE
reserved HAM BROTH
1 tbsp HONEY

TO GARNISH
6 sprigs of THYME

1 First make the broth. Pour the white wine into an open pressure cooker pan, bring to the boil and reduce by half. Add the ham stock, bay leaves, pig's ears, trotters, and ham hock, seal the pressure cooker and cook on low heat for 1¼ hours. Remove the meat and set the ears aside, then strain the broth through a fine sieve into a clean pan and set aside. Strip the meat and fat from the hock and trotters, taking as much soft fat as you can as this gives texture and taste. Discard any leftover skin and cartilage and mix the meat and fat thoroughly in a bowl.

2 For the crubeens, mix the shredded trotter and hock meat with the thyme, parsley, and mustard powder, then season to taste with salt and pepper. Press into a non-stick baking tin to a depth of 3cm (1¼in), then cover the surface with cling film. Chill for 30–45 minutes in the fridge until set. Once set, cut into even squares of about 3cm (1¼in). Dip each cube in the flour and shake off any excess, then dip in the egg and finally the panko breadcrumbs, ensuring each cube is evenly coated.

3 To make the stuffing, place all the ingredients in a large bowl and mix thoroughly until you have an even consistency – roughly that of sausage meat. Season with salt and pepper.

4 To cook the suckling pig, preheat the oven to 130°C (250°F/ Gas ½). Toast the fennel seeds in a dry frying pan until fragrant, then crush in a pestle and mortar with salt and pepper. Using a craft knife, score the skin of the saddle widthways in regular lines, roughly 5mm (¼in) apart, and rub the toasted fennel seed mixture into the skin.

5 Mould the stuffing into a sausage shape and place down the centre of the saddle. Fold the skin flaps into the centre (trim off excess if they overlap) and then sow up the belly with a larding needle and thread.

6 Heat the olive oil in a frying pan and sear the saddle until coloured on all sides, then transfer to a roasting tin. Roast for 50 minutes to 1 hour, then remove from the oven and turn the oven up to its highest temperature. Return the saddle to the oven for 10 minutes or until the skin is crisp. Remove from the oven and leave to rest for at least 30 minutes.

7 Meanwhile, to make the pickles for the salad, combine the vinegars, sugar, and spices in a saucepan. Bring to the boil, simmer for 20 minutes, then strain into a bowl. Add the celery and shallots to the pickling mixture, then leave for 30 minutes until soft. Drain and leave to cool.

8 For the pomme purée, put the potatoes in a pan with the milk, cream, and bay leaves and simmer until tender. Remove the bay leaves and discard. Drain the potatoes, reserving the cooking liquid, and transfer to a food processor along with a little of the cooking liquid. With the motor running, keep adding a little cooking liquid until you have a silky-smooth, thick purée.

Pass through a fine sieve and season to taste with salt and white pepper. Add a few drops of hickory essence, stir to combine, and keep warm.

9 Preheat the oven to 180°C (350°F/Gas 4). Scatter the thyme sprigs over the bottom of a small roasting tray and roast for 8–10 minutes until crisp, taking care not to burn them. Reserve for the garnish.

10 To make the sauce, bring the ham broth to the boil, add the honey, and reduce until syrupy. Season to taste and keep warm until serving.

11 Just before serving, deep fry the crubeens in vegetable oil for 3 minutes until golden and crisp, then drain on kitchen paper. Slice the pigs ears julienne, and roll in seasoned flour. Deep fry at 180°C (350°F) for 3 minutes or until crisp, then drain on kitchen paper.

12 Mix the pickled celery and shallots, celery leaves, chicory leaves, sorrel, and parsley in a bowl and toss to combine. Add the pig's ears and dress the salad with the lemon juice, olive oil, and salt and pepper.

TO SERVE

Place the pomme purée in a piping bag and pipe onto either plates or wooden serving boards. Carve the saddle into thick slices and arrange 3 slices on each plate or board with 3 crubeens and a small pile of the salad. Garnish with the roasted thyme and serve with the sauce in a small jug alongside.

CANNON OF VENISON WITH A RED WINE AND BLACKBERRY REDUCTION SERVED WITH POTATO AND CELERIAC MASH

Polly Oxby MasterChef 2011 contestant

PREPARATION TIME
15 minutes

COOKING TIME
40 minutes

SERVES 4

FOR THE SAUCE
400ml (14fl oz) good BEEF STOCK
200ml (7fl oz) FULL-BODIED
   RED WINE
1 SHALLOT, very finely chopped
100g (3½oz) BLACKBERRIES
2 tsp REDCURRANT JELLY

FOR THE MASHED POTATOES
1kg (2¼lb) MARIS PIPER
   POTATOES, peeled and quartered
300g (10oz) CELERIAC, cubed
100ml (3½fl oz) DOUBLE CREAM
100g (3½oz) BUTTER

FOR THE VENISON
600g (1lb 5oz) CANNON
   OF VENISON
OLIVE OIL
SALT and freshly ground
   BLACK PEPPER
30g (1oz) UNSALTED BUTTER

TO SERVE
300g (10oz) PURPLE
   SPROUTING BROCCOLI

1 For the sauce, put the beef stock, red wine, shallot, and blackberries into a small pan, bring to the boil, then reduce the heat and simmer until reduced by two-thirds. Pass the mixture through a fine sieve into a clean pan and stir in the redcurrant jelly until dissolved. Simmer for a couple of minutes to reduce and make a lovely glossy sauce. Set aside. Reheat before serving.
2 Boil the potatoes and celeriac in separate pans until tender, then drain. Mash the potatoes or pass through a ricer, add the cream and butter, and stir until smooth. Place the celeriac in a food processor and blitz until it forms a purée. Combine with the mashed potato and season to taste. Keep warm until needed.
3 While the potatoes are boiling, preheat the oven to 180°C (350°F/Gas 4). Rub the meat with olive oil and season well on all sides. Heat a frying pan and sear the venison until browned all over. Transfer to a roasting tin and smear with the butter. Roast for 8 minutes for medium rare. Remove the meat from the oven and allow to rest in a warm place before carving.
4 Steam the broccoli for 3–4 minutes until just tender. Carve the venison and serve with the mash, sauce, and broccoli.

POLLY'S CANNON OF VENISON SIMPLIFIED FOR **EVERY**DAY... ▶PAGE 170

SUCCULENT VENISON

JOHN TORODE STAYS TRUE TO THE FABULOUS FLAVOUR
OF POLLY'S VENISON IN HIS QUICK AND EASY VERSION

PREP: 15 MINS • COOK: 25–35 MINS

VENISON STEAKS

SERVES 4

2 tbsp OLIVE OIL
1 tbsp BUTTER
4 thick VENISON STEAKS
SALT and freshly ground
  BLACK PEPPER

1 Heat the oil and butter in a heavy
based frying pan then season the
venison steaks.
2 Add the venison to the pan and cook
for 3–5 minutes then flip it over and cook
for a further 3–5 minutes depending upon
the thickness of the meat and how well
done you like it. Don't overcook. Drain off
excess fat.
3 Transfer the venison to a warmed
serving dish and keep warm whilst making
the mash and the sauce.
4 Slice the venison steaks and serve on a
bed of the celeriac mash with the sauce.

"To ensure tender, succulent venison, don't overcook it. Brown on both sides, then rest in a warm place for 10 minutes. The result will almost melt in the mouth – sensational!"

+

...SERVE WITH

CELERIAC MASH

1 large POTATO, diced
1 CELERIAC, trimmed, peeled
 and diced
2 tbsp DOUBLE CREAM
50g (1¾oz) BUTTER
SALT and freshly ground BLACK PEPPER

1 Place the potato and celeriac in a large saucepan of salted cold water then bring to the boil. Reduce the heat slightly, and simmer for 12–15 minutes or until very soft.
2 Drain thoroughly, then mash together with the cream and butter, and season to taste.

BERRY SAUCE

4 tbsp REDCURRANT JELLY
150ml (5 fl oz) BEEF STOCK
5 tbsp RED WINE
½ tsp BALSAMIC VINEGAR
75g (2½oz) BLACKBERRIES
knob of BUTTER
SALT and freshly ground BLACK PEPPER

1 Put the redcurrant jelly in a small pan, break down with a spatula if very lumpy, and gently heat until the jelly has melted.
2 Add the stock and wine to the pan to deglaze it then boil rapidly for 3–4 minutes or until reduced slightly.
3 Add the balsamic vinegar, blackberries and seasoning to the pan and cook for a further 3–5 minutes or until the blackberries are soft. Stir in the butter until melted and smooth. Taste and re-season if necessary.

COD WITH GREEN LENTILS AND CHOKA

Kirsty Wark journalist and presenter and 2011 Celebrity finalist

PREPARATION TIME
30 minutes

COOKING TIME
1 hour

SERVES 4

FOR THE VEGETABLE STOCK
1 tbsp OLIVE OIL
150g (5½oz) FROZEN PEAS
2 CARROTS, chopped
2 WHITE ONIONS, chopped
1 LEEK, chopped
2 CELERY sticks, chopped
1 bunch SWISS CHARD, chopped
2 COURGETTES, chopped
2 POTATOES, chopped
100g (3½oz) SPINACH
2 GARLIC cloves, crushed

FOR THE LENTILS
1 BAY LEAF
1 sprig of ROSEMARY
1 sprig of SAGE
250g (9oz) GREEN LENTILS,
   preferably lenticchie
   di castelluccio
2 tbsp OLIVE OIL
1 WHITE ONION, finely chopped
1 CARROT, finely chopped
1 CELERY stick, finely chopped
1 small LEEK, finely chopped
100g (3½oz) piece of
   unsmoked PANCETTA

FOR THE CHOKA
200g (7oz) PLUM TOMATOES
2 tbsp SUNFLOWER OIL
1 small SWEET ONION,
   finely chopped
1 GARLIC clove, crushed
1 tbsp chopped CORIANDER
1 tsp PAPRIKA
pinch of DRIED CHILLI FLAKES
1 RED CHILLI, deseeded and
   finely chopped
SALT and freshly ground
   BLACK PEPPER

FOR THE COD
4 CENTRE-CUT COD FILLETS,
   150g (5½oz) each
SALT and freshly ground
   BLACK PEPPER
SUNFLOWER OIL
25g (scant 1oz) BUTTER
1 tbsp chopped FLAT-LEAF
   PARSLEY

1 For the vegetable stock, heat the oil in a large pot. Add the peas, stir, then mash them against the sides with the back of a wooden spoon. Add the rest of the vegetables and the garlic, stir, cover, reduce the heat, and sweat gently for 5 minutes. Cover with 1.5 litres (2¾ pints) cold water and slowly bring to almost boiling. Skim the scum from the surface, turn down the heat, and simmer for about 20 minutes until the vegetables are really soft.

2 Remove from the heat and leave to cool for a few minutes before straining. Reserve the vegetables.

3 Meanwhile, prepare the lentils. Tie the herbs together with string. Soak the lentils in cold water whilst finely chopping the vegetables. Heat the olive oil in a pan and add the chopped vegetables and the piece of pancetta. Cook gently, stirring, for 5–10 minutes until the vegetables are soft but not browned.

4 Add the drained lentils and tied herbs and cook for 5 minutes, mixing everything well. Do not season. Add enough vegetable stock to just cover the lentils. Bring to the boil, reduce the heat, and cook for 30 minutes until soft, adding more stock if it becomes dry. Remove the pancetta and herbs and set the lentils aside until needed. (Dice the pancetta. Add to the reserved vegetables with any remaining stock. Season, cool, then chill. Reheat later, with extra stock if necessary, for a hearty soup, topped with grated cheese.)

5 For the choka, heat a heavy-based frying pan until hot. Add the tomatoes and cook for 5 minutes, shaking the pan occasionally, until the skins are burnt (this gives the characteristic smoky taste to the finished sauce).

6 Put the tomatoes in a bowl, leave to cool slightly, then remove and discard the skins. Roughly crush the tomato flesh with the back of a fork.

7 Heat the oil in a saucepan, add the onion, and cook gently for 3 minutes until softened but not browned. Remove the pan from the heat, add the crushed tomatoes and the remaining ingredients, then season to taste.

8 Leave to cool slightly, then pulse in a food processor until smooth. Pass through a sieve into a clean saucepan and reheat gently before serving.

9 For the cod, season the fish generously with salt and pepper. Heat the sunflower oil in a non-stick frying pan. As it begins to smoke, add the fish skin-sides down. Press the fish down with a fish slice for 2–3 minutes until the skin turns crisp and golden brown.

10 Fry for a further 1–2 minutes, then turn the fish over. Add the butter and, when foaming, baste the fish for 2 minutes. Remove the fish from the pan and drain on kitchen paper.

11 Add the parsley to the fish pan, then spoon the butter and parsley over the lentils. Stir to combine, then gently reheat the lentils, lightly stirring to prevent sticking.

12 Spoon the lentils on 4 plates, top with the cod, then spoon over the reheated choka.

Lenticchie di castelluccio, or castelluccio lentils, are native to Umbria in Italy and are valued for their rich, earthy flavour and creamy texture. They are quick to cook and retain their shape.

PAN-FRIED COD WITH CHORIZO
Nick Pickard actor and 2011 Celebrity finalist

PREPARATION TIME
10 minutes

COOKING TIME
15 minutes

SERVES 4

4 centre-cut COD FILLETS,
   150g (5½oz) each
4 tbsp OLIVE OIL
SALT and freshly ground
   BLACK PEPPER
50g (1¾oz) UNSALTED BUTTER
juice of 1 LEMON

2 small cooking CHORIZO,
   thinly sliced
2 RED CHILLIES, thinly sliced
2 GARLIC cloves, thinly sliced
32 florets of PURPLE SPROUTING
   BROCCOLI, trimmed
   (8 per person)

1 Score the skin on each piece of the fish with 3 diagonal cuts. Rub the skin with 1 tbsp of the olive oil. Season well.
2 Place a frying pan over high heat and fry the fish skin-side down for 2–3 minutes. Carefully turn the fish over, add half the butter and the lemon juice to the pan, and continue to cook for a further 1–2 minutes, basting continuously. Remove the fish from the pan and drain on kitchen paper.
3 In a separate pan, quickly fry the chorizo slices in the remaining olive oil. Turn the slices over and remove the pan from the heat. Add the chillies, garlic, and the remaining butter, and leave to cook in the residual heat of the pan.
4 Blanch the broccoli florets in boiling water for 2 minutes. Remove with a draining spoon and transfer to the pan of chorizo.
5 Just before serving, reheat the pan of chorizo for 1 minute.
6 Lay 4 broccoli florets horizontally on the plate, topped with the other 4 laid vertically. Gently place the fish on top. Scatter a couple of chorizo pieces on top of the fish and then the remainder around the plate along with the chillies, garlic, and the pan juices.

GREGG WALLACE

"You have beautiful fish. Really beautiful – I think you cook really well."

HERB-STUFFED WILD TROUT WITH NEW POTATOES AND SPINACH

Danny Goffey musician and 2011 Celebrity semi-finalist

PREPARATION TIME
15 minutes

COOKING TIME
25 minutes

SERVES 4

FOR THE STUFFED TROUT
4 GARLIC cloves, finely chopped
4 SHALLOTS, finely chopped
25g (scant 1oz) PARSLEY,
   finely chopped
2 LEMONS, thinly sliced
SALT, for seasoning
4 WILD TROUT, 250–300g
   (9oz–10oz) each, gutted,
   backbone and pin bones removed
UNSALTED BUTTER, for greasing

FOR THE NEW POTATOES
200g (7oz) small JERSEY
   NEW POTATOES
20g (¾oz) UNSALTED BUTTER

FOR THE SAUTÉED SPINACH
1 tbsp OLIVE OIL
2 GARLIC cloves, finely chopped
400g (14oz) SPINACH, trimmed
SALT and freshly ground
   BLACK PEPPER
juice of ½ LEMON
20g (¾oz) UNSALTED BUTTER
pinch of freshly grated NUTMEG

1 Preheat the oven to 200°C (400°F/Gas 6). Combine the garlic, shallots, parsley, and lemons in a bowl and season with salt. Stuff the fish with the mixture.

2 Lay out a sheet of greaseproof paper slightly longer than the fish. Grease with the butter, then lay a fish on top. Season the skin with salt, then wrap the fish tightly in the paper, twisting the ends to seal. Repeat with the remaining fish.

3 Place the parcels on a baking tray and bake in the oven for 15 minutes. Cut open the paper to remove the baked fish.

4 While the fish is cooking, boil the potatoes in a large pan of salted water until tender, then drain thoroughly. Sauté in a knob of butter for 2–3 minutes until golden.

5 For the spinach, heat the olive oil in a pan and sauté the garlic over medium heat for 1 minute, until softened but not browned. Add the spinach, season with salt and pepper, and toss with the garlic and oil. Cover and cook for 2 minutes. Remove the lid, increase the heat, and cook for a further minute, stirring.

6 Remove the spinach from the pan and place in bowls with a squeeze of lemon juice, a knob of butter, and a good pinch of nutmeg. Serve with the baked fish and potatoes.

SEAFOOD RISOTTO
Sara Danesin Medio MasterChef 2011 finalist

PREPARATION TIME
45 minutes

COOKING TIME
1 hour

SERVES 4

500g (1lb 2oz) whole SEA BASS, scaled, filleted, and bones reserved
16 raw LANGOUSTINES
2 CARROTS, chopped into 2cm (¾in) pieces
2 CELERY sticks, chopped into 2cm (¾in) pieces
300ml (10fl oz) DRY WHITE WINE
SALT and freshly ground BLACK PEPPER
175ml (6fl oz) EXTRA VIRGIN OLIVE OIL, plus extra to deep fry
3 GARLIC cloves, finely chopped
700g (1lb 9oz) MUSSELS, cleaned and beards removed

500g (1lb 2oz) CLAMS, preferably Italian, soaked and cleaned
500g (1lb 2oz) small SQUID, cleaned, cut into 2cm (¾in) thick rings, and tentacles kept whole
3 SHALLOTS, finely chopped
350g (12oz) CARNAROLI RICE
1 tbsp TOMATO PURÉE
30g (1oz) PLAIN FLOUR
60g (2oz) UNSALTED BUTTER, chilled and diced
snipped CHIVES, to garnish

1 Cut the sea bass fillets into 3cm (1¼in) lengths and set aside.

2 Preheat the oven to 220°C (425°F/Gas 7). Peel the langoustines, reserving the heads, legs, and shells. Remove the black central vein and set the meat aside.

3 To make the stock, place the reserved langoustine casings, carrots, and celery in a deep baking tray. Roast in the oven for 15–20 minutes until the casings have coloured and the vegetables are beginning to brown. Remove from the oven and transfer to a saucepan along with the fish bones, 200ml (7fl oz) of the white wine, and enough cold water to cover. Bring to the boil, simmer for 5 minutes, then skim and continue to simmer, uncovered, for a further 30 minutes. Pass the stock through a sieve lined with muslin cloth into a clean saucepan. Season to taste with the salt and pepper and set aside in a warm place.

4 Heat 3 tbsp of the olive oil in a large pan and gently cook half of the chopped garlic for 30 seconds. Add the mussels, cover with a tightly fitting lid, turn up the heat, and cook until the shells have opened. Remove the meat from the opened shells and set aside, discarding any unopened shells. Strain the liquid into the stock, then repeat this step with the remaining garlic and the clams.

5 Heat 1 tbsp of the olive oil in a large frying pan. Quickly fry the squid rings for about 40 seconds, or until they are just cooked through, then season with salt and freshly ground black pepper and set aside.

6 In the same pan, heat the remaining oil and cook the shallots for 2–3 minutes until soft but not brown.

Add the rice and stir well for 2–3 minutes until the grains turn translucent at the edges, then stir in the tomato purée and cook for 1 minute. Pour in the remaining wine and cook until the wine has evaporated.

7 Add a ladle of the hot stock to the pan and stir continuously until all the stock has been absorbed by the rice. Repeat until the rice is almost cooked through, then stir in the langoustines and sea bass with 2 ladles of stock.

8 Meanwhile, heat enough olive oil in a small saucepan to deep fry. Season the flour with salt and freshly ground black pepper. Dust the squid tentacles and deep fry for about 1 minute or until golden brown. Remove with a slotted spoon and drain on kitchen paper.

9 Add the mussels, clams, and squid rings to the risotto along with the diced butter. Gently stir and cook for a further 2 minutes until warmed through. The risotto should be served all'onda (slightly runny). Season to taste with salt and freshly ground black pepper and serve garnished with the snipped chives and the fried squid tentacles.

A member of the lobster family, langoustines are related to Dublin Bay prawns and scampi. Most are cooked and frozen at sea; should you find them sold live, check that they are moving, since they go off rapidly once dead.

BASQUE SEAFOOD STEW
Phil Vickery MBE England rugby player and 2011 Celebrity champion

PREPARATION TIME
25 minutes

COOKING TIME
1 hour

SERVES 4

FOR THE FISH STOCK
1 FENNEL bulb, sliced
1 CARROT, chopped
1 RED ONION, chopped
½ GARLIC clove, crushed
1 tbsp VEGETABLE OIL
2 BAY LEAVES
handful of PARSLEY stalks
pinch of SAFFRON
1 tsp FISH SAUCE
500g (1lb 2oz) fresh FISH BONES
   (preferably back, no heads)
SALT and freshly ground
   BLACK PEPPER

FOR THE STEW
12 NEW POTATOES, halved
1 tbsp OLIVE OIL
175g (6oz) CHORIZO, cut in
   2cm (¾in) lengths
1 GARLIC clove, crushed
2 RED ONIONS, chopped

1 tsp SMOKED SWEET PAPRIKA
1 tsp SMOKED HOT PAPRIKA
1 RED PEPPER, deseeded
   and sliced
1 YELLOW PEPPER, deseeded
   and sliced
500g (1lb 2oz) MONKFISH FILLET
4 tbsp SEASONED FLOUR
3 tbsp VEGETABLE OIL
50g (1¾oz) UNSALTED BUTTER
12 MUSSELS

FOR THE ROUILLE
pinch of SAFFRON
2 ANCHOVY FILLETS
½ GARLIC clove
1 EGG YOLK
½ tsp DIJON MUSTARD
½ tsp TOMATO PURÉE
few drops of LEMON JUICE
4–6 drops of TABASCO
120ml (4fl oz) OLIVE OIL, in a jug

1 In a large covered pan, sweat the prepared vegetables in the oil for the stock, until soft, not brown. Add the remaining ingredients, cover with water, bring to the boil, reduce the heat, and simmer for 20 minutes, skimming often. Strain into a pan.
2 For the stew, parboil the potatoes in salted water for 5 minutes. Drain. Heat the oil in a large pan, add the chorizo, garlic, and onion. Fry for 5 minutes, stirring, until the onions are soft. Add the paprikas, peppers, potatoes, and a little of the fish stock. Cover and cook gently for 5–10 minutes until tender.
3 Make the rouille. Blitz all the ingredients except the lemon, Tabasco, and oil in a small food processor until smooth. With the machine running, add the oil in a thin stream until the mixture is thick and shiny. Add lemon juice, Tabasco and seasoning to taste.
4 Preheat the oven to 190°C (375°F/Gas 5). Dust the monkfish in the seasoned flour. Brown all over in smoking hot oil in an ovenproof pan. Add the butter and baste well. Transfer to the oven for 10–12 minutes. Remove from the oven, cover in foil, and rest for 10 minutes. Boil the stock. Add the mussels, cook for 2 minutes to open them. Remove with a slotted spoon.
5 Place the chorizo stew in the centre of large bowls. Slice the fish, place on top. Arrange the mussels around and ladle in the stock. Serve rouille on the side.

LINGUINE WITH MUSSELS AND A SPICY TOMATO SAUCE

Kirsty Wark journalist and presenter and 2011 Celebrity finalist

PREPARATION TIME
25 minutes

COOKING TIME
20 minutes

SERVES 4

"My earliest memory is going with my great uncle (with his overalls) into the tomato houses. He got me to pick a tomato and then I ate it, and ever since then it's been a really key thing in my family."

400g (14oz) TYPE "00" PASTA FLOUR
3 EGGS
2 EGG YOLKS
1 tbsp SUNFLOWER OIL
10 very ripe TOMATOES
2 tbsp OLIVE OIL

3 GARLIC cloves, finely chopped
2 WHITE ONIONS, finely chopped
1 tsp finely chopped fresh CHILLI
1 tsp DRIED CHILLI FLAKES
500g (1lb 2oz) MUSSELS, cleaned
knob of BUTTER
1 tbsp finely chopped PARSLEY

1 Pulse the pasta flour, eggs, and egg yolks in a food processor until you have a texture similar to large breadcrumbs. Remove and knead gently, then wrap in cling film and chill in the fridge for at least 20 minutes.

2 Put the sunflower oil in a pan and set over high heat. Halve 8 of the tomatoes, place them skin-side down, and cook until the skin blackens. Flip them over and cook for 3 minutes longer before taking them out of the pan and leaving them to cool.

3 Heat the olive oil in a sauté pan, add the garlic and onion and sauté gently for 5 minutes without colouring. Add the fresh chilli and chilli flakes and cook for a further 5 minutes.

4 Remove most of the blackened tomato skin and discard. Add the tomatoes to the pan with the garlic and onion and continue to cook for 15 minutes until the tomatoes have broken down. Blitz the sauce with a hand-held blender until smooth.

5 Place the mussels in a hot, dry pan with the lid on. Once they have opened, which usually takes 2–3 minutes, place them in a bowl to cool before taking all but 12 out of their shells.

6 Drop the remaining tomatoes briefly into boiling water to make it easy to remove the skins. Deseed them and chop the remaining flesh into tiny squares. Set aside until needed.

7 Remove the pasta dough from the fridge. Feed it through a pasta machine 5–6 times, starting at the lowest (thickest) setting and increasing the setting each time. Finally pass it through the linguine attachment, toss it in flour, and leave to hang for a few minutes.

8 Just before serving, cook the pasta in a large pan of salted water for 1–2 minutes, or until it rises to the top of the pan. Drain and stir in the butter before combining the pasta with the tomato sauce.

9 Stir the shelled mussels through the pasta and divide between 4 serving bowls. Sprinkle with the fresh chopped tomatoes and parsley and garnish each plate with 3 mussels in their shells.

PANCETTA-WRAPPED MONKFISH WITH ROSEMARY-INFUSED POTATOES, ARTICHOKES, AND TARTARE SAUCE

Sara Danesin Medio MasterChef 2011 finalist

PREPARATION TIME
25 minutes

COOKING TIME
1 hour

SERVES 4

FOR THE MONKFISH
1 tsp THYME leaves
1 tsp ROSEMARY leaves
40g (1¼oz) PINE NUTS, toasted
1 bulb of GARLIC
1 tbsp OLIVE OIL
2kg (4½lb) (bone in weight) WHOLE MONKFISH TAIL, skinned, and boned into 2 fillets
150g (5½oz) sliced SMOKED PANCETTA
2 tbsp SUNFLOWER OIL
SALT and freshly ground BLACK PEPPER

FOR THE POTATOES
2kg (4½lb) ROOSTER POTATOES, peeled, cut into small cubes

OLIVE OIL, for shallow frying
1 large sprig of ROSEMARY

FOR THE ARTICHOKES
SUNFLOWER OIL, for frying
2 GLOBE ARTICHOKES, hearts only, finely sliced

FOR THE TARTARE SAUCE
150ml (5½fl oz) CRÈME FRAÎCHE
2 tbsp pickled CAPERS, drained and roughly chopped
handful of PARSLEY, roughly chopped
2 tbsp snipped CHIVES
juice of ½ LEMON
splash of WHITE WINE VINEGAR

1 For the monkfish, preheat the oven to 200°C (425°F/Gas 7). Place all the ingredients apart from the fish, pancetta, and oil, in a food processor. Season and blitz to a smooth paste. Spread on the inner side of one of the monkfish fillets. Place the second fillet on top of it to create a sandwich.

2 Overlap the pancetta slices on a piece of cling film; the width of the pancetta needs to be a little greater than the length of the monkfish fillet sandwich. Place it in the middle of the pancetta. Draw up the end of the cling film closest to you and use it to wrap the fish in the pancetta slices. Secure with string.

3 Heat the oil in a frying pan and add the wrapped monkfish. Brown on all sides before removing to a baking tray and roasting for a further 20–25 minutes, or until fully cooked through.

4 Boil the potatoes until just tender. Drain and cool completely. Heat some oil in a frying pan, add the rosemary, and fry to impart its flavours before adding the potatoes. Cook until golden on all sides, turning frequently. Remove and drain on kitchen paper.

5 Fry the artichokes in hot oil until golden. Drain on kitchen paper. For the tartare, mix all the ingredients together.

6 To serve, place potatoes in the centre of the plates. Cut the monkfish in portions. Set on top of the potatoes. Surround with the artichokes and tartare sauce.

SARA'S PANCETTA MONKFISH SIMPLIFIED FOR **EVERY**DAY... ▶ PAGE 182

HERBY **MONKFISH**

JOHN TORODE PROVIDES A TASTY AND SPEEDY TWIST ON SARA'S PANCETTA-WRAPPED MONKFISH

PREP: 25–30 MINS • COOK: 45–50 MINS

SERVES 4

675g (1½lb) BABY NEW POTATOES
2–3 tbsp OLIVE OIL
1 sprig of ROSEMARY, leaves only
a small handful of SEA SALT FLAKES
4 x 150g (5½oz) MONKFISH FILLETS
salt and freshly ground
  BLACK PEPPER
2 tbsp THYME leaves
1 tsp finely chopped ROSEMARY
8 slices PANCETTA
6 GARLIC cloves, bruised
2 tbsp OLIVE OIL
a squeeze of fresh LEMON juice
a splash of WHITE WINE

1 Preheat the oven to 200°C (400°C/Gas 6). Toss the potatoes in the oil in a roasting tin and cook in the oven for 35 minutes, shaking occasionally. Roughly chop the rosemary with the salt, scatter over the potatoes and roast a further 10–15 minutes, turning occasionally until crisp and golden.
2 Meanwhile, season the monkfish and sprinkle with the thyme and rosemary. Wrap 2 slices of pancetta around each fillet and arrange in a lightly greased ovenproof dish. Scatter the bruised garlic cloves around, drizzle with oil, lemon juice, and wine, and then bake for 25–30 minutes or until the fish is cooked through and the pancetta is crisp.
3 To serve, remove the pancetta-wrapped monkfish from the dish using a fish slice, and serve on warmed plates with the rosemary roasted potatoes and a generous spoonful of the herby green sauce or the lemon, wine, and herb sauce.

"The combination of fragrant herbs and salty pancetta works equally well with chicken breasts."

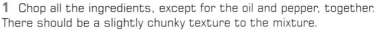

HERBY GREEN SAUCE

4 canned ANCHOVIES, finely chopped
4 GHERKINS, roughly chopped
2 tbsp roughly chopped FLAT-LEAF PARSLEY
2 tbsp roughly chopped BASIL
2 tbsp roughly chopped CHIVES
2 tbsp roughly chopped DILL
4 tbsp CAPERS, drained well
approx 120ml (4fl oz) EXTRA VIRGIN OLIVE OIL
freshly ground BLACK PEPPER

1 Chop all the ingredients, except for the oil and pepper, together. There should be a slightly chunky texture to the mixture.
2 Spoon into a bowl then gradually drizzle in the oil, stirring constantly, until all is incorporated and you have a nice spoonable sauce. Season to taste.

LEMON, WINE, AND HERB SAUCE

20g (¾oz) BUTTER
1 small SHALLOT, very finely chopped
100ml (3½fl oz) CHICKEN STOCK
300ml (10fl oz) WHITE WINE
squeeze of LEMON JUICE
10g (¼oz) BUTTER, softened
2 tbsp PLAIN FLOUR
3 tbsp DOUBLE CREAM
1 tbsp freshly chopped DILL
1 tbsp THYME leaves
SALT and freshly ground BLACK PEPPER

1 Sauté the shallots in the butter for 2–3 minutes or until softened. Add the stock, wine, and lemon juice, bring to a simmer, and cook for 5–6 minutes.
2 In a bowl, blend the softened butter with the flour to a paste, then to whisk into the sauce base, until dissolved and the sauce has thickened slightly. Add the cream and simmer for a further 3–5 minutes. Stir in the dill, thyme, and seasoning to taste.

CLASSIC MARIANNA FISH PIE
Margi Clarke actress and 2011 Celebrity contestant

PREPARATION TIME
25 minutes

COOKING TIME
20 minutes

SERVES 4

FOR THE MASH
6 large POTATOES, cut in chunks
30g (1oz) UNSALTED BUTTER
3 tbsp WHOLE MILK
SALT and freshly ground
  BLACK PEPPER

FOR THE FILLING
300ml (10fl oz) WHOLE MILK
1 tsp ENGLISH MUSTARD
1 BAY LEAF
SALT and freshly ground
  BLACK PEPPER
200g (7oz) SMOKED
  HADDOCK FILLET

200g (7oz) COD FILLET
200g (7oz) SALMON FILLET
2 CANNED ANCHOVIES, chopped
200g (7oz) cooked,
  peeled PRAWNS
30g (1oz) UNSALTED BUTTER
3 tbsp PLAIN FLOUR
2 tbsp CRÈME FRAÎCHE

FOR THE TOPPING
50g (1¾oz) WHITE BREADCRUMBS
75g (2½oz) GRUYÈRE CHEESE,
  grated

1 Preheat the oven to 180°C (350°F/Gas 4). Boil the potatoes in a large pan of salted water until soft. Drain thoroughly, then mash until smooth. Beat in the butter and 3 tbsp of the milk, then season to taste with salt and pepper.
2 Meanwhile, make the filling. Place the milk, mustard, bay leaf and seasoning into a pan and add all of the fish except the prawns. Simmer gently for 3 minutes. Remove the fish to a buttered casserole dish and reserve the poaching milk. Discard the bay leaf. Flake the fish and discard the skin. Add the prawns.
3 Melt the butter in a saucepan and stir in the flour. Cook gently for 2 minutes, stirring. Remove from the heat. Stir in the reserved cooking liquid. Return to the heat, bring to the boil, then simmer gently for 3–4 minutes, stirring continuously, until thick and smooth. Remove from the heat, then add the crème fraîche.
4 Pour the mixture over the fish. Top with the mashed potato, then the breadcrumbs, followed by the cheese.
5 Bake in the oven for 25 minutes, or until the top is golden.

Simplify for EVERYDAY

• Use just inexpensive white fish, like pollack, and some prawns.
• Top with par-boiled sliced potatoes, instead of the mash, before adding the breadcrumbs and cheese.

BREAD-CRUSTED MACKEREL WITH RHUBARB SAUCE AND AN APPLE, RADISH, AND FRISÉE SALAD

Paul Elder MasterChef 2011 contestant

PREPARATION TIME
25 minutes

COOKING TIME
30 minutes

SERVES 4

"They said it was like restaurant standard and they're happy to put me through."

FOR THE MACKEREL
4 slices of WHITE BREAD, crusts removed
4 MACKEREL FILLETS, all bones removed
small bunch of DILL, chopped
SALT and freshly ground BLACK PEPPER
2 tbsp GROUNDNUT OIL
25g (scant 1oz) UNSALTED BUTTER

FOR THE RHUBARB SAUCE
2 RHUBARB sticks, cut into 5cm (2in) pieces
100g (3½oz) CASTER SUGAR
juice of ½ LEMON

FOR THE SALAD
5 tbsp GROUNDNUT OIL
2½ tbsp CHARDONNAY VINEGAR or other WHITE WINE VINEGAR
SALT and freshly ground BLACK PEPPER
8 RADISHES, leaves attached
2 GRANNY SMITH APPLES
1 head of FRISÉE, inner leaves picked

1 Using a rolling pin, or pasta machine, roll the slices of bread out as thinly as possible into rectangles. Place a mackerel fillet in the middle of each piece of bread and scatter a little dill over the fish. Season well, then wrap up tightly to form a parcel. Repeat with the rest of the bread and fish. Chill in the fridge.

2 Place the rhubarb in a saucepan with the sugar and a splash of water. Bring to the boil, reduce the heat, then simmer until soft. Allow to cool slightly, then transfer to a food processor and blitz until smooth. Pass through a sieve into a clean pan and add the lemon juice to taste. Keep warm until ready to serve.

3 Make the salad. Whisk the oil and vinegar together and season to taste. Finely slice the radishes, reserving the trimmed leaves. Core and finely slice the apple. Combine with the frisée and radish leaves in a large bowl, then toss with the dressing.

4 Heat 2 tbsp of groundnut oil in a large frying pan, then add the mackerel parcels. Fry for 2 minutes until the bread is turning golden, then turn them over and fry for a further minute. Add the butter and baste the parcels until evenly golden and crisp. Remove from the pan and drain on kitchen paper.

5 Slice the parcels in half and serve with the rhubarb sauce and the apple, radish, and frisée salad.

Atlantic mackerel has firm, oily, strong-flavoured flesh, which goes well with acidic sauces such as rhubarb or gooseberry. Look for fresh fish with bright eyes and firm bodies, or choose good-sized moist fillets.

HAKE WITH SALSA VERDE AND CRUSHED NEW POTATOES

Aggie MacKenzie journalist and 2011 Celebrity semi-finalist

PREPARATION TIME
20 minutes

COOKING TIME
20 minutes

SERVES 4

FOR THE POTATOES
400g (14oz) small
 NEW POTATOES
1 tbsp EXTRA VIRGIN OLIVE OIL
1 bunch of SPRING ONIONS,
 finely sliced
1 tbsp PARSLEY, chopped
SALT and freshly ground
 BLACK PEPPER

FOR THE SALSA VERDE
20g (¾oz) PARSLEY, chopped
20g (¾oz) BASIL, chopped
20g (¾oz) MINT, chopped
3 canned ANCHOVIES, drained
 and chopped

1 tbsp DIJON MUSTARD
100ml (3½fl oz) EXTRA VIRGIN
 OLIVE OIL
2 tbsp RED WINE VINEGAR
1 GARLIC clove, finely chopped

FOR THE FISH
4 HAKE FILLETS, each weighing
 appox. 175g (6oz)
SEASONED FLOUR, to dredge
1 tbsp GROUNDNUT OIL
25g (scant 1oz) BUTTER

TO SERVE
LEMON wedges

1 Boil the potatoes in a large pan of salted water until tender. Drain, roughly crush, then add the olive oil, spring onions, and parsley. Season to taste and toss gently.

2 Meanwhile, mix together the ingredients for the salsa verde, season to taste, then set aside.

3 Toss the fish in the seasoned flour, then shake off any excess.

4 Heat the groundnut oil in a frying pan, then add the fish, skin-side down, and fry for 3–4 minutes until the skin is crisp. Turn over the fish, add the butter, and cook for a further 2 minutes, basting the fish with the butter continuously.

5 Remove from the pan and drain on kitchen paper.

6 To serve, place the fish on plates with the salsa verde spooned over, and the crushed potatoes to one side. Serve with lemon wedges to squeeze over the fish.

FRESH SARDINES WITH PINE NUTS AND ANCHOVIES

Linda Lusardi actress and 2011 Celebrity semi-finalist

PREPARATION TIME
15 minutes

COOKING TIME
30 minutes

SERVES 4

40g (1¼oz) SULTANAS
5 tbsp OLIVE OIL, plus extra
  for greasing
250g (9oz) fresh
  WHITE BREADCRUMBS
40g (1¼oz) PINE NUTS
2 tbsp chopped PARSLEY
40g can ANCHOVIES, drained
  and chopped
pinch of freshly grated NUTMEG
SALT and freshly ground
  BLACK PEPPER

12 fresh SARDINES, scaled,
  gutted, and heads and
  back bones removed
12 BAY LEAVES
4 tbsp LEMON JUICE
2 large POTATOES
15g (½oz) BUTTER
4 large CARROTS, sliced
LEMON wedges, to garnish

1 Preheat the oven to 180°C (350°F/Gas 4). Put the sultanas in a bowl and cover with boiling water. Leave them to soak for 10 minutes, then drain.

2 Heat the oil in a frying pan. Add half the breadcrumbs and fry over medium heat, turning them frequently, until light golden brown.

3 Remove from the heat and add the sultanas, pine nuts, 1 tbsp of the parsley, the anchovies, nutmeg, salt, and pepper.

4 Place a little of the mixture inside each sardine and press the sides together to close. Brush a large oven-proof dish with olive oil. Arrange the sardines side by side in a single layer in the dish. Place a bay leaf between each fish.

5 Sprinkle the remaining breadcrumbs over the top, drizzle with a little extra olive oil, and bake in the oven for 20 minutes. Sprinkle with the lemon juice before serving.

6 Meanwhile, boil the potatoes in a large pan of salted water until soft. Drain and mash with the butter and remaining parsley.

7 Boil the carrots in a separate pan of salted water for 10 minutes, or until tender, then drain.

8 Serve the sardines with the mashed potatoes, carrots, and garnished with lemon wedges.

JOHN TORODE

"I think that everything on the plate is cooked very, very well. It's very homely, I feel like I'm at home."

PAN-FRIED HALIBUT WITH BEURRE NOISETTE ON A BED OF KALE

Danny Goffey musician and 2011 Celebrity semi-finalist

PREPARATION TIME
10 minutes

COOKING TIME
15 minutes

SERVES 2

2 HALIBUT FILLETS, 100g (3½oz) each, skin on
SALT and freshly ground BLACK PEPPER
2 tbsp OLIVE OIL
16 CLAMS
a splash of WHITE WINE

210g (7½oz) SALTED BUTTER
12 CAPERS
juice of ½ LEMON
small bunch of PARSLEY, chopped
100g (3½oz) KALE
2 GARLIC cloves
2 LEMON wedges, to serve

1 Season the halibut fillets with salt and pepper. Heat 1 tbsp olive oil in a frying pan, add the halibut fillets, and cook skin-side down for 5 minutes. Turn the fillets over and add the clams and a splash of white wine to the pan. Cover with a lid and cook until the clams open, for about 3–4 minutes.

2 Meanwhile, put 200g (7oz) butter in a pan, brown to a noisette, then add the capers, lemon juice, and chopped parsley.

3 Put the kale in a pan of salted boiling water and simmer for 5–6 minutes, then drain and squeeze out the excess water. Return to the pan and sauté with the remaining oil and the garlic for a few minutes, and then mix in the remaining butter to finish.

4 To serve, place the kale in the middle of the plates, place the halibut fillets on top and arrange the clams in a ring around. Stir the fish pan juices into the noisette and spoon over the halibut. Serve with a wedge of lemon on the side.

SOUS VIDE SEA TROUT, SCALLOP MOUSSE, FENNEL CONFIT, AND SMOKED MUSSEL CREAM SAUCE

Tom Whitaker Masterchef 2011 finalist

PREPARATION TIME
1 hour

COOKING TIME
1 hour 30 minutes

SERVES 4

GREGG WALLACE

"It's a beautiful blend of everything that is great about seafood. That's really, really, really, top, top notch."

FOR THE TROUT FILLET
500g (1lb 2oz) SEA TROUT FILLET, pin-boned, with skin
juice of ½ LEMON
4 sprigs of DILL
knob of UNSALTED BUTTER
200g (7oz) SEA PURSLANE, woody stalks removed, and washed
SALT and freshly ground BLACK PEPPER
1 tbsp VEGETABLE OIL

FOR THE SCALLOP MOUSSE
8 large SCALLOPS, cleaned and corals removed
100ml (3½fl oz) DOUBLE CREAM
SALT and WHITE PEPPER

FOR THE FENNEL CONFIT
2 bulbs of FENNEL, green fronds reserved for garnish

cold-filtered RAPESEED OIL
SEA SALT
juice of 1 LEMON

FOR THE MUSSELS
500g (1lb 2oz) LIVE MUSSELS, cleaned and debearded
WOOD CHIPS, for smoking
300ml (10fl oz) DOUBLE CREAM

FOR THE WATERCRESS OIL
100g (3½oz) fresh WATERCRESS
3 tbsp OLIVE OIL

TO GARNISH
small jar of fresh SALMON ROE
a few PEA SHOOTS (optional)

1   Preheat the oven to 180°C (350°F/Gas 4). For the sous vide trout, remove the skin from the trout fillet, scrape off any excess flesh, and reserve.
2   Add the fillet to a sous vide bag with the lemon juice, and dill, and then vacuum seal the bag.
3   Set a water bath to 52.5°C (126.5°F). Add the trout fillet to the bath for 28 minutes. Remove from the bath and leave to cool.
4   Meanwhile, make the scallop mousse. Place the scallops in a food processor and blitz until smooth. With the motor still running, gradually add the cream and season with salt and white pepper. Transfer to a bowl, cover with cling film, and chill until firm.
5   Next prepare the fennel confit. Finely slice the fennel bulbs using a mandolin and add to a pan. Add enough rapeseed oil to just cover completely and heat very gently over low heat for 1 hour until very soft. Drain through a sieve, tip into a bowl and mash the soft fennel with a little salt and lemon juice (reserve the oil for frying). Keep warm until ready to serve.
6   Bring a little water to the boil in a large pan, add the mussels, cover and cook for 20 seconds until the shells open, then drain.

7 Carefully remove the meat from the mussels and reserve the shells.

8 Prepare the smoker by adding the wood chips and placing over a gas hob on medium heat.

9 Add the shells on one side of the smoker and the mussels on the other, and allow to infuse with smoke for 20 minutes. Remove from the heat and set aside until needed.

10 Place the smoked shells into a saucepan with the double cream. Heat gently for 10 minutes until the cream has thickened slightly and has taken on a smoky flavour. Strain, then season to taste. Reheat gently before serving.

11 Put the grill on high, rub the reserved fish skin with a little butter and place on a baking tray under the grill – it should cook for about 5 minutes on each side but watch carefully so that it doesn't burn. Leave the crisp skin to cool, then cut into 12 small squares. Set aside for garnish.

12 Prepare the watercress oil. Remove the leaves from the watercress, add to a food processor, and blitz. With the machine running, add the olive oil in a gentle stream until fully blended. Transfer to a squeezy bottle.

13 When nearly ready to serve, quenelle the scallop mousse using a teaspoon and add to a baking tray lined with baking parchment – you will need 2 quenelles per person. Place chefs rings over quenelles of mousse and cover with foil – this will stop them from colouring. Bake at 180°C (350°F/Gas 4) for 15 minutes until set.

14 Add the prepared purslane to a pan of simmering water, and cook until tender (about 3–4 minutes).

15 Carefully remove the trout from the bag and cut into 12 cubes. Heat a frying pan with some seasoning and oil to medium heat. Add the cubes of fish gently to the pan and colour lightly – they are already cooked so should not be in the pan for more than a few minutes.

TO SERVE

To assemble the dish, on each of 4 square plates add 3 spoonfuls of fennel mash diagonally. Place a cube of sea trout on top of each. Between each piece add the baked scallop quennelles. Add a piece of crispy skin on top of each piece of fish, with some salmon roe and a tiny sprig of fennel frond (or pea shoots) on top of that. In 4 places on the plates add a 2cm (¾in) squeeze of the smoked sauce and then a smaller dot of the watercress oil in the middle. Finally, garnish with the sea purslane and the smoked mussels.

SEA TROUT WITH HERBY TOPPING

CAPTURE ALL THE FLAVOUR OF TOM'S FISH DISH WITH THIS EASY SEA TROUT EN PAPILLOTE **PREP: 25–30 MINS • COOK: 45–55 MINS**

SERVES 4

40g (1¼oz) BUTTER, softened
2 tbsp freshly chopped FLAT-LEAF PARSLEY
finely grated zest of ½ LEMON
4 SEA TROUT fillets
4 slices of LEMON
drizzle of OLIVE OIL
SALT and freshly GROUND BLACK PEPPER
50g (1¾oz) fresh WHITE BREADCRUMBS
2 tbsp PINE NUTS, chopped

1 Preheat the oven to 190°C (375°F/Gas 5). Mix together 25g (scant 1oz) butter, half the parsley, and half the lemon zest. Prepare the trout en papillote (below) and cook in the oven for 10–12 minutes.

2 For the topping, mix the remaining softened butter, parsley, and lemon zest with the breadcrumbs until well combined, then stir in the pine nuts. When you have removed the trout fillets from the parcels, transfer them to a lightly greased sheet of foil lining the grill pan. Spread with the crumb topping and finish under a medium-hot grill for 2–3 minutes or until the topping is crisp and turning golden.

3 SIMPLE STEPS EN PAPILLOTE

Lay out each trout fillet on a large disc of parchment. Top with butter-mix, lemon and oil, and season well.

Wrap the paper over the trout and fold the edges to seal tightly. Place on a baking tray. Bake as above in the main recipe.

Unwrap the fish carefully, when it is cooked. Take care as you do so – hot steam will be released.

...CHOOSE FROM

PEA, POTATO, AND BACON FRICASSÉE

500g (1lb 2oz) SALAD POTATOES, quartered
150g (5½oz) SMOKED BACON LARDONS
225g (8oz) FROZEN PEAS, thawed
5 tbsp CHICKEN STOCK
SALT and freshly ground BLACK PEPPER
2 tbsp DOUBLE CREAM

1 Boil the potatoes in salted water until tender and drain.
2 Dry fry the lardons in a non-stick pan until crisp. Drain off excess fat.
3 Add the potatoes and sauté for 3–4 minutes then stir in the peas and stock, season, and simmer for 3–5 minutes. Stir in the cream, bubble for 1–2 minutes and serve as a base for the fish.

NEW POTATO AND CAPER SALAD

500g (1lb 2oz) waxy SALAD POTATOES
2 tbsp MAYONNAISE
2 tbsp CRÈME FRAÎCHE
1 tsp WHOLEGRAIN MUSTARD
juice of ½ LEMON
½ small RED ONION, very finely chopped
3 tbsp SMALL CAPERS, rinsed and drained
SALT and freshly ground BLACK PEPPER

1 Boil the potatoes in salted water until tender. Drain and cut into thick slices.
2 Mix the remaining ingredients together and season to taste.
3 Toss the potatoes in the dressing and serve with the fish on top.

PRAWN CURRY WITH BASMATI RICE
Shobu Kapoor actress and 2011 Celebrity contestant

PREPARATION TIME
15 minutes

COOKING TIME
20 minutes

SERVES 4

"The secret of
a good curry?
It's a secret!
I can't tell you."

FOR THE MARINADE
400g can COCONUT MILK
1 tsp CUMIN SEEDS
SALT, to taste
½ tsp RED CHILLI POWDER
½ tsp GARAM MASALA
½ tsp GROUND TURMERIC
½ tsp GROUND CORIANDER
½ tsp GROUND CUMIN
2 GARLIC cloves, crushed
1–2 DRIED KAFFIR LIME LEAVES
1–2 GREEN CHILLIES, deseeded
   and finely chopped

FOR THE RICE
1 tbsp OLIVE OIL
75g (2½oz) FROZEN PETIT POIS
300ml (10fl oz) boiling WATER
200g (7oz) BASMATI RICE
½ tsp GROUND TURMERIC

FOR THE PRAWNS
300g (10oz) raw, shelled
   KING PRAWNS, deveined
2 tbsp VEGETABLE OIL
2 ONIONS, chopped
2 TOMATOES, chopped

TO GARNISH
handful of chopped CORIANDER

1 First, combine all the marinade ingredients in a large bowl. Place the prawns in the marinade, cover, and set aside for 10 minutes.
2 Meanwhile, cook the rice. Heat the oil in a pan, add the petit pois, and cook for 2 minutes until soft. Add the water, rice, and turmeric and bring back to the boil. As soon as the boiling water boils, cover with a lid and reduce the heat to the lowest setting. Cook for 10 minutes, then remove the pan from the heat and allow the rice to rest, covered, until the curry is ready. Fluff up the rice with a fork just before serving.
3 To cook the prawns, heat 1 tbsp of the vegetable oil in a large frying pan. Remove the excess marinade from the prawns, reserving the marinade, and flash fry them on medium-high heat for about 1 minute until pink. Remove the prawns from the pan with a slotted spoon and place on kitchen paper to drain.
4 Add the remaining oil to the same pan and fry the onions for 5 minutes until softened. Add the tomatoes and cook for a further 5 minutes until soft. Add the remaining marinade and let the sauce cook and thicken for a few minutes.
5 Once the sauce is thick, return the fried prawns to the pan and cook for 2 minutes until orange in colour. Remove the kaffir lime leaves from the pan before serving.
6 Serve the rice topped with the prawns, and sprinkle with the chopped coriander, to garnish.

TIGER PRAWNS AND LOCH FYNE SMOKED SALMON IN A WHITE WINE SAUCE
Linda Lusardi actress and 2011 celebrity semi-finalist

PREPARATION TIME
25 minutes

COOKING TIME
40–45 minutes

SERVES 4

FOR THE FISH
16 whole raw TIGER PRAWNS
400g (14oz) piece of unsliced
    LOCH FYNE SMOKED SALMON

FOR THE SAUCE
8 SHALLOTS, sliced
25g (scant 1oz)
    UNSALTED BUTTER
pinch of CHILLI POWDER
1 tsp TOMATO PURÉE
2 tbsp BRANDY
300ml (10fl oz) DRY WHITE WINE

300ml (10fl oz) DOUBLE CREAM
juice of ½ LEMON
SALT and freshly ground
    BLACK PEPPER
4 PLUM TOMATOES, skinned,
    deseeded, and finely chopped
1 CUCUMBER, peeled, deseeded,
    and cut into batons
1 tbsp chopped FLAT-LEAF
    PARSLEY
1 tbsp snipped CHIVES

1 Shell and devein the prawns, reserving the heads for the sauce.
2 Slice the smoked salmon into thick batons, roughly the same size as the prawns.
3 To make the sauce, gently fry the shallots in the butter for 10 minutes until caramelized. Add the prawn heads and fry for a further 2 minutes. Add the chilli powder, tomato purée, brandy, and white wine, and bring to the boil. Simmer for 30 minutes until reduced and syrupy. Add the cream and cook slowly for 5–10 minutes until the sauce coats the back of a spoon. Add the lemon juice and pass through a fine sieve. Season to taste and put to one side until needed.
4 Blanch the tomatoes, cucumber, and flat-leaf parsley in boiling salted water for 1 minute. Refresh in iced salted water and set aside.
5 Just before serving, reheat the sauce, add the prawns, and cook for 2–3 minutes until pink. Then add the salmon, cucumber, tomato, and parsley at the very end to heat.
6 To serve, spoon into a bowl and sprinkle with the chives.

Tiger prawns can be bought both cooked and raw. If you buy them raw and shell-on, you will need twice the weight of shell-off prawns. Look for moist prawns that smell fresh; avoid those that look dry and have a fishy aroma.

VANILLA MISO YELLOWTAIL WITH CAVOLO NERO, PARSNIPS DAUPHINOISE, AND SEAWEED SALAD

Tim Anderson MasterChef 2011 champion

PREPARATION TIME
25 minutes

COOKING TIME
40 minutes

SERVES 4

Vanilla and miso yellowtail

50g (1¾oz) CASTER SUGAR
50g (1¾oz) WHITE MISO PASTE
50g (1¾oz) RED or BROWN MISO
   PASTE, preferably hatcho miso
5 tbsp MIRIN
5 tbsp SAKE
5cm (2in) fresh ROOT GINGER,
   grated

½ VANILLA POD, seeds only
½ tsp grated NUTMEG
freshly ground WHITE PEPPER
4 YELLOWTAIL AMBERJACK or
   TUNA STEAKS, each about
   175g (6oz)
OLIVE OIL, for drizzling

1 Mix the first nine ingredients together in a large bowl to make a marinade, then add the fish fillets. Mix well, cover, and chill for 1 hour.
2 Preheat the grill. Arrange the marinated fish on a non-stick baking tray, drizzle with a little oil, and grill for 6–8 minutes, turning halfway through cooking. Rest on a warm plate until serving.

Parsnips and dauphinoise

BUTTER, for greasing
850g (1lb 14oz) PARSNIPS,
   peeled and sliced at an angle
   about 3mm (⅛in) thick
175ml (6fl oz) WHOLE MILK
175ml (6fl oz) DOUBLE CREAM
2 tsp DRIED YUZU PEEL
4 SHALLOTS, finely diced
50g (1¾oz) PARMESAN
   CHEESE, finely grated

100g (3½oz) GRUYÈRE or
   COMTÉ CHEESE, grated
175g (6oz) CAVOLO NERO,
   roughly chopped
50g (1¾oz) ROASTED
   HAZELNUTS, chopped
SALT and freshly ground
   BLACK PEPPER

1 Preheat the oven to 160°C (325°F/Gas 3). Grease a deep 20cm (8in) square baking tin with the butter and line with greaseproof paper. Blanch the sliced parsnips in boiling salted water for 3 minutes, then drain and pat dry on kitchen paper.
2 Meanwhile, in a small saucepan, heat the milk, cream, yuzu, and shallots. Bring to the boil and simmer, uncovered, for 15 minutes. Remove from the heat and cover with a lid to

infuse for 15 minutes. Strain the mixture through a fine sieve into a clean saucepan. Heat gently, then stir in the Parmesan cheese and 50g (1¾oz) of the Gruyère cheese. Remove from the heat and leave to cool slightly.

3 Layer the parsnips, cavolo nero, and nuts in the lined tin, seasoning with salt and black pepper as you go. Pour the cheese sauce over, scatter with the remaining Gruyère cheese, and bake for 1 hour or until golden brown.

Seaweed salad

10g (¼oz) DRIED WAKAME
10g (¼oz) DRIED HIJIKI
10g (¼oz) DRIED DULSE
10g (¼oz) DRIED ARAME
175ml (6fl oz) SAKE
SALT, to taste
360ml (12fl oz) PILSNER BEER
RAPESEED OIL for deep frying
140g (5oz) PLAIN FLOUR
1 EGG
30g (1oz) toasted WHITE
   SESAME SEEDS
50g (1¾oz) PURPLE KALE or
   RED KALE, stem removed,
   leaves torn
50g (1¾oz) SAMPHIRE

85g (3oz) DAIKON, sliced
   into julienne
6 GREEN BATAVIA LETTUCE
   leaves, torn
6 RED BATAVIA LETTUCE
   leaves, torn
small handful of GREEN or PURPLE
   SHISO leaves
2 SPRING ONIONS, thinly sliced

1 Rehydrate the wakame, hijiki, dulse, and arame in a bowl with the sake, 175ml (6fl oz) water, a little salt, and 150ml (5fl oz) of the beer. Once tender, drain and dry completely on kitchen paper.

2 Heat the oil for deep frying to 180°C (350°F). Make a thin batter from the remaining beer, the flour, egg, and sesame seeds. Using a fork, carefully drip the batter into the hot oil so that it forms small, crunchy beads. Remove from the oil with a slotted spoon, and drain on kitchen paper.

3 Steam the kale leaves and samphire for 2–3 minutes until tender. Refresh in iced water, then pat dry on kitchen paper.

4 Just before serving, in a large mixing bowl, toss the kale, samphire, lettuces, and shiso together with the onions, rehydrated seaweeds, and tempura beads.

Miso and ginger dressing

1 tbsp WHITE MISO PASTE
5cm (2in) piece of fresh
   GINGER, peeled and grated
1 tsp CASTER SUGAR
2 tbsp MIRIN
1 tbsp UMEZU

juice of 1 LEMON
1 tbsp SESAME OIL
2 tbsp AVOCADO OIL
2 tbsp PILSNER BEER
SALT and freshly ground
   BLACK PEPPER

1 To make the dressing, mix all the ingredients together and season to taste with salt and freshly ground black pepper.

TO SERVE
Cut the fish in thick slices, and the dauphinoise into sqares. Serve the fish with the dauphinoise, and seaweed salad. Arrange on 4 sqaure plates, with the dressing in small dishes alongside.

With a velvety texture and a fruity, herby flavour, avocado oil is suitable for salad dressings as well as for cooking; the strength of the flavour is variable, so if possible, taste before you buy and use the lighter oil for cooking.

SPICY FISH PIE

JOHN TORODE'S ECLECTIC FISH PIE SIMPLIFIES TIM'S
RECIPE TO MAKE IT A MEAL FOR EVERYDAY COOKING

PREP: 30–35 MINS • COOK: 35–40 MINS

SERVES 4

750g (1lb 10oz) PARSNIPS or SWEET POTATOES,
  cut into thin slices
75g (3oz) CAVOLO NERO, finely shredded
225ml (7½fl oz) COCONUT MILK
1 stalk LEMONGRASS, finely chopped
2cm (¾in) fresh GALANGAL or GINGER,
  finely grated
1 GARLIC clove, crushed
30g (1oz) butter
1 small SHALLOT, finely chopped
30g (1oz) PLAIN FLOUR
225ml (7½fl oz) WHITE WINE
1 tbsp SOY SAUCE
350g (12oz) FRESH TUNA, cut into chunks
175g (6oz) peeled raw TIGER PRAWNS
2 tbsp freshly chopped CORIANDER
25g (scant 1oz) BUTTER, melted
25g (scant 1oz) PARMESAN CHEESE, grated
25g (scant 1oz) GRUYÈRE CHEESE, grated
30g (1oz) ROASTED HAZELNUTS, chopped

FLAVOUR INFUSIONS

Galangal is a rhizome like ginger, and is used in the
same way. It has a fragrant sourness – a bit like
ginger and cardamom combined. Available fresh,
dried, and ground.
Lemongrass The flavour of lemongrass is tart,
peppery, and citrus-like. Fresh stalks should be firm,
not wrinkled or dry. In the absence of fresh, you can
also buy freeze-dried and air-dried lemongrass.
Coconut milk Made from the white flesh of the
coconut, the milk can be bought as liquid in cans,
or as powder, or in blocks (as cream), for
dissolving in boiling water. It has a mild, but
sweet taste.

"Fish pie is a very traditional English dish, but the Asian flavours in this simplified version make it international and bang up to date."

1 Preheat the oven to 180°C (350°F/Gas 4). Simmer the parsnips or sweet potatoes in a pan of salted water for 3–4 minutes or until just tender. Drain well and cool slightly.

2 Blanch the cavolo nero in boiling water for 2 minutes then drain and refresh under cold running water. Drain again thoroughly.

3 To make the sauce, place the coconut milk in a pan with the lemongrass, ginger, and garlic then bring to just below the boil. Remove from the heat and leave to infuse.

4 Melt the butter in a pan and sauté the shallot for 2–3 minutes until softened. Add the flour and cook for 1 minute, stirring. Remove from the heat and gradually blend in the wine. Stir in the infused coconut milk and soy sauce, return the pan to medium heat and simmer for 2–3 minutes, stirring well.

5 Stir a few tablespoons of the sauce in with the blanched cavolo nero, then spoon into an ovenproof dish. Mix the remaining sauce in with the tuna, prawns, and coriander and spoon on top of the cavolo nero, spreading it over evenly. Arrange the par-boiled parsnip or sweet potato slices on top and brush with the butter.

6 Mix together the Parmesan, Gruyère cheese, and hazelnuts. Sprinkle over the top and bake for 35–40 minutes until golden brown, and the parsnips or sweet potatoes are cooked through.

SEA BREAM WITH CRUSHED NEW POTATOES AND CRAB, ROAST TOMATOES, AND A TOMATO-BUTTER SAUCE

Annie Assheton MasterChef 2011 final 6

PREPARATION TIME
15 minutes

COOKING TIME
30 minutes

SERVES 4

JOHN TORODE

"Your fish is cooked beautifully – lovely crispy skin and really wonderful soft, succulent flesh. I think it's a very good dish."

FOR THE ROAST TOMATOES
200g (7oz) BABY PLUM TOMATOES, halved
1 tbsp OLIVE OIL
SALT and freshly ground BLACK PEPPER

FOR THE POTATOES
3 tbsp OLIVE OIL
1½tbsp WHITE WINE VINEGAR
400g (14oz) NEW POTATOES
3 SPRING ONIONS, finely sliced
150g (5½oz) fresh WHITE CRABMEAT

FOR THE SAUCE
100ml (3½fl oz) OLIVE OIL
125g (4½oz) VINE CHERRY TOMATOES
1 tsp CASTER SUGAR
1 tsp SHERRY VINEGAR
100ml (3½fl oz) DOUBLE CREAM
25g (scant 1 oz) UNSALTED BUTTER

FOR THE FISH
4 SEA BREAM FILLETS, skin on
SEASONED FLOUR, for dusting
3 tbsp OLIVE OIL

1 Preheat the oven to 150°C (300°F/Gas 2). Place the halved baby plum tomatoes cut-side up on a baking tray. Drizzle with a little olive oil and season with salt and pepper. Transfer to the oven and roast for 20 minutes. Remove from the oven and keep warm until serving.

2 For the potatoes, make a simple vinaigrette by whisking the olive oil and white wine vinegar, and season well. Bring a pan of salted water to the boil, add the potatoes, and cook for 10–15 minutes or until soft. Drain well, then crush them with a fork and dress with the vinaigrette. Stir through the spring onions and crabmeat and season to taste.

3 For the sauce, warm the oil in a pan and sauté the tomatoes very gently for 10 minutes. Allow to cool, then transfer to a blender and liquidize with the sugar and vinegar. Pass through a sieve and put into a clean pan with the double cream and some seasoning. Reheat and whisk in the butter just before serving.

4 Lightly dust the fish fillets with the seasoned flour. Heat the oil in a frying pan and gently fry the fish, skin-side down, until the skin is golden brown and the fish is nearly cooked through. Turn the fish over, fry briefly, then remove from the pan.

5 Place a small mound of the potatoes in the centre of the plate and top with a piece of fish. Arrange the roasted tomatoes and sauce around them.

WILD MUSHROOM AND SPINACH TART WITH MUSTARD LEEKS AND FONDANT POTATO

Kennedy Leitch MasterChef 2011 contestant

PREPARATION TIME
35 minutes

COOKING TIME
1 hour

SERVES 4

FOR THE PASTRY
150g (5½oz) UNSALTED
  BUTTER, cubed
300g (10oz) PLAIN FLOUR
½ tsp SALT
1 EGG plus 1 EGG YOLK, beaten

FOR THE MUSHROOM MIX
25g (scant 1oz) DRIED PORCINI
100g (3½oz) BUTTER
2 SHALLOTS, finely chopped
2 GARLIC cloves, crushed
800g (1¾lb) WILD MUSHROOMS
  (morels, girolles, ceps,
  chestnut etc.), cleaned and
  larger ones quartered or halved
100ml (3½fl oz) DRY WHITE WINE
1 tbsp finely chopped
  THYME leaves
2 tsp TRUFFLE OIL
75ml (2½fl oz) DOUBLE CREAM,
  plus extra to taste
1 tbsp snipped CHIVES
1 tbsp chopped TARRAGON

SALT and freshly ground
  BLACK PEPPER

FOR THE FONDANT POTATO
2 large DÉSIRÉE POTATOES
100g (3½oz) UNSALTED BUTTER
400ml (14fl oz) VEGETABLE STOCK
2 GARLIC cloves
2 sprigs of THYME

FOR THE LEEKS
50g (1¾oz) UNSALTED BUTTER
2 tbsp OLIVE OIL
2 LEEKS, cut into
  4cm (½in) lengths
100ml (3½fl oz) DRY WHITE WINE
1 tbsp WHOLEGRAIN MUSTARD

FOR THE SPINACH
knob of BUTTER
1 GARLIC clove, crushed
150g (5½oz) SPINACH

1 Preheat the oven to 180°C (350°F/Gas 4) and grease four 10–12cm (4–5in) loose-bottomed tartlet tins. Rub the butter and flour together with the salt. Slowly add the beaten egg to form a dough, adding 1–2 tbsp water if needed. Turn out onto a floured surface and knead until smooth. Wrap the pastry in cling film and chill in the fridge for 30 minutes. Roll out the pastry and line the tart tins. Place in the fridge for 10 minutes.
2 Line the tarts with greaseproof paper and fill with baking beans. Bake for 15 minutes, then remove the beans and paper and bake for a further 5 minutes. Cool slightly before filling.
3 Place the dried porcini for the mushroom mix in a bowl and cover with boiling water. Leave to soak for 20 minutes to rehydrate them and then strain, reserving the liquid.
4 Peel and halve the potatoes and cut into 4 equal-sized cylinder shapes, ensuring that the ends are flat. Heat the butter in a deep frying pan and add the potatoes, standing them on end. Fry until the undersides are golden, then add the stock, garlic, and thyme.

Bring to the boil, then reduce to a simmer. Cover the pan with a piece of greaseproof paper and continue to simmer until the potatoes are tender.

5   Heat the butter and oil in a pan and sauté the leeks until softened. Add the white wine and reduce by two-thirds, then stir in the mustard. Season and set aside until needed.

6   To prepare the mushroom mix, melt the butter in a pan, add the shallots and garlic, and cook for 2–3 minutes. Add all the mushrooms and cook until they begin to brown. Add the wine, thyme, and seasoning and a little of the reserved porcini liquid. Cook until most of the wine has evaporated, then add the truffle oil and cook for 30 seconds. Stir in the cream, chives, and tarragon and season to taste.

7   For the spinach, gently heat the butter and garlic in a frying pan. Add the spinach, stir until wilted, then season to taste.

8   To finish the tarts, remove them from the tins, put a layer of spinach at the bottom and top with the mushroom mix. Place the tarts on the plates and arrange the leeks and potato next to them.

KENNEDY'S MUSHROOM TART SIMPLIFIED FOR **EVERY**DAY… ▶ PAGE 208

FAST FILO TART

THIS SIMPLE TWIST ON KENNEDY'S WILD MUSHROOM AND SPINACH TART USES QUICK AND EASY FILO AND NO PRE-BAKING **PREP: 25–30 MINS •COOK: 35–40 MINS**

SERVES 4

25g (scant 1oz) dried PORCINI MUSHROOMS
200g (7oz) BABY SPINACH leaves
25g (scant 1oz) BUTTER
1 tbsp OLIVE OIL
2 SHALLOTS, chopped
1 large LEEK, sliced
2 GARLIC cloves, crushed
400g (14oz) mixed CULTIVATED and WILD
    MUSHROOMS, wiped and quartered,
    or halved if small
1 tbsp THYME leaves
125g (4½oz) RICOTTA CHEESE
100ml (3½fl oz) SOURED CREAM
115g (4oz) PARMESAN CHEESE, grated
1 large EGG, beaten
2 tsp WHOLEGRAIN MUSTARD
SALT and freshly ground BLACK PEPPER
270g pack FRESH FILO PASTRY
OLIVE OIL for brushing

1 Preheat the oven to 180° (350°F/Gas 4). To make the filling, add the dried porcini to a jug, pour over just enough boiling water to cover, and leave to soak for 15–20 minutes. Blanch the spinach in a large pan of boiling water for about 10 seconds, then drain thoroughly, refresh under cold running water, drain again and leave to cool.

2 Heat the butter and oil together and sauté the shallots, leek, and garlic for 2–3 minutes. Add the mushrooms and thyme and sauté for a further 5 minutes or until softened, then continue to cook until any excess moisture from the mushrooms has evaporated. Add the soaked porcini.

3 Mix together the ricotta cheese, soured cream, 100g (3½oz) of the Parmesan, the egg, mustard, and seasoning to taste. Stir into the mushroom mixture along with the spinach.

4 Lay the first square of filo in a greased 18cm (7in) cake tin and brush with oil. Repeat with 2 more squares, then spoon a third of the mushroom mix over. Repeat, ending with a top layer of 3 filo squares. Brush with oil, scatter with the remaining Parmesan, and bake for 35–40 minutes or until very crisp and golden. Cool slightly before cutting into portions.

QUICK AND EASY FILO LAYERS

Measure the correct size for the filo. Put the sheets of filo on a worksurface and lay the tin on top.

Cut with a sharp knife, carefully around the base of the tin, tilting the knife inwards.

Brush a coating of oil with a pastry brush onto each sheet of filo pastry before adding the next layer.

AUTUMN VEGETABLE TEMPURA BENTO BOX
Tim Anderson MasterChef 2011 champion

PREPARATION TIME
40 minutes

COOKING TIME
1 hour 40 minutes

SERVES 4

FOR THE DASHI
30cm (12in) square of
  DRIED KONBU
20 DRIED SHIITAKE MUSHROOMS

FOR THE JELLY
120ml (4fl oz) UMESHU
½ tbsp AGAR-AGAR FLAKES
1 VICTORIA PLUM, stoned
  and quartered
2 tbsp CLOTTED CREAM
1 tbsp WHIPPING CREAM
1 tbsp KINAKO (soybean flour)
1 tsp ICING SUGAR
4 BLACKBERRIES, to decorate

FOR THE PICKLES
1 CARROT
1 COURGETTE,
12 RADISHES
SALT
100ml (3½fl oz) UMEZU
  (UME VINEGAR)
3 tbsp RICE VINEGAR
3 tbsp prepared DASHI
1 tbsp SAKE

FOR THE ROASTED ROMANESCO
1 small ROMANESCO, in florets
3 tbsp WALNUT OIL
1 tbsp SANSHO or SZECHUAN
  PEPPERCORNS
1 tsp WASABI POWDER

FOR THE RICE
1 tsp chopped FRESH GINGER,
1 wedge SAVOY CABBAGE
100g (3½oz) JAPANESE SHORT-
  GRAIN RICE, washed
150ml (5fl oz) prepared DASHI
1 tsp HOJICHA or KUKICHA TEA
3 tbsp pure YUZU JUICE

8 GREEN SHISO leaves, chopped
5 reserved SHIITAKE MUSHROOMS
1 tbsp SESAME SEEDS

FOR THE QUAIL EGGS
8 QUAILS' EGGS
3 tbsp RICE VINEGAR
1 tbsp MATCHA TEA
1 tbsp SENCHA TEA

FOR THE KINPIRA CARROTS
2 tbsp VEGETABLE OIL
4 CARROTS, cut into julienne
2 RED BIRD'S EYE CHILLIES,
  deseeded and cut into julienne
2 tbsp SOY SAUCE
1 tbsp MIRIN
1 tbsp CASTER SUGAR
1 tbsp SESAME OIL
2 tbsp toasted SESAME SEEDS

FOR THE VEGETABLE TEMPURA
½ AUBERGINE, cut into 5mm
  (¼in) slices
RAPESEED OIL, for deep frying
175g (6oz) PLAIN FLOUR
1 EGG
250ml (8fl oz) ice cold
  SPARKLING WATER
1 small FENNEL bulb, trimmed
  and cut into 5mm (¼in) slices
½ BUTTERNUT SQUASH,
  peeled, deseeded and cut into
  5mm (¼in) slices
4 florets of PURPLE
  CAULIFLOWER

FOR THE SAUCE
4 tbsp SOY SAUCE
2 tbsp YUZU JUICE
2 tsp MIRIN
1 tbsp prepared DASHI

1 Make the dashi. Put the konbu and mushrooms into a saucepan with 2 litres (3½ pints) water. Gradually bring to the boil and simmer for 10 minutes. Strain the dashi into a bowl and set aside. Reserve the mushrooms too.

2 For the jelly, gently heat the umeshu and agar-agar flakes, without stirring, until boiling. Add the quartered plum, bring back to the boil, then simmer for 4 minutes. Spoon into sake cups or small ramekins, leave to cool, then chill in the fridge for at least 20 minutes until set. Whisk together the creams, kinako, and icing sugar until light and smooth, then refrigerate until serving.

3 For the pickles, thinly slice the vegetables, preferably on a mandolin. Rub them with a little salt and put into a mixing bowl. Combine the umezu, vinegar, 2 tbsp water, the measured prepared dashi, and sake, and season with salt. Pour over the vegetables and mix gently with your hands. Cover and chill in the fridge until serving, then strain just before use.

4 Next, preheat the oven to 180°C (350°F/Gas 4). Prepare the roasted romanesco. Toss the romanesco florets in the oil, 2 tsp salt, the sansho, and wasabi powder. Spread out evenly on a baking tray and roast in the oven for 20 minutes until browned and tender. Keep warm until serving.

5 Meanwhile, cook the rice. Blitz the ginger and cabbage in a food processor until minced. Put the cabbage mixture, rice, dashi, tea, and yuzu juice into a saucepan and bring to the boil. As soon as the liquid is boiling, cover the pan with a tight-fitting lid and reduce the heat to the lowest setting. Cook gently for 10 minutes, then remove from the heat and leave to rest, covered, for a further 10 minutes. Chop 5 of the shiitake mushrooms. Add to the rice with the shiso, and sesame seeds, and stir to combine. Shape the rice into triangles and keep warm until serving.

6 Boil the eggs for 2 minutes in 350ml (12fl oz) water and the vinegar. Drain, refresh in cold water, then carefully remove the shells and set the eggs aside. Grind 1 tbsp salt and the teas together with a mortar and pestle until you have a fine powder. Set aside, ready to sift over the eggs just before serving.

7 For the carrots, heat the vegetable oil in a wok or frying pan. Add the carrots and chillies and sauté, stirring, for 2 minutes until the carrots begin to soften. Add the soy sauce, mirin, sugar, and sesame oil and cook for a further 2–3 minutes until glazed and sticky. Mix in the sesame seeds and leave to cool.

8 To make the vegetable tempura, first prepare the aubergine. Sprinkle the aubergine slices with salt, place in a colander, and leave for 10 minutes to draw the water out. Rinse thoroughly under cold water, then pat dry completely on kitchen paper.

9 Heat the rapeseed oil for deep frying to 180°C (350°F), or until a cube of day-old bread browns in 30 seconds.

10 Quickly make the batter. Place the flour and egg in a bowl. Gradually whisk in the sparkling water until the batter is the consistency of double cream; don't worry if there are a few lumps in the mixture.

11 Dip the prepared aubergine, fennel, butternut squash and purple cauliflower florets, a few at a time, in the batter. Shake off excess. Fry in batches for 3–4 minutes until crisp and golden. Drain on kitchen paper. Keep warm whilst frying the remainder.

12 Mix together all the ingredients for the sauce and divide between 4 dipping bowls.

TO SERVE

Take 8 bento boxes (2 per person). In the first 4 boxes, plate the tempura and dipping sauce, the romanesco, and a few pickles. In the second 4 boxes, plate the rice, carrots, eggs, pickles, and jelly. To finish, top each jelly with the chilled cream and a blackberry to decorate.

With spiralling, fresh green florets, romanesco is the most attractive of the cauliflowers and has an excellent nutty, slightly sweet taste. It is best steamed or lightly roasted as the curds disintegrate easily if boiled.

TIM'S BENTO BOX SIMPLIFIED FOR **EVERY**DAY... ▶ PAGE 214

BENTO **TO GO**

THIS EASY TAKE ON TIM'S BENTO BOX MAKES A TASTY MEAL WITH RICE AND DIPPING SAUCE

PREP: 40–45 MINS • COOK: 30–45 MINS

VEGETABLE TEMPURA

SERVES 4

2 EGGS, separated
175ml (6fl oz) ICED WATER
2 tbsp VEGETABLE OIL
100g (3½oz) PLAIN FLOUR
200g (7oz) CAULIFLOWER, broken into
   very small florets and blanched for 2 minutes
100g (3½oz) AUBERGINE, cut into thin slices
VEGETABLE OIL for deep frying

1 Whisk the egg yolks, water and vegetable oil, then whisk into the flour in a large bowl, but don't overmix.
2 Whisk the egg whites until stiff and then fold into the batter with a metal spoon.
3 Dip a few pieces of vegetable in the batter, drain off the excess, and deep-fry in hot oil for 3–4 minutes or until crisp, puffy, and golden. Drain on kitchen paper. Keep warm. Repeat with the remaining vegetables until all are cooked.

CRISP FRIED TOFU

SERVES 4

2 x 200g blocks TOFU, cubed
1 EGG, beaten
3 tbsp WHOLEWHEAT FLOUR
2 tsp GARLIC POWDER
VEGETABLE OIL for frying
2 tbsp TAMARI

1 Toss the tofu in the beaten egg, drain off excess, then toss in the flour mixed with the garlic.
2 Sauté in a little hot oil, turning until golden. Drain on kitchen paper and sprinkle with the tamari.

...SERVE WITH

SUSHI RICE

SERVES 4

1 x 500g bag SUSHI RICE
75ml (3fl oz) MIRIN (Japanese rice wine)
1 tbsp CASTER SUGAR
½ tsp SALT
few CHIVE STALKS

1 Cook the rice according to the packet directions.
2 Meanwhile, in a small saucepan, combine the mirin, sugar, and salt, and heat them gently until the sugar has dissolved.
3 When the rice is cooked, stir in the mirin dressing and fluff up with a fork.
4 Spoon into small bowls and serve, garnished with a few chive stalks, with the tempura, tofu, and the dipping sauce.

DIPPING SAUCE

SERVES 4

100ml (3½floz) SOY SAUCE
100ml (3½floz) RICE WINE VINEGAR
2 tbsp CLEAR HONEY
1 GARLIC clove, crushed
1 tbsp finely grated FRESH GINGER
1 tsp SESAME SEEDS
1 tsp SESAME OIL

1 Combine all the ingredients in a small saucepan, heat through for 2–3 minutes until well mixed and the honey has melted.
2 Serve with the tempura, tofu, and rice.

SPICED PUMPKIN TART WITH BROAD BEAN AND BASIL PURÉE AND CARAWAY CABBAGE ON A FONDANT POTATO

Tom Whitaker MasterChef 2011 finalist

PREPARATION TIME
45 minutes, plus chilling

COOKING TIME
1 hour 30 minutes

SERVES 6

FOR THE PASTRY
1 EGG, beaten
pinch of SALT
1½ tsp CASTER SUGAR
125g (4½oz) UNSALTED BUTTER,
　at room temperature, plus
　extra for greasing
250g (9oz) PLAIN FLOUR

FOR THE TART FILLING
1 PUMPKIN, peeled, deseeded,
　and cut into 2cm (¾in) cubes,
　peeled weight 900g (2lb)
1 tsp FENNEL SEEDS
1 tsp CUMIN SEEDS
pinch of CAYENNE PEPPER
pinch of WHITE PEPPER
½ tsp grated NUTMEG
½ tsp ground TURMERIC
1 tsp BLACK MUSTARD SEEDS
50g (1¾oz) UNSALTED BUTTER
150g (5½oz) PUMPKIN SEEDS

FOR THE FONDANT POTATOES
3 large POTATOES
1 tbsp OLIVE OIL
75g (2½oz) UNSALTED BUTTER

FOR THE CABBAGE
2 ONIONS, finely sliced
1½ tsp CARAWAY SEEDS
25g (scant 1oz)
　UNSALTED BUTTER
1 small WHITE CABBAGE, cored
　and finely sliced

FOR THE BROAD BEAN PURÉE
375g (13oz) shelled
　BROAD BEANS
juice of ½–1 LEMON
120ml (4fl oz) CRÈME FRAÎCHE
½–1 tsp MUSTARD POWDER
small bunch of BASIL

FOR THE CHIVE BUTTER
75g (2½oz) UNSALTED BUTTER
small bunch of CHIVES,
　finely snipped

1 Preheat the oven to 180°C (350°F/Gas 4). Make the pastry by creaming the egg, salt, caster sugar, and butter with an electric hand whisk. Gradually draw in the flour with your hands until the mixture resembles rough breadcrumbs. Add 1½–2 tbsp water and bring the mixture together to form a soft, but not sticky dough. Transfer to a floured surface and knead gently until smooth, making sure you don't overwork the mix. Wrap in cling film and chill in the fridge for 30 minutes.

2 For the filling, steam the diced pumpkin for 10 minutes until just soft, then leave to cool. Meanwhile, toast the fennel and cumin seeds in a dry frying pan until fragrant, then crush in a pestle and mortar. Combine with the rest of the spices in a large bowl, then add the steamed pumpkin. Coat the pumpkin pieces in the spice mix, season well, then fry them in batches in the butter until lightly coloured. Leave to cool.

3 Toast the pumpkin seeds in a dry frying pan until coloured, then transfer to a bowl to stop them from cooking further. Add 50g (1¾oz) of the toasted pumpkin seeds to a coffee grinder or mini processor and blitz until roughly powdered.

4 Grease a 25cm (10in) loose-bottomed tart tin with a little butter. Roll out three-quarters of the pastry until 3mm (⅛in) thick and use it to line the tart tin. Roll out the remaining pastry and cut into long, thin strips. Put the pumpkin, toasted pumpkin seeds, and some of the pumpkin seed powder into the pastry case. Create a lattice effect on top with the strips of pastry, then sprinkle with more pumpkin seed powder. Bake in the oven for 30 minutes until golden, then remove and place on a wire rack to cool slightly.

5 Meanwhile, make the fondant potatoes. Peel and trim the potatoes until about 4cm (1½in) high, then cut two 5.5cm (2¼in) rounds from each potato using a pastry cutter. Heat the olive oil in an ovenproof pan over medium heat, then add the potatoes and fry until golden brown on one side. Turn them over, then add the butter, 300ml (10fl oz) water, and plenty of salt and white pepper. Transfer to the oven and cook for 30 minutes or until soft. Remove from the oven and keep warm until serving.

6 To cook the cabbage, gently fry the sliced onion and caraway in the butter until soft but not browned. Meanwhile, steam the cabbage for 10 minutes or until tender. Combine the cabbage with the onions, season with salt and pepper, and keep warm until you are ready to serve.

7 Steam the broad beans for 10 minutes, leave to cool slightly, then remove the skins. Put the broad beans, lemon juice, crème fraîche, mustard powder, and basil in a food processor and blend until smooth. Season to taste.

8 Finally, make the chive butter. Clarify the butter by gently melting it in a heavy-based saucepan and skimming off all the froth from the surface. You will then see a clear yellow layer on top of a milky layer beneath. Carefully pour the clear fat into a bowl or jug, leaving the milky residue in the pan. Discard the milky residue and add the clarified butter to the chives. Brush the warm tart with chive butter.

9 Serve slices of tart with a quenelle of broad bean and basil purée and a fondant potato topped with the cabbage.

Pumpkin seeds have a high oil content, dried pumpkin seeds rapidly go rancid. Store them in an airtight container and consume them as soon as possible; in the fridge they will remain fresh for several weeks, or you can keep them in the freezer for up to 6 months.

SEASONAL VEGETABLE DUMPLINGS IN A SPICY YOGHURT CURRY SERVED WITH CACHUMBA SALAD AND CRISPY PURI BREADS

Jackie Kearney MasterChef 2011 final 4

PREPARATION TIME
25 minutes

COOKING TIME
1 hour 30 minutes

SERVES 6

Seasonal vegetable dumplings

250g (9oz) BEETROOT, leaves
  trimmed
½ BUTTERNUT SQUASH, peeled,
  deseeded, and cut into 1cm
  (½in) cubes, weight 250g (9oz)
1½ tbsp GHEE
1 WHITE ONION, finely sliced
SALT
1½ tbsp CUMIN SEEDS
1 tbsp FENNEL SEEDS

1 tbsp dried POMEGRANATE
  SEEDS
2–3 fresh, small GREEN CHILLIES,
  chopped (deseed if you prefer
  a milder taste)
125g (4½oz) GRAM FLOUR
½ tsp ASAFOETIDA
bunch of CORIANDER, chopped
½ tsp BICARBONATE OF SODA
SUNFLOWER OIL, for deep frying

1 Boil the beetroot for 20–30 minutes until soft. Peel away the skins, chop the flesh into 1cm (½in) cubes, and set aside. Boil the squash for about 8 minutes until just softened, then drain and set aside.

2 While the beetroot and squash are cooking, heat the ghee in a frying pan and fry the onion with a little salt, stirring, until soft and golden. Set aside.

3 Toast the cumin seeds, fennel seeds, and pomegranate seeds in a dry frying pan until fragrant, then add the chopped chillies. Cook for 1 minute, then add the softened onions. Stir to combine, remove from the heat, and set aside.

4 In a large bowl, combine the gram flour, asafoetida, chopped coriander, bicarbonate of soda, and a pinch of salt. Gradually whisk in water to form a batter – it should have the consistency of porridge – then add the beetroot, squash, and onion mixture and gently fold in.

5 Heat the oil in a large pan. Test the temperature by adding a little blob of the mixture – when it rises to the surface, the oil is hot enough. Add dessertspoons of the mixture to the oil and gently fry the dumplings for 8–10 minutes until golden brown. Drain on kitchen paper.

While beetroot is available in different shapes and colours, the familiar round, red roots are the ones you are most likely to find. This beetroot is available all year, but at its best from midsummer to late autumn. Look for glossy, fresh leaves and hard roots that are free of mould and abrasions.

Kadhi yogurt curry

1 tsp CHILLI POWDER
1 tsp ground TURMERIC
1 tbsp ground CORIANDER
65g (2¼oz) GRAM FLOUR
750ml (1¼ pints) PLAIN
    GREEK-STYLE YOGURT
SALT

2–3 hot RED CHILLIES, finely
    chopped (deseed if you prefer
    a milder taste)
3 GARLIC cloves, finely sliced
1 tbsp BLACK MUSTARD SEEDS
2 tbsp GHEE

1 Toast the chilli powder, turmeric, and coriander in a dry frying pan until fragrant. Whisk the gram flour with a splash of water to make a loose paste, then add the yogurt and whisk until smooth. Add to the spice mixture and cook over medium heat for 10–15 minutes until reduced and thickened. Season to taste with salt.
2 While the curry cooks, fry the chopped red chillies, sliced garlic, and mustard seeds in the ghee until the seeds start popping and the garlic is golden brown. Add to the yogurt curry and stir to combine.
3 Add the vegetable dumplings to the yogurt curry and reheat gently for 5–10 minutes to soften, being careful not to break the dumplings. Keep warm until serving.

Cachumba salad

½ CUCUMBER, deseeded and
    chopped into 1cm (½in) pieces
2 TOMATOES, deseeded and
    chopped into 1cm (½in) pieces
1 small ONION, chopped into
    ½cm (¼in) pieces
juice of ½ LEMON

handful of CORIANDER, chopped
handful of MINT, chopped
SALT

1 Combine all the ingredients for the salad and season to taste with salt. Set aside until serving.

Puri bread

125g (4½oz) fine CHAPATI
  FLOUR or fine WHOLEMEAL
  FLOUR
½ tsp SALT

1 tsp CAROM SEEDS
PLAIN FLOUR, for dusting
SUNFLOWER OIL, for deep frying

1 Mix the flour, salt, and carom seeds in a bowl and gradually add
warm water until the mixture starts to come together – about
100ml (3½fl oz). Turn out onto a lightly floured surface and knead
well for 5–10 minutes until smooth. Place in a bowl, cover with a
damp cloth and leave to rest in a warm place for 20 minutes.
2 Divide the dough into 18 small balls, then roll each ball into
a thin disc, about 7cm (2¾in) in diameter and 3mm (⅛in) thick.
3 Heat the oil to 180°C (350°F), then deep fry the puri in
batches. Use a spoon to baste the puri with hot oil, then turn
them in the pan – the basting and turning help them to puff
up. Cook until crisp on each side, then drain on kitchen paper. The
puri can be kept warm in the oven before serving.

TO SERVE
Place 2–3 dumplings on each plate and spoon the sauce over
them. Add a large spoonful of cachumba salad and 2–3 crispy
puri breads to each plate.

SAAG PANEER ON A PUMPKIN ROSTI WITH TAMARIND GLAZE AND COCONUT CREAM

Jackie Kearney MasterChef 2011 final 4

PREPARATION TIME
50 minutes

COOKING TIME
35 minutes

SERVES 4

FOR THE ROSTI
1 small PUMPKIN, deseeded
 and peeled
1 large POTATO, peeled
1 GREEN CHILLI, deseeded and
 finely diced
1 RED CHILLI, deseeded and
 finely diced
small bunch of CORIANDER, finely
 chopped
SALT and freshly ground
 BLACK PEPER
2 tbsp SUNFLOWER OIL

FOR THE SAAG PANEER
500g (1lb 2oz) BABY SPINACH
SALT
SUNFLOWER OIL
4 tbsp GHEE
1 tsp BLACK MUSTARD SEEDS
1 tsp CUMIN SEEDS
1 small WHITE ONION, finely sliced

1 GREEN CHILLI, deseeded and
 finely diced
1 RED CHILLI, deseeded and
 finely diced
½ tbsp GINGER PASTE
1 tbsp GARLIC PASTE
2 tbsp GARAM MASALA
12 CHERRY TOMATOES, halved
500g (1lb 2oz) PANEER, cut
 into 4cm (1½in) cubes

FOR THE TAMARIND GLAZE
2 tbsp SUGAR
2 tbsp RED WINE VINEGAR
100g (3½oz) TAMARIND PASTE

FOR THE COCONUT CREAM
100g (3½oz) CREAMED COCONUT
3 tbsp WARM WATER

TO GARNISH
4 small CORIANDER leaves
4–8 EDIBLE FLOWERS

1 Preheat the oven to 180°C (350°F/Gas 4). Using a coarse grater, grate both the pumpkin and potato into a large bowl. Add the green and red chillies and the coriander. Season.
2 Heat the oil over medium to high heat in a large frying pan. Remove excess liquid from the pumpkin mixture by squeezing in a clean tea towel over the sink. Divide the mixture into 4 equal patties and shape to make rostis. Carefully place the patties in hot oil and fry on both sides for about 3 minutes or until lightly golden. Transfer to a baking tray and place in the oven for about 15 minutes, or until fully cooked.
3 Meanwhile, make the saag paneer. Bring a large pan of water to the boil, add the spinach. Blanch for about 30 seconds. Drain immediately and rinse under cold water. Purée the spinach with either a hand-held blender or in a food processor, adding salt and a little sunflower oil if needed. Reserve.
4 Melt 3 tbsp of the ghee in a saucepan over medium heat. Add the seeds and fry for 1 minute, stirring. Reduce the heat, add the onions, and fry for 4–5 minutes until softened.

5 Add both the chillies, and the garlic and ginger pastes, and continue to cook for 2–3 minutes until the garlic and ginger are both golden, taking care not to let them burn. Sprinkle in the garam masala and cook for 1 minute.

6 Finally add the spinach and tomatoes, and cook, stirring, for a further 2–3 minutes, until all the flavours are amalgamated.

7 In a separate pan, heat the remaining ghee over medium to high heat. Once melted, fry the paneer pieces until golden around the edges. Do this in batches if necessary. Once fried, transfer the pieces with a slotted spoon to kitchen paper to drain excess oil, then keep warm until ready to serve.

8 Make the tamarind glaze. Place all the ingredients in a saucepan with a little water and boil over high heat until reduced by about two-thirds and syrupy. Strain through a fine sieve to reach a smooth consistency. Transfer to a squeezy bottle ready to use for garnishing the plates.

9 Using the back of a fork, gently crush the coconut cream into the warm water until dissolved, and it is the consistency of smooth, thick, cream.

TO SERVE

Zig zag 4 serving plates with the tamarind glaze. Place the rosti on top in the centre of the plates. Layer the paneer and saag on top, finishing with a layer of paneer. Add a spoonful of the coconut cream to the top of each stack. Garnish with small coriander leaves, and finally finish with 1 or 2 edible flowers arranged to one side of each plate.

CURRY IN A HURRY

JOHN TORODE CAPTURES THE AUTHENTIC FLAVOURS OF JACKIE'S SAAG PANEER WITH THIS SPEEDY ALTERNAIVE

PREP: 20 MINS • COOK: 35 MINS

 +  +

SERVES 4

225g (8oz) peeled, deseeded PUMPKIN, cubed
25g (scant 1oz) BUTTER
1 tbsp OLIVE OIL
400g (14oz) PANEER, cubed
400g (14oz) BABY SPINACH
2 tbsp OLIVE OIL
1 ONION, chopped
2 GARLIC cloves, crushed
1 tsp grated FRESH GINGER
1 green CHILLI, deseeded and finely chopped

1 tsp GARAM MASALA
1 tsp each of CHILLI POWDER and GROUND CORIANDER
2 tsp GROUND CUMIN
4 TOMATOES, chopped
2 tbsp chopped CORIANDER
SALT and freshly ground BLACK PEPPER
4 tbsp COCONUT CREAM

FLAVOUR INFUSIONS

Chillies come in various colours, shapes and sizes, adding fruity, nutty, smoky, or floral flavour as well as varying degrees of heat.
Coriander seeds have a woody, almost floral fragrance with a peppery aftertaste. They add a sweet, mellow warmth and are used whole or ground. The herb adds pungent fragrances.
Cumin seeds (particularly toasted), and ground cumin have a woody, earthy, pungent smell and add a rich, slightly bitter-sweet flavour and warmth.

"The wonderful, fragrant spices enhance the sweetness of the pumpkin. You could use any winter squash or even sweet potatoes."

1 Preheat the oven to 200ºC (400ºF /Gas 6). Place the pumpkin in a roasting tin, dot over the butter and roast in the oven turning occasionally for about 20 minutes, or until just tender.

2 Meanwhile, heat 1 tbsp of the oil in a sauté pan, add the diced paneer and sauté for 4–5 minutes, stirring and turning or until golden brown on the outside. Transfer the paneer to a plate, then add half the spinach to the pan, cover with a lid and cook for 2 minutes until wilted. Transfer the spinach to a colander and leave to drain. Repeat with the remaining spinach, and add this to the colander to drain.

3 Heat the remaining 2 tbsp olive oil in the pan, add the onion, garlic, ginger, and chilli and sauté, stirring, for 2–3 minutes or until softened. Add the garam masala, chilli, cumin, and coriander, and sauté for a further 3 minutes stirring constantly.

4 Add the chopped tomatoes and cook for 8–10 minutes until pulpy.

5 Meanwhile squeeze all the liquid from the spinach and roughly chop. Add to the pan with the spices, chopped coriander, paneer, and roasted pumpkin. Heat until piping hot, then season to taste, stir in 3 tbsp water and the coconut cream, heat through again, then serve.

HIGH TEA MENU
Tom Whitaker MasterChef 2011 finalist

PREPARATION TIME
1 hour 5 minutes

COOKING TIME
55 minutes

**MAKES 18 CUPAKES,
2 SLICES CLAFOUTIS**

Tier 1

FOR THE CUPCAKES
125g (4½oz) CASTER SUGAR
125g (4½oz) BUTTER, softened
1 tbsp ROSEWATER
½ tsp PURE ALMOND EXTRACT
2 large EGGS
125g (4½oz) SELF-RAISING
  FLOUR
25g (scant 1oz) GROUND
  ALMONDS
a dash of MILK, if required

FOR THE ICING
250g (9oz) FONDANT ICING SUGAR
125g (4½oz) BUTTER,
  at room temperature
1 tsp PURE VANILLA EXTRACT
few drops of ORANGE and PINK
  FOOD COLOURING

1 For the cupcakes, preheat the oven to 200°C (400°F/Gas 6). Cream together the sugar and butter in a mixing bowl with an electric whisk until light and fluffy. Add the rose water, almond extract, and eggs, and beat until well combined.
2 Mix together the flour and ground almonds and gently fold in with a metal spoon to form a soft dropping consistency, adding a dash of milk if necessary.
3 Half-fill the cupcake cases with the mixture and bake in the oven for 20 minutes, or until the centres spring back when lightly pressed. Transfer to a wire rack to cool completely.
4 For the icing, mix together all the ingredients until smooth. If the mixture is too stiff, add a few drops of warm water to loosen to the consistency of warm butter. Place the icing in a piping bag fitted with a star nozzle. Pipe whorls of the icing onto the cupcakes starting from the outside and working in.
5 Store any remaining cakes in an airtight container.

FOR THE CHERRY CLAFOUTIS
125g (4½oz) PLAIN FLOUR, sifted
75g (2½oz) BUTTER
25g (scant 1oz) CASTER SUGAR
½ tsp SALT
1 EGG YOLK
1½ tbsp cold MILK
ICING SUGAR, to serve

FOR THE FILLING
1 EGG
30g (1oz) CASTER SUGAR

40g (1¼oz) PLAIN FLOUR
40g (1¼oz) BUTTER, melted
  and cooled
1 tbsp KIRSCH
5 tbsp cold MILK
1 VANILLA POD, split and seeds
  scraped out
425g can PITTED BLACK
  CHERRIES, drained and dried
  on kitchen paper

1 For the tart cases, preheat the oven to 180°C (350°F/Gas 4). Place the flour and butter in a bowl. Rub lightly with your fingers until a crumb-like texture is reached. Add the sugar, salt, egg, and milk. Mix to combine. If necessary, tip the mixture out onto a lightly floured surface and knead it together. Wrap in cling film and chill in the fridge for 20 minutes.

2 Remove the pastry from the fridge and take out of the cling film. On a lightly floured surface roll the pastry out to 5mm (¼in) thickness. Cut the pastry into 2 squares. Use to line two 10cm (4in) tart cases, leaving some of the pastry to hang over the edge. Line with greaseproof paper and fill with baking beans.

3 Bake in the oven for 20 minutes, or until the edges have darkened and the pastry is cooked through. Remove from the oven, take out the baking beans, and leave to cool.

4 When cool enough to handle, trace the edge of the tart case with a sharp knife, cutting off the excess pastry.

5 For the filling, crack the egg into a bowl. Add the sugar and flour. Whisk lightly until combined. Add all the remaining ingredients to the mixture, apart from the cherries. Mix to combine.

6 Divide the cherries equally between the tart cases. Pour over the mixture and place in the preheated oven. Cook for 15 minutes, or until the custard has set. Remove and leave to cool slightly.

7 To serve, remove the tarts from the cases, dust with the icing sugar, and cut each tart into 6 pieces.

PREPARATION TIME
1 hour 15 minutes,
plus resting

COOKING TIME
33–40 minutes

**MAKES 22 MACAROONS,
20 WHOOPIE PIES,
12 SCONES**

Tier 2

FOR THE PINK MACAROONS
175g (6oz) ICING SUGAR
125g (4½oz) GROUND ALMONDS
3 large EGG WHITES
pinch of SALT
75g (2½oz) CASTER SUGAR
PINK FOOD COLOURING

FOR THE FILLING
150g (5½oz) BUTTER, at
  room temperature
75g (2½oz) ICING SUGAR, sifted
PINK FOOD COLOURING

1 For the macaroons, preheat the oven to 160°C (325°F/Gas 3). Line 2 baking trays with baking parchment. Using a food processor, blitz together the icing sugar and ground almonds.
2 In a separate bowl whisk the egg whites with a pinch of salt until softly peaking. Whisk in the caster sugar, whisking well after each addition. Add a few drops of pink food colouring until the desired colour is reached.
3 Fold the almond mixture into the meringue using a metal spoon. Place the mixture in a piping bag fitted with a 1cm (½in) plain nozzle. Pipe small rounds, about 3cm (1¼in) diameter onto the prepared trays, leaving a small gap between each. Using the back of a spoon, smooth the surface of the mixture. Leave to rest for 15 minutes.
4 Bake in the oven for 12–15 minutes. The macaroons should feel dry to the touch. Leave to cool.
5 For the filling, beat together the butter and icing sugar. Beat in a few drops of food colouring to the desired colour.
6 To serve, sandwich the macaroons together in pairs with the filling. Store any remaining macaroons in an airtight container.

FOR THE WHOOPIE PIES
250g (9oz) PLAIN FLOUR
75g (2½oz) COCOA POWDER
1 tsp BAKING POWDER
¼ tsp BICARBONATE OF SODA
¼ tsp SALT
175g (6oz) UNSALTED BUTTER, at
  room temperature
150g (5½oz) GRANULATED SUGAR
1 large EGG
1 tsp VANILLA EXTRACT
4 tbsp BUTTERMILK
100ml (3½fl oz) warm
  strong COFFEE

FOR THE FILLING
50g (1¾oz) VEGETABLE
  SHORTENING
50g (1¾oz) UNSALTED BUTTER,
  at room temperature
115g (4oz) ICING SUGAR
1½ tsp pure VANILLA EXTRACT
120ml (4fl oz) GLUCOSE or CORN
  SYRUP

1 For the chocolate whoopie pies, preheat the oven to 190°C (375°F/Gas 5). Sift together the flour, cocoa powder, baking powder, bicarbonate of soda, and salt. Set aside.

2 Place the butter and sugar in a separate bowl. Beat well with an electric whisk until the mixture is pale and fluffy. Beat in the egg and vanilla extract. Using a wooden spoon, mix in the buttermilk and coffee until thoroughly blended.

3 Add the flour mixture, a quarter at a time, to the bowl. Work in well after each addition until a firm dough is formed.

4 Line 2 baking trays with baking parchment.

5 Spoon heaped tablespoons of the mixture onto the lined trays, leaving a 4cm (1¾in) gap.

6 Bake in the oven for 9–10 minutes. The cookies should have flattened out to a smooth disk. Remove from the oven and transfer to a wire rack to cool whilst preparing the filling.

7 For the vanilla filling, beat together all the ingredients until well combined with an electric whisk.

8 To serve, spread one of the cookies with the filling. Top with another. Repeat until all the cookies are filled. Store any remainder in an airtight container.

FOR THE SCONES
225g (8oz) SELF-RAISING FLOUR
½ tsp BAKING POWDER
pinch of SALT
50g (1¾oz) BUTTER
25g (scant 1oz) CASTER SUGAR
150ml (5fl oz) MILK

TO SERVE
500g (1lb 2oz) CLOTTED CREAM,
pot of good quality
    RASPBERRY JAM

1 Preheat the oven to 220°C (400°F/Gas 6). Sift the flour, baking powder, and salt in a bowl. Add the butter and rub in until the mixture resembles breadcrumbs. Add the sugar and milk. Draw together to form a soft, but not sticky dough.

2 Tip the mixture out onto a lightly floured surface. Using the palm of your hand flatten the mixture out until it is about 2cm (¾in) thick. Using a 5cm (2in) fluted cutter, cut out your scones.

3 It will be necessary to reform the dough 2–3 times.

4 Place the scones onto a baking sheet lined with baking parchment. Bake in the oven for 12–15 minutes, until risen, golden, and the bases sound hollow when tapped. Remove, then cool on a wire rack.

5 To serve, split and fill with clotted cream and raspberry jam.

PREPARATION TIME
30 minutes

COOKING TIME
15 minutes

MAKES 24

Tier 3

12 slices WHITE BREAD,
  crusts removed, cut into
  perfect squares
BUTTER, at room temperature

**FOR THE SALMON
SANDWICHES**
150g (5½oz) SALMON FILLET,
  skinned
3 DILL sprigs
SALT and freshly ground
  BLACK PEPPER
6 tbsp DOUBLE CREAM

FOR THE BEEF SANDWICHES
150g (5½oz) thinly sliced, rare,
  roast BEEF TOPSIDE
made ENGLISH MUSTARD
handful of LAMB'S LETTUCE

**FOR THE CUCUMBER
SANDWICHES**
100g (3½oz) CREAM CHEESE
60g (2oz) SOFT GOAT'S CHEESE
squeeze of LEMON JUICE
¼ CUCUMBER, peeled and
  thinly sliced

1 For the salmon and dill sandwiches, poach the salmon in a
little water with a sprig of the dill and a little salt and pepper
for 5–10 minutes, until just cooked through.
2 Remove with a slotted spoon and allow to cool. Flake the
salmon into a bowl, discarding any bones. Finely chop the
remaining dill. Add with the cream, mix gently, taste, and season.
3 Butter 4 slices of the bread and sandwich together with the
salmon mixture. Cut into 8 triangles.
4 For the roast beef and mustard sandwiches, butter 4 slices of
the remaining bread and spread thinly with the English mustard.
Top 2 bread slices with slices of beef, top with some lamb's
lettuce, then the remaining buttered bread. Cut into 8 triangles.
5 For the cheese and cucumber sandwiches, beat the 2 cheeses
together. Season and add the lemon juice. Mix again. Spread the
mixture on to the remaining 4 bread slices. Top 2 of the bread
slices with slices of cucumber then cover with the remaining
bread. Cut into 8 triangles.

TO SERVE
Place the sandwiches attractively on the base of a cake stand.
Arrange the macaroons, scones, and whoopie pies on the middle
tier, and place the cupcakes and clafoutis on the top tier.

MINI HIGH TEA

GREGG WALLACE TAKES TOM'S HIGH TEA MENU
AND SIMPLIFIES IT FOR EVERYDAY AFTERNOONS

PREP: 45 MINS · COOK: 30 MINS

SANDWICHES

SERVES 4

BUTTER, to spread
8 slices fresh WHITE BREAD
6 tbsp CREAM CHEESE
1 tbsp MAYONNAISE
2 tbsp freshly chopped DILL
1 tsp fresh LEMON JUICE
freshly ground BLACK PEPPER
4 slices SMOKED SALMON

1 Butter the bread slices and set aside. Mix the cream cheese with the mayonnaise until softened, then stir in the dill, lemon juice, and seasoning.

2 Divide the dill cream cheese between 4 slices of the bread then top equally with the smoked salmon. Top each sandwich with another slice of bread, cut off the crusts and serve in triangles.

"Everyone loves a traditional afternoon tea – and this one is as traditional as it gets!"

CHERRY SCONES

MAKES 8

350g (12oz) SELF-RAISING FLOUR
1 tsp BAKING POWDER
85g (3oz) cold BUTTER, diced
30g (1oz) CASTER SUGAR
about 175ml (6fl oz) WHOLE MILK, warmed
1 tsp PURE VANILLA EXTRACT
60g (2oz) GLACÉ CHERRIES, rinsed, dried,
  and chopped
MILK or beaten EGG for brushing
CLOTTED CREAM and CHERRY JAM to serve

1 Preheat the oven to 220°C (425°F/Gas 7).
In a bowl, mix the flour, baking powder, and butter together, rubbing in the butter with your fingertips until the mixture resembles fine breadcrumbs. Stir in the sugar. Add the milk, vanilla extract, and cherries, and stir together until the mixture has formed a soft dough – do not over-mix the dough as this will result in tough scones.
2 Transfer the dough to a lightly floured surface and shape into a round about 4cm (1½in) thick. Using an 8cm (3¼in) round cutter, cut out 8 scones, reshaping the dough as necessary.
3 Place the scones on a lightly floured baking tray, brush with a little extra milk or beaten egg and cook in the oven for 10–12 minutes or until golden and well risen. Leave to cool, then serve while still slightly warm, split, and sandwiched with clotted cream and cherry jam.

CHOCOLATE CUPCAKES

MAKES 12

175g (6oz) unsalted BUTTER
100g (3½oz) DARK CHOCOLATE,
  (minimum 70% cocoa solids), chopped
175g (6oz) CASTER SUGAR
100g (3½oz) SELF-RAISING FLOUR
20g (¾oz) COCOA POWDER
4 EGGS
50g (1¾oz) BUTTER
3 tbsp WHOLE MILK
200g (7oz) ICING SUGAR, sifted
30g (1oz) COCOA POWDER, sifted

1 Preheat the oven to 180°C (350°F/Gas 4).
Line a 12-hole muffin tin with paper cake cases. Melt the butter, chocolate, and sugar in a bowl over a pan of simmering water. Cool 5 minutes.
2 Sift together the flour and cocoa. Beat the chocolate for 2–3 minutes then beat in the eggs one at a time. Fold in the flour with a metal spoon. Spoon into the paper cases until three-quarters full. Bake for about 20 minutes or until the centres spring back when pressed. Cool slightly then transfer to a wire rack until cold.
3 To make the icing, melt the butter and milk in a bowl over a pan of simmering water beat in the icing sugar and cocoa. Chill until spreadable.
4 Swirl the chocolate fudge icing on to the cupcakes with a spatula, or use a piping bag fitted with a star-shaped nozzle.

DESSERTS

DATE PARCELS STUFFED WITH FRANGIPANE AND POMEGRANATE

Jackie Kearney MasterChef 2011 final 4

PREPARATION TIME
45 minutes, plus chilling

COOKING TIME
20 minutes

SERVES 4

FOR THE DATE PARCELS
18 large MEDJOOL DATES,
  stoned and halved
6 sheets of FILO PASTRY,
  halved widthways
40g (1¼oz) SOYA MARGARINE
  or BUTTER, melted
SUNFLOWER OIL

FOR THE FRANGIPANE
1 tbsp ROSEWATER
20g (¾oz) CASTER SUGAR

75g (2½oz) ground ALMONDS
30g (1oz) fresh
  POMEGRANATE SEEDS

TO DECORATE
50g (1¾oz) SHELLED
  PISTACHIOS, roughly chopped
50g (1¾oz) fresh
  POMEGRANATE SEEDS

1 Arrange 12 date halves, cut-side up, tight together, in 3 rows on each of 3 large sheets of lightly oiled greaseproof paper. Flatten each, by hand, to a rectangle, then top with further sheets of oiled greaseproof. Using a rolling pin, roll firmly to flatten and press into thin slabs, doubled in size. Carefully transfer to baking trays and chill in the fridge for 30–40 minutes.
2 Meanwhile, make the frangipane. Gently heat the rosewater, sugar, and 6 tbsp water in a small pan to dissolve the sugar. Add the ground almonds and beat to a thick paste.
3 To assemble, take the date sheets out of the fridge and set on a flat board. Peel off the top layer of paper. Trim each to 12 x 8cm (5 x 3¼in). Loosen with a palette knife. Divide the frangipane between the date sheets, spreading it down the length in the middle of each and leaving a small gap at each end. Sprinkle over the pomegranate seeds and roll each piece lengthways. Using a sharp knife, trim the ends and cut each roll into 4 pieces.
4 Preheat the oven to 190°C (375°F/Gas 5). Take a piece of filo pastry and brush the edges with the melted fat. Roll up a date piece in the pastry, twisting each end like a wrapped sweet to seal. Trim the ends with a sharp knife. Repeat with the remaining pastry and date pieces, then chill in the fridge for 15 minutes.
5 Meanwhile, lightly toast the chopped pistachios on a non-stick baking tray in the oven for 6–8 minutes. Leave to cool.
6 Heat sunflower oil for deep frying in a deep pan to 180°C (350°F) or until an offcut of pastry sizzles and rises to the top of the oil when dropped in. Fry the date parcels in batches for about 4 minutes or until golden brown, then drain on kitchen paper. Leave the parcels to cool slightly before serving.
7 To serve, lay out the date parcels onto a serving platter and sprinkle with the chopped pistachios and pomegranate seeds.

Simplify for **EVERY**DAY

• Use 12 whole stoned dates. Sprinkle the inside with rosewater, then stuff with a few pomegranate seeds and some white marzipan. Make these into the filo parcels.
• Quickly toast the nuts, stirring, in a non-stick frying pan instead of in the oven.

BOOZY CHOCOLATE-ORANGE PROFITEROLES
Nicky French MasterChef 2011 contestant

PREPARATION TIME
25 minutes, plus cooling

COOKING TIME
25 minutes

SERVES 4–6

"Cooking is just such a big part of my life, it's a big part of my family life. Any spare time that I have, I tend to be in the kitchen."

The most popular commercial orange variety is the Valencia, both for its long growing season and for its ease of peeling, comparative lack of seeds, and sharp but sweet, juicy flesh. For preference, buy unwaxed oranges if you plan to use the zest or peel.

FOR THE PROFITEROLES
100g (3½oz) UNSALTED BUTTER, cubed
pinch of SALT
125g (4½oz) PLAIN FLOUR, sifted
30g (1oz) CASTER SUGAR
4 large EGGS
400ml (14fl oz) DOUBLE CREAM
30g (1oz) ICING SUGAR

FOR THE SAUCE
100ml (3½fl oz) DOUBLE CREAM
zest of 1 large ORANGE
100g (3½oz) MILK CHOCOLATE, broken into pieces
3 tbsp COINTREAU (optional)

1 Preheat the oven to 200°C (400°F/Gas 6). Put 300ml (10fl oz) water, the butter, and salt into a heavy-based saucepan and heat gently until the butter melts. Increase the heat and bring to the boil. Add the flour and caster sugar and, using a wooden spoon, beat vigorously over medium heat until you have a smooth, silky paste that leaves the sides of the pan clean. Transfer the paste to a bowl and leave to cool for 10 minutes.

2 Break the eggs into a jug and beat lightly. Add the egg to the paste, a little at a time, beating well after each addition until you have a smooth, glossy paste that holds its shape (you may not need all the egg).

3 Line 2 or 3 baking trays with baking parchment. Fill a piping bag fitted with a 1cm (½in) plain nozzle with the paste, then pipe 30–32 small, 5cm (2in) diameter balls, leaving plenty of space between each one. Wet your finger and gently smooth the top of each ball of paste.

4 Bake in the oven for 20–25 minutes until golden and crisp. This may have to be done in batches. Once cooked, transfer to a wire rack and leave to cool.

5 Whilst the profiteroles are baking, whip the cream and add the icing sugar to taste. Chill until needed.

6 For the sauce, in a medium saucepan, bring the cream and orange zest to the boil. Then remove from the heat. Add the chocolate and stir until it has all melted and the sauce is smooth, then add the Cointreau to taste, if using. Keep warm.

7 Fill a piping bag fitted with a 1cm (½in) nozzle with the whipped cream. Using a sharp knife, cut a small slit in the bottom of each profiterole, then pipe the cream inside. Pile in dessert dishes or in a large stack on a large serving plate. Serve with the warm chocolate sauce poured over the top.

ASSIETTE OF CHOCOLATE
Alice Taylor MasterChef 2011 contestant

PREPARATION TIME
1–2 hours

COOKING TIME
30 minutes–1 hour

SERVES 6

Bitter chocolate ginger torte

FOR THE TORTE
½ packet GINGER BISCUITS,
 finely crushed in
 a food processor
1 large piece of STEM GINGER
 in syrup, finely chopped
45g (1½oz) melted BUTTER
225g (8oz) DARK CHOCOLATE,
 85% cocoa solids, broken
 into pieces
2½ tbsp LIQUID GLUCOSE

2½ tbsp ORANGE LIQUEUR
300ml (10fl oz) DOUBLE CREAM
100g (3½oz) DARK CHOCOLATE,
 for garnish

FOR THE ORANGE SAUCE
120ml (4fl oz) ORANGE JUICE
2 tsp CORNFLOUR
juice and zest of 1 ORANGE
1½ tsp CASTER SUGAR
2 tbsp ORANGE LIQUEUR

1 Preheat oven to 200°C (400°F/Gas 6). Set 6 cook's rings on a baking tray. Base-wrap each in cling film, making sure it is easy to remove once the rings are filled. For the torte, mix together the biscuit crumbs, ginger, and butter. Sprinkle the biscuit mixture evenly over the bases of the rings and press down firmly.
2 Place the chocolate in a heatproof bowl together with the liquid glucose and the orange liqueur. Place the bowl over a pan of barely simmering water, making sure the bottom of the bowl does not touch the water, and leave until the chocolate has melted and become quite smooth. Stir, then take off the heat and leave the mixture to cool for 5 minutes. Don't worry if the chocolate looks a little grainy at this point as it will recover with the addition of the cream.
3 In a separate bowl, whip the cream until very slightly thickened. Fold into the chocolate mixture. When it is smoothly blended, spoon it into the prepared rings. Very gently tap the baking tray on the work surface to even the mixture out, then place in the fridge to set.
4 For the orange sauce, in a small saucepan mix 2 tablespoons of the measured orange juice with the cornflour until smooth. Stir in the remaining juice and the freshly squeezed juice. Slowly bring to the boil, and cook for 1 minute, stirring all the time, until thickened, then stir in the sugar until dissolved, and the orange liqueur. Pour into a plastic squeezy bottle and chill until serving.

White chocolate mousse

FOR THE MOUSSE
150g (5½oz) WHITE CHOCOLATE,
    broken into pieces
4 EGGS, whites only
75g (2½oz) CASTER SUGAR
150ml (5fl oz) DOUBLE CREAM

FOR THE COULIS
200g (7oz) RASPBERRIES
MINT sprigs, to garnish

1 For the mousse, melt the chocolate in a bowl set over a pan of simmering water. Whisk the egg whites until softly peaking, then fold in the sugar, 1 tbsp at a time. In a separate bowl, whip the cream until softly peaking. Fold the 2 mixtures together, then add the melted chocolate. Fold gently until completely combined, then pipe or spoon into shot glasses and refrigerate immediately.
2 For the coulis, rub the raspberries through a fine sieve. Set the coulis aside until ready to serve.

Milk chocolate choux bun

FOR THE CHOUX BUNS
60g (2oz) STRONG WHITE FLOUR
1 tsp CASTER SUGAR
50g (1¾oz) SALTED BUTTER
2 EGGS, beaten

FOR THE VANILLA CREAM
200ml (7fl oz) DOUBLE CREAM
1 VANILLA POD, split and seeds
    scraped out

FOR THE CHOCOLATE SAUCE
3 tbsp DOUBLE CREAM
200g (7oz) MILK CHOCOLATE,
    broken into pieces
20g (¾oz) SALTED BUTTER

1 Preheat oven to 200°C (400°F/Gas 6) For the choux buns, fold a sheet of baking parchment to make a crease and then open it up again. Sift the flour straight on to the square of paper and add the sugar.
2 Place 150ml (5fl oz) water and the butter into a medium-sized saucepan. Heat gently until the butter has melted. Bring to the boil, remove from the heat, then tip all the flour in and immediately beat the mixture vigorously with a wooden spoon until smooth, and the mixture leaves the sides of the pan clean.
3 Beat the eggs into the mixture, a little at a time, beating well after each addition until you have a smooth glossy paste.
4 Lightly grease a baking tray, then rinse under cold water. (This will help create steam, which helps the pastry rise). Spoon the mixture into a piping bag fitted with a 1cm (½in) plain nozzle and pipe walnut-sized balls, well apart, onto the prepared baking tray.

5 Use a wet palette knife to cut the mixture away from the nozzle each time so you are left with a flat surface on each bun. Alternatively, dip your finger in water and pat each one down to remove the peak. The buns will double in size as they cook, so leave plenty of space between each one.

6 Bake in the oven for 10 minutes, then increase the heat to 220°C (425°F/Gas 7) and bake for a further 15 minutes until the buns are crisp and golden brown. Make a small slit towards the base of each bun with the tip of a sharp knife to let out steam and cool on a wire rack.

7 To make the vanilla cream, whip the cream with the vanilla seeds until it is fairly stiff, then spoon into a piping bag fitted with a small nozzle. Pipe a little cream into each bun and set them aside until ready to serve.

8 To make the chocolate sauce, melt half the cream and all the milk chocolate in a bowl set over a pan of simmering water, until smooth. Spoon half into a piping bag fitted with a fine writing nozzle and set aside. Stir the remaining cream and the butter into the melted chocolate mixture until it forms a smooth, glossy sauce. Remove the pan from the heat and set aside, keeping warm, until ready to serve.

TO SERVE

To one side of each plate, pipe the chocolate sauce in a flower shape, large enough to hold the torte in the centre. Remove the cling film from the sides of the cooks rings. Run a blow torch round the outsides to loosen the tortes. Invert, crumb-sides up in the centres of the piped flowers and remove the cling film and rings. Fill the 'petals' of the flowers with the reserved orange sauce in the squeezy bottle. Place the white chocolate mousses in the middle of the plates. Spoon some warm raspberry coulis on top of each one. Arrange 3 choux buns next to each glass and spoon some warm chocolate sauce over. Use 2 teaspoons to shape quenelles of vanilla cream and place on on top of each torte and one on top of the buns. Decorate each plate with a mint sprig and serve straight away.

ALICE'S ASSIETTE OF CHOCOLATE SIMPLIFIED FOR **EVERY**DAY... ▶ PAGE 242

TOP-CHOC TART

GREGG WALLACE OFFERS A FUN TWIST ON ALICE'S CHOCOLATE TORTE, WITH A TRIO OF TASTY TOPPINGS

PREP: 45–50 MINS • CHILL: 1½ HRS

CHOCOLATE TART

SERVES 4–6

300g (10oz) GINGER NUT BISCUITS
100g (3½oz) BUTTER, melted for the base
200ml (7fl oz) DOUBLE CREAM
100g (3½oz) butter, cut into small pieces
  for the filling
300g (10oz) DARK CHOCOLATE, minimum
  of 70% cocoa solids, broken in pieces
2 pieces STEM GINGER, drained and very
  finely chopped

1 To make the tart base, crush the ginger nuts in a food processor or in a plastic bag with a rolling pin. Mix in the melted butter. Press the mixture into the base and sides of a greased 23cm (9in) round fluted flan tin.
2 To make the filling, place the cream, butter, and chocolate in a bowl over a saucepan of gently simmering water. Stir frequently until melted and smooth.
3 Remove from the heat and whisk for a few minutes until very smooth and creamy. Then stir in the chopped stem ginger.
4 Pour the chocolate mixture into the biscuit base, smooth over the surface and then chill until set.
5 Top slices of pie with vanilla cream, dust with cocoa powder, and serve with the orange sauce and raspberry topping.

"For less decadence, serve this lovely tart with just the vanilla cream."

...SERVE WITH

RASPBERRY TOPPING

150g (5½oz) fresh RASPBERRIES
2–3 tbsp CHAMBORD or AMARETTO LIQUEUR
1–2 tbsp ICING SUGAR, sifted

1 Place the raspberries in a bowl. Add enough chosen alcohol to just moisten.
2 Stir in the icing sugar and leave to macerate for 1 hour.

ORANGE SAUCE

Finely grated rind and juice of
   1 large ORANGE
pure ORANGE JUICE
1 tbsp CASTER SUGAR
2 tsp CORNFLOUR

1 Make the freshly squeezed orange juice up to 200ml (7fl oz) with pure juice. Heat, stirring, until the sugar has dissolved.
2 Blend the cornflour with a little cold water. Bring the sauce to a simmer then stir in the blended cornflour and boil for 1–2 minutes, stirring, until thickened.

VANILLA CREAM

100g (3½oz) MASCARPONE cheese
150g (5½oz) ICING SUGAR, sifted
1 tsp PURE VANILLA EXTRACT
COCOA POWDER for dusting

1 Beat the mascarpone, icing sugar, and vanilla together until it forms soft peaks.
2 Chill for at least 1 hour before using.

MARBLED CHOCOLATE SLICE WITH RICH CHOCOLATE SAUCE, ROSÉ SORBET, AND SABLÉ BISCUITS

James Perry MasterChef 2011 final 5

PREPARATION TIME
30 minutes, plus chilling

COOKING TIME
40 minutes

SERVES 6

FOR THE ROSÉ SORBET
115g (4oz) CASTER SUGAR
250ml (8fl oz) WATER
350ml (12fl oz) ROSÉ WINE
5 MINT leaves, to decorate

FOR THE MARBLE SLICE
3 EGGS
100g (3½oz) CASTER SUGAR
finely grated zest of 1 ORANGE
100g (3½oz) PLAIN FLOUR
1 tbsp BAKING POWDER
100g (3½oz) UNSALTED
  BUTTER, chopped, plus
  extra for greasing
100g (3½oz) DARK
  CHOCOLATE, chopped
100g (3½oz) WHITE
  CHOCOLATE, chopped

FOR THE SABLÉ BISCUITS
50g (1¾oz) PLAIN FLOUR, sifted
40g (1¼oz) chilled UNSALTED
  BUTTER, diced
50g (1¾oz) CASTER SUGAR
finely grated zest of ½ LEMON
1 EGG YOLK
1 tbsp ICING SUGAR, for dusting

FOR THE CHOCOLATE SAUCE
100g (3½oz) DARK CHOCOLATE,
  minimum 70% cocoa solids
25g (scant 1oz) UNSALTED
  BUTTER, diced
5 tbsp WHOLE MILK
1½ tbsp DOUBLE CREAM

1 To make the sorbet, mix the sugar and water in a saucepan, stirring until the sugar has dissolved, then bring to the boil and gently simmer for 5 minutes. Leave to cool slightly, then add the rosé wine. When completely cold, transfer to an ice-cream machine and churn until smooth and set. Transfer to a plastic container with a lid and keep in the freezer until ready to serve. Alternatively, pour the mixture in a freezerproof container and freeze until mushy. Whisk until the ice crystals are broken up. Return to the freezer and repeat the process twice.
2 Meanwhile, make the marble slice. Preheat the oven to 160°C (325°F/Gas 3). Grease the sides and line the base of a 20cm (8in) square cake tin with baking parchment.
3 Place the eggs, sugar, and orange zest in a large bowl and beat using an electric whisk for 3–4 minutes until light and frothy. Sift the flour and baking powder in a separate bowl, then add to the egg mixture and beat for a further 30 seconds until smooth. Divide the mixture between 2 bowls. Melt the 2 chocolates in separate bowls set over pans of simmering water with 50g (1¾oz) of butter in each. Using the electric whisk, beat the melted white chocolate into one bowl of cake batter and the dark chocolate into the other.

Spearmint is the most popular for everyday culinary use. While it is cheap to buy in supermarkets, it is so easy to grow that it is worth buying a pot from a garden centre. Keep fresh cut mint in water for 2 days, dried mint in an airtight container.

4 Pour the cake batters into the prepared cake tin and swirl a wooden skewer or sharp knife through the 2 mixtures to create a marbled effect. Bake in the preheated oven for 20–25 minutes until cooked – a skewer should come out clean when inserted into the centre of the cake. Leave to cool in the tin for 5 minutes before transferring to a wire cooling rack to cool completely.

5 To make the sablé biscuits, place all ingredients except the icing sugar into a food processor and pulse until the mixture forms a dough. Turn out onto a lightly floured surface and knead gently until smooth. Wrap in cling film and chill in the fridge for 30 minutes. Increase the oven temperature to 180°C (350°F/Gas 4) and line a baking tray with baking parchment.

6 Place the sablé dough between 2 pieces of baking parchment and roll out to a thickness of 3mm (⅛in). Using a 7.5cm (3in) round biscuit cutter, cut discs of the dough and transfer to the baking tray. Place in the freezer for 5 minutes, then bake for 6–8 minutes. Leave to cool and dust with icing sugar before serving.

7 For the chocolate sauce, melt the dark chocolate and butter gently in a saucepan. Gradually whisk in the milk and cream until smooth and glossy. Set aside, then reheat gently before serving.

8 To serve, trim the cake and cut into 6 rectangular slices. Serve with the sauce, sablé biscuits, and sorbet decorated with mint.

Simplify for **EVERY**DAY

• Make a quick chocolate sauce by using a good quality dark chocolate spread, and just heating it with a splash of milk or single cream to a smooth, pouring consistency. • The dessert would go well with raspberry sorbet instead of the rosé wine sorbet too.

CHILLI-SPICED CHOCOLATE FONDANT
Sharon Maughan actress and 2011 Celebrity semi-finalist

PREPARATION TIME
20 minutes

COOKING TIME
10 minutes

SERVES 6

"I'm really proud of my effort today."

85g (3 oz) DARK CHOCOLATE (70% cocoa), broken into pieces
85g (3oz) UNSALTED BUTTER, cubed, plus a little extra for greasing
2 EGGS
85g (3oz) CASTER SUGAR
½ RED CHILLI, deseeded and finely diced

30g (1oz) PLAIN FLOUR
2 tbsp COCOA POWDER
¼ tsp CAYENNE PEPPER
ICING SUGAR for dusting
2 RED CHILLIES, deseeded and sliced, to decorate

1 Preheat the oven to 200°C (400°F/Gas 6) and grease 6 dariole moulds. Place the chocolate and butter in a bain-marie or a bowl set over a pan of simmering water, making sure that the base of the bowl is clear of the water. When the chocolate and butter have melted and combined, remove from the heat and leave to stand for 5 minutes.

2 Using an electric whisk, beat together the eggs and sugar in a bowl until thick and pale. Slowly whisk in the chocolate and butter mixture. When it is well incorporated, fold in the chilli. Sift the flour, cocoa powder, and cayenne pepper over and fold in gently with a metal spoon.

3 Divide the mixture between the dariole moulds, place in the oven and cook for 10 minutes until firm on top and starting to come away from the sides of the moulds. Remove and leave to stand for 2 minutes before loosening the edges and turning out onto the plates. Dust with the icing sugar and lay some slices of chilli on the plates to decorate, before serving.

MOIST CHOCOLATE CAKE WITH VANILLA WHIPPED CREAM AND RASPBERRY COULIS

Nick Pickard actor and 2011 Celebrity finalist

PREPARATION TIME
15 minutes

COOKING TIME
35 minutes

SERVES 6–8

GREGG WALLACE

"You've gone for classic flavour combinations that are absolutely right. That tastes great."

FOR THE CHOCOLATE CAKE
4 large EGGS
225g (8oz) CASTER SUGAR
2 drops of PURE VANILLA EXTRACT
125g (4½oz) UNSALTED BUTTER, plus extra for greasing
150g (5½oz) DARK CHOCOLATE (70% cocoa), broken into small pieces
50g (1¾oz) GROUND ALMONDS
25g (scant 1oz) PLAIN FLOUR, sifted

FOR THE VANILLA CREAM
150ml (5fl oz) WHIPPING CREAM
150ml (5fl oz) DOUBLE CREAM
1 VANILLA POD, split and seeds scraped out
50g (1¾oz) ICING SUGAR

FOR THE RASPBERRY COULIS
200g (7oz) RASPBERRIES
2 tbsp ICING SUGAR

1 Preheat the oven to 160°C (325°F/Gas 3). Grease a 20cm (8in) round loose-bottomed cake tin and line with baking parchment.
2 Using an electric whisk, whisk together the eggs, caster sugar, and vanilla extract until fluffy.
3 Place the butter, chocolate, and 3 tbsp water in a large bowl and heat over simmering water until melted. Stir together until thoroughly smooth.
4 Using a metal spoon, fold both the mixtures together. Stir in the ground almonds and flour, then pour the mixture into the lined tin. Bake in the preheated oven for 30–35 minutes until firm to the touch. Remove from the oven and leave to cool slightly before turning out onto a wire rack.
5 For the vanilla cream, place the whipping cream, double cream, vanilla seeds, and icing sugar in a bowl and whisk together until soft peaks form. Set aside until needed.
6 For the raspberry coulis, place the raspberries, icing sugar, and 2 tbsp water into a small pan and set over a medium heat for 4–5 minutes until the raspberries have broken down. Remove from the heat and rub through a fine sieve.
7 To serve, cut slices of the cake, place on plates with dots of the raspberry coulis around the edge. Serve the vanilla cream separately or place quenelles on top of the cake.

SALTED CHOCOLATE TARTS WITH CARAMELIZED PECANS

Annie Assheton MasterChef 2011 final 6

PREPARATION TIME
20 minutes, plus
chilling

COOKING TIME
30 minutes

SERVES 4

FOR THE PASTRY
90g (3¼oz) softened BUTTER
40g (1¼oz) CASTER SUGAR
1 EGG YOLK
125g (4½oz) PLAIN FLOUR
2 tsp COCOA POWDER

FOR THE FILLING
175g (6oz) DARK CHOCOLATE
  (70% cocoa solids)
175ml (6fl oz) DOUBLE CREAM
175g (6oz) LIGHT
  MUSCOVADO SUGAR
1½ tsp MALDON SEA SALT

FOR THE PECANS
100g (3½oz) CASTER SUGAR
12 PECAN HALVES
pinch of MALDON SEA SALT

TO SERVE
chilled CRÈME FRAÎCHE

1 First make the pastry. Cream together the butter and sugar with an electric whisk, then add the egg yolk and beat until well blended. Sift the flour and cocoa together, then gradually work in to form a soft but not sticky dough. Wrap in cling film and leave to rest in the fridge for 45 minutes.

2 Preheat the oven to 200°C (400°F/Gas 6). Roll out the pastry and use to line four 8–10cm (3½–4in) loose-bottomed tartlet tins, making sure there aren't any holes. Line the tarts with greaseproof paper, fill with baking beans, and bake for 15 minutes. Remove the beans and paper, and cook for another 5 minutes. Allow to cool.

3 To make the filling, put the chocolate, cream, muscovado sugar, and salt in a large bowl over a saucepan of gently simmering water. Make sure the bottom of the bowl does not come into contact with the water. Stir occasionally until the mixture is melted and completely smooth. Spoon the filling into the pastry cases and put in the fridge for about 2 hours until set.

4 Meanwhile, make the caramelized pecans. Put the caster sugar and 2 tbsp water into a saucepan and dissolve completely over very low heat, shaking the pan occasionally. Turn up the heat and boil until it turns golden brown. Working quickly, stir through the pecans and sea salt, then transfer onto a baking sheet lined with baking parchment. Spread out as much as possible with a wet spatula. When cool, break up the pecans, trying to keep each one whole. When the tarts have almost set, top each one with 3 pecans. Serve with very cold crème fraîche.

Simplify for **EVERY**DAY

• Use bought sweet shortcrust instead of making your own.
• Decorate with bought chocolate-coated pecans and a few grains of the salt, instead of the home-made caramel ones.

WARM CHOCOLATE FONDANT WITH CHOCOLATE SAUCE AND CHANTILLY CREAM

Michelle Mone OBE entrepreneur and 2011 Celebrity contestant

PREPARATION TIME
20 minutes

COOKING TIME
10 minutes, plus chilling

SERVES 6

"I couldn't have done any more."

FOR THE FONDANTS
50g (1¾oz) melted BUTTER,
    for brushing
1 tbsp COCOA POWDER, plus
    extra for dusting
150g (5½oz) DARK CHOCOLATE
    (70% cocoa), broken into
    small pieces
125g (4½oz) UNSALTED BUTTER
4 whole EGGS
2 EGG YOLKS
130g (4½oz) CASTER SUGAR
60g (2oz) PLAIN FLOUR

FOR THE CHOCOLATE SAUCE
150ml (5fl oz) MILK
2 tbsp DOUBLE CREAM
30g (1oz) CASTER SUGAR
200g (7oz) extra bitter
    DARK CHOCOLATE
30g (1oz) UNSALTED BUTTER

FOR THE CHANTILLY CREAM
300ml (10fl oz) DOUBLE CREAM
2 tbsp ICING SUGAR
1 VANILLA POD, split and seeds
    scraped out

1 For the chocolate fondants, brush the inside of six 150ml (5fl oz) moulds with plenty of melted butter, then dust with cocoa powder. Transfer to the fridge to set.
2 Melt the chocolate and butter in a bowl set over a pan of simmering water, making sure the base of the bowl does not touch the water. Remove from the heat and stir until smooth.
3 In a separate bowl, whisk the eggs, yolks, and sugar together until thick and pale, then combine with the melted chocolate.
4 Sift the flour and cocoa powder into the mixture, then stir to combine. Pour the mixture into the prepared moulds and place in the fridge to set for at least 20 minutes.
5 Preheat the oven to 180° (350°F/Gas 4). Once the fondants are set, place them on a baking tray and bake in the oven for 8–10 minutes. Remove from the oven and leave to rest for at least 15 seconds before turning out.
6 To make the chocolate sauce, combine all the ingredients in a pan and heat gently until the sugar has melted. Remove from the heat and pass through a fine sieve.
7 For the Chantilly cream, combine the cream, icing sugar, and vanilla seeds and whisk to soft peaks.
8 To serve, place the fondants on six plates. Pour some sauce over the top of each one and serve with the Chantilly cream.

FROZEN WHITE CHOCOLATE PARFAIT WITH MACERATED STRAWBERRIES AND A CHOCOLATE AND PECAN TUILE

James Perry MasterChef 2011 final 5

PREPARATION TIME
50 minutes

COOKING TIME
8–9 minutes

SERVES 6

"I worked hard in there and I got those plates out. If I go home I'll be gutted."

FOR THE PARFAIT
150g (5½oz) WHITE CHOCOLATE, broken into pieces
115g (4oz) CASTER SUGAR
500ml (16fl oz) DOUBLE CREAM
6 large EGG YOLKS

FOR THE STRAWBERRIES
3–4 tbsp KIRSCH
2 tbsp ICING SUGAR
200g (7oz) hulled STRAWBERRIES, quartered

FOR THE TUILES
2 EGG WHITES
60g (2oz) BUTTER, softened
115g (4oz) CASTER SUGAR
100g (3½oz) PECANS, ground
1 tbsp COCOA POWDER

TO SERVE
12 perfect PECAN halves, toasted

1 For the parfait, melt the chocolate in a bowl over a pan of gently simmering water. Bring 100ml (3½fl oz) water and the sugar to the boil in a small pan. Whip the cream to soft peaks.
2 In a large bowl whisk the egg yolks until pale and slightly thickened. Whisk in the sugar syrup in a steady stream. Continue to whisk for 1 minute until thick and pale. Whisk in the melted white chocolate, then quickly fold in the whipped cream.
3 Transfer the mixture into 6 moulds about 6cm (2½in) wide and 4cm (1½in) deep, placed on a flat plate lined with greaseproof paper. Cover with cling film. Freeze for at least 2 hours until firm.
4 For the strawberries, in a small saucepan heat the Kirsch and icing sugar together, stirring. Add the strawberries. Mix well. Transfer into a bowl, cover, and set aside to macerate.
5 For the tuiles, preheat the oven to 180°C (350°F/Gas 4). In a large mixing bowl, beat together all the ingredients until a smooth paste is formed. On a non-stick, flat baking tray spread the mixture as thinly as possible using a palette knife.
6 Place onto the baking tray in the oven and bake for 8–9 minutes. Remove from the oven on to a cooling rack. Whilst still warm and pliable use a 6cm (2½in) cutter or a spare parfait mould to cut circular shapes.(At least 1 tuile for every parfait.) Transfer to a wire rack to cool and harden.
7 To serve, remove cling film from parfaits. Using a blowtorch lightly warm the outsides of the moulds until the parfaits will slip out. Turn them out onto the centres of the serving plates. Top each with a tuile and the toasted pecans. Surround with the macerated strawberries.

JAMES'S PARFAIT SIMPLIFIED FOR **EVERY**DAY... ▶ PAGE 254

PERFECT PARFAIT

GREGG WALLACE PUTS A SIMPLE SPIN ON THE SWEETLY NUTTY FLAVOURS OF JAMES'S PARFAIT

PREP: 40 MINS • CHILL: 4–5 HRS

PARFAIT

SERVES 6–8

200ml (7fl oz) SINGLE CREAM
6 EGG YOLKS
100g (3½oz) CASTER SUGAR
150g (5½oz) WHITE CHOCOLATE,
  chopped
200ml (7fl oz) DOUBLE CREAM
2 tsp PURE VANILLA EXTRACT

1 To make the parfait, place the single cream in a small pan and heat until just simmering. Set aside. Whisk the egg yolks and sugar together in a bowl until thick and pale, then slowly pour on to the warmed cream, whisking constantly.
2 Place the chopped chocolate in a heatproof bowl and set over a pan of gently simmering water. Melt the chocolate, stirring frequently until very smooth and glossy. Meanwhile, whisk the double cream with the vanilla until it just forms soft peaks and set aside.
3 Pour the cream and egg mixture into the chocolate mixture, stirring constantly until well mixed and smooth. Stir into the whipped double cream until smooth and well mixed. Pour the mixture into a 900g (2lb) loaf tin lined with cling film and smooth over the surface. Transfer to a freezer and freeze for at least 4–5 hours or until firm. The parfait will not become completely solid on freezing but will have a softness to it and will indent slightly when pressed.
4 To serve the parfait, carefully remove it from the tin and discard the cling film. If the parfait does not release from the tin easily, dip the base of the tin in a bowl of hot water for just a few seconds. Cut into slices and serve with the strawberry topping and pecan praline.

"Creamy parfait, sticky-sweet strawberry sauce, and crunchy praline flakes – simply irresistible!"

...SERVE WITH

PECAN PRALINE

BUTTER for greasing
50g (1¾oz) PECAN NUTS
100g (3½oz) CASTER SUGAR
2 tbsp WATER

1 Line a baking tray with baking parchment, brush the parchment with a little butter, scatter the pecan nuts over and set aside.
2 Heat the sugar and water together in a saucepan for 3–4 minutes until dissolved, then bring to the boil and cook for a further 4–5 minutes or until deep caramel in colour. Remove from the heat and pour over the pecans, making sure they are all covered. Leave to cool and set, then break into pieces.

STRAWBERRY TOPPING

400g (14oz) fresh
   STRAWBERRIES, hulled
2 tbsp ICING SUGAR
freshly squeezed juice of ½ LEMON
1–2 tsp KIRSCH

1 To make the strawberry topping, place the strawberries in a food processor with the icing sugar and lemon juice, then process until smooth.
2 Pass the purée through a sieve into a bowl to remove any seeds. Stir in the Kirsch until well mixed. Cover and chill until required.

CHOCOLATE AND COCONUT TEMPURA
Colin McAllister property developer and 2011 Celebrity contestant

PREPARATION TIME
20 minutes, plus freezing

COOKING TIME
10 minutes

SERVES 4

FOR THE ICE CREAM
4 ripe MANGOES, peeled and
  rougly chopped
300g (10oz) FROZEN
  RASPBERRIES
600ml (1 pint) DOUBLE CREAM

FOR THE TEMPURA
125g (4½oz) TEMPURA FLOUR
1 large EGG
150ml (5fl oz) SPARKLING
  WATER, chilled
SALT and freshly ground
  BLACK PEPPER

300ml (10fl oz) ice cold WATER
1 litre (1¾ pints) neutral-
  flavoured oil, such as
  SUNFLOWER OIL
4 BOUNTY BARS, kept in the
  fridge overnight

TO DECORATE
1 ripe MANGO, peeled and sliced
100g (3½oz) DARK CHOCOLATE
  (70% cocoa), grated
4 MINT leaves

1 Make the ice cream by combining the mangoes, raspberries, and double cream, using a hand-held blender. Add the mixture to an ice-cream maker and churn according to the manufacturer's instructions. Transfer to a plastic container with a lid and freeze until needed. Alternatively, place the mixture in a freezerproof container and freeze until mushy. Whisk until the ice crystals are broken up. Return to the freezer and repeat twice.
2 For the tempura, put the flour, egg, sparkling water, and a pinch of salt and pepper in a bowl and stir together in light, quick motions until most of the lumps are gone.
3 Set the bowl in a bowl of iced water to keep the batter light (if the temperature of the batter increases, it will become thicker and stickier than desired).
4 Heat the oil to about 170–180°C (340–350°F). If you do not have a thermometer, drop a little batter into the oil – if it begins to bubble as soon as it hits the oil and stays on the surface rather than sinking to the bottom, the oil is hot enough.
5 Coat the Bounty Bars with the batter, drop them in the oil, and fry until golden. Remove from the oil and place on kitchen paper on a wire rack to drain.
6 To serve, place a Bounty Bar on each plate and accompany with the ice cream and slices of mango, decorated with grated chocolate and a mint leaf.

Simplify for EVERYDAY

• Use bought raspberry or mango sorbet or ice cream instead of making your own.
• For the batter simply whisk 115g (4oz) self-raising flour with a pinch of salt and very cold water to make a creamy batter. Dip the bounty bars in straight away and deep-fry in hot oil.

TIRAMISU
Shobu Kapoor actress and 2011 Celebrity contestant

PREPARATION TIME
15 minutes, plus 1 hour chilling

SERVES 6–8

500g (1lb 2oz)
  MASCARPONE CHEESE
400g (14oz) can SWEETENED
  CONDENSED MILK
1 tsp PURE VANILLA EXTRACT
3 tbsp BRANDY

150ml (5fl oz) ESPRESSO COFFEE
115g (4oz) SAVOIARDI
  FINGER BISCUITS
2 tbsp COCOA
  POWDER, sifted

1 Put the mascarpone into a large mixing bowl and beat with an electric hand whisk until smooth. Add the condensed milk and vanilla extract, then whisk again until combined. Set aside until needed.

2 Mix the brandy with the espresso coffee in a shallow bowl. Quickly dip each of the biscuits into the coffee mixture, ensuring that they do not become soggy.

3 Line a 2 litre (3½ pint) trifle dish with one layer of the soaked biscuits. Spoon half of the mascarpone mixture over the biscuits, then dust with half of the sifted cocoa powder.

4 Add another layer of the biscuits followed by the remaining mascarpone mixture, and finally dust with the remaining cocoa powder.

5 Transfer to the fridge and chill for at least 1 hour before serving.

LEMON DRIZZLE CAKE WITH THYME CHANTILLY CREAM

Phil Vickery MBE England rugby player and 2011 Celebrity champion

PREPARATION TIME
20 minutes

COOKING TIME
35 minutes

SERVES 8

FOR THE CAKE
150g (5½oz) CASTER SUGAR
150g (5½oz) BUTTER
2 VANILLA PODS, split and seeds
    scraped out
zest of 1 LEMON
3 EGGS
150g (5½oz) SELF-RAISING
    FLOUR, sifted

FOR THE LEMON SYRUP
juice of 2 LEMONS
50g (1¾oz) CASTER SUGAR

FOR THE CHANTILLY CREAM
1 tbsp CASTER SUGAR
2 sprigs of THYME, leaves only,
    finely chopped
300ml (10fl oz) WHIPPING CREAM

TO SERVE
16 STRAWBERRIES, hulled and
    sliced in half
ICING SUGAR, for dusting

1 To make the cake, preheat the oven to 180°C (350°F/Gas 4). Using an electric hand whisk, beat together the sugar, butter, vanilla seeds, and lemon zest until well combined.
2 With the electric whisk still running, add the eggs one by one. When all the eggs are combined, gently fold in the flour. Pour the mixture into a greased 23cm (9in) springform cake tin, place in the oven and bake for 35–40 minutes. The cake is done when a skewer inserted comes out clean.
3 Once the cake is cooked, remove from the tin and place on a wire rack. Using a skewer, make plenty of holes all over the top of the cake.
4 For the syrup, place the lemon juice and sugar in a saucepan. Bring to the boil, stirring, until well combined and the sugar is fully dissolved. Leave the syrup to cool for 5 minutes, then pour it over the cake and leave to soak in.
5 For the cream, add the sugar and thyme to the whipping cream. Whisk to soft peaks.
6 To serve, put a slice of cake on each plate with a dollop of the cream and a couple of halved strawberries. Dust with icing sugar to finish.

PEACH UPSIDE-DOWN CAKE WITH CHANTILLY CREAM AND SPUN SUGAR TWISTS

Polly Oxby MasterChef 2011 contestant

PREPARATION TIME
15 minutes

COOKING TIME
1 hour 20 mins

SERVES 8–10

"I thought I'd better come and be true to myself and a sponge is about as true as it gets."

Peaches are now generally available in several varieties, from the traditional yellow-fleshed type to white-fleshed and the new, sweet-flavoured 'doughnut' peach, named for its shape. When ripe, the fruit will be fragrant and the flesh will yield to gentle pressure; avoid fruit with dull, blemished, or wrinkled skin and hard flesh.

FOR THE CAKE
125g (4½oz) GRANULATED SUGAR
125g (4½oz) BUTTER, softened, plus extra for greasing
2 EGGS
250g (9oz) SELF-RAISING FLOUR, sifted
4 ripe PEACHES, stoned and thinly sliced
100g (3½oz) DEMERARA SUGAR
2 tbsp PEACH JAM

FOR THE SPUN SUGAR TWISTS
75g (2½oz) CASTER SUGAR

FOR THE CHANTILLY CREAM
300ml (10fl oz) DOUBLE CREAM
1 tsp PURE VANILLA EXTRACT
1 tbsp ICING SUGAR

1 Preheat the oven to 160°C (325°F/Gas 3). Grease an 18cm (7in) non-stick cake tin and line with baking parchment. Place the granulated sugar and butter in a bowl and cream with an electric hand whisk until pale and fluffy. Beat in the eggs, one at a time, then fold in the flour.

2 Place the peach slices in a bowl with the demerara sugar and toss until evenly coated. Layer the slices in the bottom of the lined tin and carefully pour the cake batter over the top. Bake for 1 hour, or until a skewer inserted into the middle of the cake comes out clean. Remove from the oven and leave to rest for 10 minutes before turning out. Leave to cool.

3 While the cake cools, make the spun sugar twists. Place the caster sugar in a large, heavy frying pan over medium heat. Melt the sugar, without stirring, until it turns a deep golden colour, then leave to cool and thicken slightly. Using a spoon, slowly drizzle it over a knife-sharpening steel while rotating it to form a spring shape. Carefully slide off the steel and leave to cool on a sheet of greaseproof paper.

4 Once the cake has cooled, heat the peach jam in a small pan until fluid, then pass through a sieve. Using a pastry brush, lightly brush the surface of the cake with the jam to glaze.

5 Whip the cream, vanilla, and icing sugar together to soft peaks. Serve slices of the cake with the Chantilly cream and garnish with a spun sugar twist.

S'MORE MILLE FEUILLES WITH FOREST FRUIT COULIS AND CAMPFIRE SORBET

Tim Anderson MasterChef 2011 champion

PREPARATION TIME
1 hour, plus chilling

COOKING TIME
25 minutes

SERVES 4

FOR THE SORBET
15g (½oz) BUTTER
1 RED BIRD'S EYE CHILLI, finely chopped
1 tsp LAPSANG SOUCHONG TEA LEAVES
250ml (8fl oz) fresh APPLE JUICE
100ml (3½fl oz) CLEAR HONEY
100ml (3½fl oz) very smoky HIGHLAND or ISLAY WHISKY
4 sachets STRAWBERRY-FLAVOURED POPPING CANDY

FOR THE BASE
125g (4½oz) CASTER SUGAR
100g (3½oz) PLAIN FLOUR
85g (3oz) cold UNSALTED BUTTER, cubed
10 DIGESTIVE BISCUITS
50g (1¾oz) HAZELNUTS
50g (1¾oz) PISTACHIOS

FOR THE CREAM
2 EGG WHITES
150ml (5fl oz) LIGHT CORN SYRUP or GOLDEN SYRUP
150ml (5fl oz) ICING SUGAR, sifted
pinch of SALT
1 tsp PURE VANILLA EXTRACT

FOR THE GANACHE
1 tbsp JUNIPER BERRIES
picked leaves from 1 sprig of ROSEMARY
1 small BAY LEAF

2 tbsp CASTER SUGAR
200ml (7fl oz) DOUBLE CREAM
1 tbsp GIN
400g (14oz) MILK CHOCOLATE
30g (1oz) UNSALTED BUTTER, cubed

FOR THE PASTRY
100g (3½oz) BUTTER, diced
2 EGG WHITES
50g (1¾oz) ICING SUGAR
8 sheets FILO PASTRY

FOR THE FOREST FRUIT COULIS
100g (3½oz) RASPBERRIES
100g (3½oz) BLACKBERRIES
50g (1¾oz) REDCURRANTS
50g (1¾oz) BLACKCURRANTS
50g (1¾oz) BLUEBERRIES
100g (3½oz) ICING SUGAR
juice of 2 LEMONS

TO SERVE
100ml (3½fl oz) RAPESEED OIL
10 MINT leaves
1 sachet STRAWBERRY-FLAVOURED POPPING CANDY
50g (1¾oz) ICING SUGAR
freshly grated NUTMEG

Simplify for **EVERY**DAY

• Instead of marshmallow cream you could use basic meringue.
• Use a 400g bag of frozen forest fruits, just thawed, for the coulis. • It would also go well with a whiskey sorbet and a splash of Drambuie drizzled over. Top with a sprinkling of cayenne.

1 Preheat the oven to 180°C (350°F/Gas 4). Grease and line the base and sides of a 30 x 23cm (12 x 9in) non-stick baking tin with baking parchment.
2 To make the sorbet, melt the butter in a pan over medium heat, then sauté the chilli and tea leaves for 2 minutes until tender. Stir in the apple juice, honey, 2 tbsp water, and whisky. Heat and flambé, until the flames die down. Strain into a jug and leave to cool.

3 Pour the mixture into an ice-cream machine and churn until smooth and set. Transfer to a plastic container with a lid and freeze until needed. Alternatively, pour the mixture in a freezerproof container and freeze until mushy. Whisk until the ice crystals are broken up. Return to the freezer and repeat the process twice.

4 Meanwhile, place all the ingredients for the biscuit base into a food processor, then blitz until well combined. Press the mixture evenly and firmly into the lined tin, using the back of a spoon.

5 Bake for 10–12 minutes until just set. Allow to cool in the tin for 15 minutes before carefully turning onto a wire rack to cool completely. Cut the cooled biscuit into four 10 x 5cm (4 x 2in) rectangles. Reserve until needed.

6 To prepare the marshmallow cream, whip the egg whites, corn (or golden) syrup, sugar, and salt with an electric whisk on medium speed for 2–3 minutes until well combined. Increase to highest speed for 12–15 minutes until thick and stiff, then fold in the vanilla extract.

7 Fit a piping bag with a 1cm (^{1}/$_2$in) round nozzle and spoon in the mixture. Transfer to the fridge to set for at least 20 minutes before using.

8 Meanwhile make the ganache. Crush the juniper berries, rosemary, bay leaf, and sugar together in a mortar and pestle. Add to a small saucepan along with cream and gin, bring the mixture to the boil, reduce the heat, then simmer for 10 minutes. Remove from the heat and cover with a lid, then leave the mixture to infuse for a further 20 minutes. Strain the mixture into a clean pan, then bring up to a gentle simmer. Whisk in the chocolate and butter until smooth, then remove from the heat.

9 Leave the ganache to cool until the mixture has thickened, and will just hold its shape, then spoon into a piping bag fitted with a 1cm (^{1}/$_2$in) round nozzle. Transfer to the fridge to firm slightly, to the consistency of whipped cream.

10 Prepare the filo stacks for the mille feuilles. Put the butter, egg whites, and sugar in a small saucepan over medium heat. Stir until the butter has melted and the mixture has thickened. Cut the filo pastry sheets into quarters. Brush each filo layer with a little of the melted butter mixture and arrange into stacks of 8 sheets. Cut into eight 10 x 5cm (4 x 2in) rectangles. Place on a lightly greased baking tray, then bake for 12 minutes until crisp and golden. Transfer the filo stacks to a wire rack to cool completely.

11 Meanwhile, make the coulis by blitzing all the ingredients together in a small food processor. Rub through a fine sieve into a bowl to remove the seeds. Chill before serving.

12 Prepare the decoration. Heat the rapeseed oil in a frying pan. Fry the mint leaves for 1 minute until crisp and bright green (take care not to overcook or they will go brown), then drain on kitchen paper and leave to cool.

13 Put the popping candy and icing sugar in a mortar and grind to a fine powder with a pestle.

TO SERVE

Set a biscuit base on each of 4 plates with a tiny amount of the ganache. Pipe the remaining ganache onto the bases in a layer about 1cm (½in) thick. Top each with 1 filo stack, then pipe on the marshmallow cream. Using a blowtorch, toast the top of the marshmallow cream lightly until golden brown. Top with another filo stack. Spoon a small pool of the forest fruit coulis to one side of the mille feuilles. Quickly stir the remaining popping candy through the sorbet. Scoop 4 quenelles of sorbet, using a dessertspoon, and place in tiny serving dishes. Dust the top of the mille feuilles with the icing sugar and popping candy mixture, then decorate the top with a little grated nutmeg and the fried mint leaves. Serve the millle feuilles straight away with the little dishes of sorbet placed alongside.

JOHN TORODE

"The idea of a biscuit with chocolate and marshmallow around a campfire – a wonderful thing."

JAM DOUGHNUTS AND CUSTARD
Aggie MacKenzie journalist and 2011 Celebrity semi-finalist

PREPARATION TIME
30 minutes, plus rising

COOKING TIME
30 minutes

SERVES 4–6

FOR THE JAM
200g (7oz) fresh RASPBERRIES
200g (7oz) GRANULATED SUGAR

FOR THE DOUGHNUTS
5 tbsp MILK
1 EGG
½ tsp LIQUID GLUCOSE
1½ tsp DRIED FAST ACTION YEAST
10g (¼oz) UNSALTED BUTTER
200g (7oz) TYPE "00" PASTA
   FLOUR, plus extra for dusting
½ tsp BAKING POWDER

pinch of GROUND NUTMEG
SALT
1 tsp CASTER SUGAR, plus extra
   for rolling
SUNFLOWER OIL, for frying

FOR THE CUSTARD:
300ml (10fl oz) DOUBLE CREAM
100ml (3½fl oz) WHOLE MILK
1 VANILLA POD, split
5 EGG YOLKS
50g (1¾oz) CASTER SUGAR

1 Make the jam. Heat the raspberries in a pan until the juices run. Bring to the boil. Remove from the heat. Add sugar and stir until dissolved. Bring back to the boil, and boil for 4–5 minutes until thickened. To test for a set, put a teaspoonful of the jam onto a cold plate. If it wrinkles when pushed with a fingertip, it is ready. Sieve into a jug, then pour into a squeezy bottle. Set aside.
2 For the doughnuts, warm the milk gently in a pan to blood temperature. Remove from the heat. Add the egg, glucose, yeast, and butter, and whisk until smooth.
3 Sift the flour, baking powder, nutmeg, and salt into a mixing bowl, add the sugar, then make a well in the centre. Pour in the milk mixture, stirring, to form a dough. Knead on a lightly floured surface for 5 minutes until smooth. Transfer to an oiled bowl, cover, and leave for 20–30 minutes in a warm place to rise.
4 Re-knead the dough, divide into 15 pieces, and roll into smooth balls. Space out on a lightly oiled baking tray, cover with cling film, and leave for a further 20 minutes in a warm place.
5 Meanwhile, make the custard. Heat the cream, milk, and vanilla pod in a saucepan until almost boiling, then remove from the heat. Whisk the yolks and sugar until pale, then add the hot milk, whisking all the time. Strain into a clean pan. Cook gently, stirring, until the mixture coats the back of a spoon. Pour into a jug and cover with a circle of wet greaseproof paper. This will prevent a skin forming. Set aside.
6 Heat the oil to 180°C (350°F). Fry the doughnuts, a few at a time, for 2 minutes on each side or until golden and cooked through. Reheat the oil between batches. Remove with a slotted spoon, drain on kitchen paper, and roll in sugar whilst still warm.
7 Make a small hole in each and squeeze in the raspberry jam.
8 Serve the doughnuts whilst still warm, with the jug of custard.

RHUBARB FOOL WITH GINGER BISCUITS
Tim Lovejoy television presenter and 2011 Celebrity semi-finalist

PREPARATION TIME
15 minutes

COOKING TIME
25 minutes

SERVES 4–6

FOR THE RHUBARB FOOL
300g (10oz) RHUBARB, chopped
  into 2.5cm (1in) pieces
200g (7oz) CASTER SUGAR
1 CINNAMON stick
1 STAR ANISE
85g (3oz) ICING SUGAR, sifted
200ml (7fl oz) thick
  GREEK YOGURT
1 VANILLA POD, split and
  seeds scraped out
400ml (14fl oz) DOUBLE CREAM,
  whipped to soft peaks

FOR THE GINGER BISCUITS
125g (4½oz) UNSALTED BUTTER,
  at room temperature
175g (6oz) CASTER SUGAR
1 tbsp GOLDEN SYRUP
1 EGG, beaten
250g (9oz) PLAIN FLOUR
½ tsp BICARBONATE OF SODA
2 tsp GROUND GINGER
1 tsp finely grated FRESH GINGER
1 tbsp finely chopped
  CRYSTALLIZED GINGER

Seasonal rhubarb appears in the shops in early to mid spring and again in July. To buy the freshest, look for glossy, firm stalks and check the ends to see if they look recently cut. Out of season, hothouse rhubarb is available and is usually sweeter and more highly coloured.

1 Preheat the oven to 190°C (375°F/Gas 5).
2 Place the chopped rhubarb on a flat baking tray. Scatter with the caster sugar, pour over 3 tbsp water, and add the cinnamon and star anise. Place into the oven and cook for 10–15 minutes until the rhubarb is tender, but still holding its shape.
3 Remove and leave to cool to room temperature. Discard the cinnamon stick and star anise before chilling in the fridge. Reduce the oven temperature to 180°C (350°F/Gas 4).
4 Whisk the icing sugar, yogurt, and vanilla seeds into the softly whipped double cream. Remove the cooked rhubarb from the fridge and gently fold through the cream mixture. Divide portions amongst bowls and chill in the fridge until needed.
5 For the ginger biscuits, beat together the butter and caster sugar in a bowl. Add the golden syrup and egg. Mix thoroughly with a wooden spoon, or preferably with an electric hand whisk.
6 Sieve together the flour, biarbonate of soda, and the ground ginger. Add this to the butter mixture with the fresh and crystallized ginger, and beat together until mixed well.
7 Roll into small balls, about the size of large marbles, and place well-apart on a flat baking tray lined with baking parchment.
8 Bake in the oven for 8–10 minutes. Cool slightly, then transfer to a wire rack to firm up and cool completely.
9 Serve the chilled rhubarb fool along with the ginger biscuits. Store any remaining biscuits in an airtight container.

Simplify for **EVERY**DAY

• Use drained, canned rhubarb for the fool and add a good pinch of ground cinnamon. • Use pure vanilla extract with seeds instead of scraping your own.
• Serve with bought thin ginger biscuits or brandy snaps.

PISTACHIO MERINGUES WITH ROSE CREAM, ROSE AND CARDAMOM PANNA COTTA WITH HIBISCUS SYRUP, AND CARDAMOM CRISPS

Kirsty Wark journalist and presenter and 2011 Celebrity finalist

PREPARATION TIME
30 minutes

COOKING TIME
1 hour 30 minutes, plus cooling

SERVES 4

JOHN TORODE

"The whole thing is beautifully made. For me, gorgeous. Love it."

FOR THE PANNA COTTA
600ml (1 pint) DOUBLE CREAM
150ml (5fl oz) WHOLE MILK
100g (3½oz) CASTER SUGAR
3 GELATINE LEAVES
a few drops of ROSEWATER
½ tsp GROUND CARDAMOM

FOR THE HIBISCUS SYRUP
50g (1¾oz) CASTER SUGAR
1 tbsp HIBISCUS CORDIAL
1 tsp LIQUID GLUCOSE

FOR THE MERINGUES
3 EGG WHITES
squeeze of LEMON JUICE
140g (5oz) VANILLA SUGAR

1 tbsp CORNFLOUR
75g (2½oz) shelled
   PISTACHIO NUTS, finely chopped
300ml (10fl oz) DOUBLE CREAM
1 tbsp ICING SUGAR

FOR THE CARDAMOM CRISPS
125g (4½oz) UNSALTED BUTTER
175g (6oz) CASTER SUGAR
1 EGG
50g (1¾oz) DESICCATED COCONUT
175g (6oz) SELF-RAISING FLOUR
zest of 1 LEMON
¼ tsp crushed CARDAMOM SEEDS
ICING SUGAR, for dusting

1 Put the cream, milk, and sugar in a pan and slowly bring to the boil. Simmer for 5 minutes until reduced by a third. Soak the gelatine in cold water for 5 minutes until soft. Drain and squeeze out excess water. Take the cream off the heat, then stir in the rosewater, cardamom, and gelatine. Pour the mixture into four 100ml (3½fl oz) dariole moulds, then chill for 2 hours.
2 To make the syrup, mix all the ingredients with 1 tbsp water in a pan and bring to the boil. Simmer until syrupy, then leave to cool.
3 For the meringues, preheat the oven to 110°C (225°F/Gas ¼). Whisk the egg whites with the lemon juice to soft peaks, then gradually whisk in the sugar until glossy. Fold in the cornflour and 50g (1¾oz) pistachios, then transfer to a piping bag with a 1cm (½in) round nozzle. Pipe sixteen 5cm (2in) rounds onto a baking sheet lined with silicone paper and place in the oven for 1½ hours. When cool, whip the cream and icing sugar to soft peaks and use to sandwich the meringues. Roll them in the remaining pistachios.
4 For the crisps, preheat the oven to 190°C (375°F/Gas 5). Cream the butter and sugar until light and fluffy. Add the egg, beat until smooth, then stir in the remaining ingredients. shape into 2cm (¾in) balls and place well apart on a non-stick baking tray. Flatten a little with a palette knife. Bake for 10 minutes until lightly golden, then flatten again. Leave to cool and then dust with icing sugar.
5 To serve, put three crisps, a panna cotta and one or two meringues on each plate, with the syrup swirled around the edge.

SFOGLIATINA OF FIGS WITH PASSITO DI PANTELLERIA ZABAYON AND RASPBERRY COULIS

Sara Danesin Medio MasterChef 2011 finalist

PREPARATION TIME
40 minutes

COOKING TIME
35 minutes

SERVES 4

FOR THE COULIS
250g (9oz) RASPBERRIES
60g (2oz) CASTER SUGAR

FOR THE SFOGLIATINA
200g (7oz) PUFF PASTRY
40g (1¼oz) ICING SUGAR
8 ripe fresh ITALIAN FIGS, cut
  vertically into 1cm (½in) slices
1 tbsp CASTER SUGAR

FOR THE ZABAYON
5 EGG YOLKS
3 tbsp CASTER SUGAR
3 tbsp PASSITO DI PANTELLERIA,
  or other sweet white wine

TO DECORATE
4 MINT leaves
4 sprigs of fresh REDCURRANTS
8–12 BLACKBERRIES

1 First make the coulis. Place the raspberries and sugar in a food processor and blend until smooth. Pass through a fine sieve and set aside.

2 For the sfogliatina, preheat the oven to 220°C (425°F/Gas 7). On a well-floured surface, roll out the puff pastry to 5mm (¼in) thick. Cut into four 7cm (2¾in) squares. Sprinkle with icing sugar, place on a baking tray lined with baking parchment, and bake in the oven for 2–3 minutes. Remove from the oven, sprinkle with icing sugar again, and return to the oven for another 3–4 minutes until the puff pastry is shiny and golden. Remove from the oven and leave to cool on a wire rack. Once they are cool, carefully slice the puff pastry squares in half horizontally.

3 Sprinkle a non-stick pan with 1 tbsp of caster sugar and gently warm the figs in it. Increase the heat and lightly caramelize the figs, turning once, taking care not to overcook them – they need to keep their shape. Leave to cool.

4 To make the zabayon, place the egg yolks, sugar, and sweet wine in a large bowl over a pan of boiling water, making sure the base of the pan doesn't touch the water. With an electric whisk, whisk the mixture over the heat for about 10 minutes until a thick, fluffy, creamy consistency is reached. Remove from the heat and place in a cool bowl.

5 To serve, spoon some of the raspberry coulis on to a serving plate. Place a square of the pastry on the plate followed by a layer of figs and then top with pastry and pour the zabayon over. Decorate with a small leaf of mint, a sprig of redcurrants, and 2–3 blackberries.

ORANGE CAKE WITH POMEGRANATE ICE CREAM, CARAMELIZED ORANGES, AND ORANGE AND POMEGRANATE SYRUP

Annie Assheton MasterChef 2011 final 6

PREPARATION TIME
30 minutes, plus freezing

COOKING TIME
1 hour

SERVES 8–10

"It's a very special cake and the combination of pomegranate and orange is really fantastic."

FOR THE CAKE
BUTTER, for greasing
60g (2oz) crustless WHITE
    BREAD, 2 days old
200g (7oz) CASTER SUGAR
100g (3½oz) GROUND ALMONDS
1½ tsp BAKING POWDER
4 EGGS
200ml (7fl oz) SUNFLOWER OIL
½ tbsp POMEGRANATE MOLASSES
zest of 2 ORANGES

FOR THE ICE CREAM
30g (1oz) ICING SUGAR
juice of ½ ORANGE
1 tbsp POMEGRANATE MOLASSES
300ml (10fl oz) DOUBLE CREAM

FOR THE ORANGES IN SYRUP
juice of 2 ORANGES
85g (3oz) CASTER SUGAR
1½ tbsp POMEGRANATE
    MOLASSES
3 whole ORANGES
juice of ½ POMEGRANATE

FOR THE ORANGE CARAMEL
50g (1¾oz) CASTER SUGAR
juice of ½ ORANGE

TO SERVE
seeds from 1½ fresh
    POMEGRANATES

1 Line a 20cm (8in) square cake tin with baking parchment and grease the sides. Make the breadcrumbs by whizzing 60g (2oz) of slightly stale white bread to crumbs in a mini processor.
2 In a large bowl, combine the breadcrumbs with the caster sugar, ground almonds, and baking powder. In another bowl, whisk together the eggs, sunflower oil, and molasses, and then stir this mixture into the dry ingredients. Finally, grate in the orange zest and stir. Pour the cake mix into the prepared tin and put into a cold oven. Set the temperature to 180°C (350°F/Gas 4) and leave to cook for 40–50 minutes until firm to the touch.
3 Meanwhile, make the ice cream. Whisk the icing sugar with the orange juice and pomegranate molasses until dissolved. Stir in the double cream and whisk until the mixture is thick and peaking. Shape into quenelles with 2 tablespoons and place onto a baking tray lined with baking parchment. Put in the freezer until hardened (about 45 minutes), then cover with cling film.
4 To make the syrup, put the orange juice, 85g (3oz) of caster sugar, and the pomegranate molasses into a small pan and heat gently until the sugar has completely dissolved. Simmer for 2–3 minutes until the liquid becomes syrupy.
5 When the cake is cooked, remove from the oven and stand the cake tin on a board. Using a metal skewer, make lots of holes down through the cake. Gradually pour over about half the syrup.

Use a pastry brush to spread the syrup evenly. Leave to soak in for 5 minutes, then carefully turn it out onto the board. Rest a wire rack on top immediately and, holding the board and rack, invert the cake onto the rack instead. Leave until slightly warm.

6 Now peel and segment 3 oranges. Cut each segment in half and add to the remaining orange and pomegranate syrup with the pomegranate juice. Simmer for 2 or 3 minutes, then remove the orange segments with a slotted spoon and set aside. Continue to simmer the syrup until thickened but take care not to let it start to discolour and burn.

7 Dissolve 50g (1¾oz) of caster sugar into the juice of ½ an orange. Place over low heat until completely dissolved, without boiling. Once dissolved, bring to the boil and cook until it becomes a deep caramel colour. Remove from the heat and leave to thicken for 1–2 minutes. Take a dessert spoon of caramel and drizzle in pretty curly patterns onto baking parchment. Leave to harden.

TO SERVE

To assemble the pudding, put the cake on a board and cut off the edges with a bread knife. Then divide the cake into rectangles. Put a piece of cake on each plate, slightly off centre. Spoon a few segments of caramelized orange onto the top of the cake and some syrup round the edge of the plate. Arrange some pomegranate seeds on top of the syrup. Finally, place a quenelle of ice cream next to the plate and top with a shard of orange caramel.

ANNIE'S ORANGE CAKE SIMPLIFIED FOR **EVERY**DAY... ▶ PAGE 272

QUICK-MIX CAKE

GREGG WALLACE'S SIMPLE VERSION OF ANNIE'S DESSERT STILL HAS THE WOW FACTOR AND PACKS A LOT OF FLAVOUR. **PREP: 45 MINS • COOK: 30 MINS**

ORANGE CAKE

SERVES 8

Finely grated zest of 3 ORANGES
5 tbsp freshly squeezed ORANGE JUICE
100ml (3½fl oz) SUNFLOWER OIL
120ml (4fl oz) MILK
3 EGGS
250g (9oz) PLAIN FLOUR
2 tsp BAKING POWDER
200g (7oz) CASTER SUGAR
100g (3½oz) GROUND ALMONDS

1 Preheat the oven to 180°C (350°F/Gas 4). Grease and line a 23cm (9in) springform cake tin with baking parchment. In a jug mix together the orange rind, orange juice, oil, and milk, then beat in the eggs.
2 Sift together the flour, baking powder, and sugar then stir in the almonds. Make a well in the centre, then pour in the orange mixture and beat with an electric hand whisk until smooth and well mixed. Transfer to the prepared tin, and level the surface.
3 Cook for about 1 hour (cover with foil if over-browning), or until a skewer inserted into the centre comes out clean. Cool slightly, and remove the tin. Slice the warm cake, top with a dollop of the cream, a drizzle of syrup, and pomegranate seeds.

"It's the almonds that give the cake its superb moistness. You could make the cake with limes instead of oranges for a new take on zest and zing!"

...SERVE WITH

POMEGRANATE SYRUP

ORANGE CREAM

85g (3oz) CASTER SUGAR
juice of 2 small ORANGES
120ml (4fl oz) PURE POMEGRANATE JUICE
small knob of BUTTER
POMEGRANATE SEEDS, to decorate (optional)

175g (6oz) MASCARPONE CHEESE
5 tbsp DOUBLE CREAM
50g (1¾oz) ICING SUGAR, sifted
finely grated rind of 1 ORANGE

1 Heat the sugar and juices gently until the sugar
has dissolved. Bring to the boil and boil until
reduced slightly and syrupy. Whisk in a small knob
of butter. Pour into a jug and set aside.

1 Beat the mascarpone with the double cream
and icing sugar until very smooth and well mixed.
2 Stir in the orange rind and chill until required.

LEMON CAKE WITH GINGER CREAM
Danny Goffey musician and 2011 Celebrity semi-finalist

PREPARATION TIME
30 minutes

COOKING TIME
20 minutes

SERVES 6–8

FOR THE CAKE
SUNFLOWER OIL, for greasing
115g (4oz) UNSALTED BUTTER
115g (4oz) DEMERARA SUGAR
1 EGG, beaten
finely grated zest of 1 LEMON
115g (4oz) SELF-RAISING FLOUR

FOR THE DRIZZLE
juice of 1 LEMON
60g (2oz) CASTER SUGAR

FOR THE GINGER CREAM
300ml (10fl oz) DOUBLE CREAM
2 pieces STEM GINGER
   in syrup, finely chopped
2 tbsp GINGER SYRUP from jar

TO DECORATE
a little ICING SUGAR, sifted

1 Preheat the oven to 180°C (350°F/Gas 4). Grease a 20cm (8in) deep, round cake tin and line the base with a circle of greased greaseproof paper.
2 Make the cake. Heat the butter and demerara sugar in a pan until dissolved. Allow to cool, then stir in the egg and lemon zest.
3 Sift the flour over the surface and fold in gently with a metal spoon.
4 Transfer to the prepared tin and bake in the oven for 20 minutes until golden, and the centre springs back when lightly pressed.
5 Leave to cool in the tin for 5 minutes, then turn out onto a wire rack and remove the paper.
6 While the cake is still warm, heat the lemon juice and caster sugar for the drizzle, over low heat until the sugar has dissolved. Make tiny holes with a skewer over the surface of the cake and drizzle the heated lemon and sugar over. Leave to cool.
7 Whisk together the cream, finely chopped stem ginger, and the ginger syrup until softly peaking.
8 Dust the cake with a little sifted icing sugar to decorate, and serve, cut into slices with a generous dollop of the ginger cream.

Simplify for EVERYDAY

• Bake an all-in-one sponge cake using 115g (4oz) of soft butter, caster sugar, and self-raising flour with 1 tsp baking powder and 2 eggs instead of the more complicated melted cake. • Make the lemon drizzle the same way but serve with ginger or vanilla ice cream instead of the ginger cream.

STICKY TOFFEE PUDDING WITH TOFFEE SAUCE AND VANILLA ICE CREAM

Nick Pickard actor and 2011 Celebrity finalist

PREPARATION TIME
20 minutes, plus freezing

COOKING TIME
40 minutes

SERVES 4

FOR THE VANILLA ICE CREAM
270ml (9fl oz) WHOLE MILK
270ml (9fl oz) WHIPPING CREAM
1 VANILLA POD, split and seeds
  scraped out
85g (3oz) CASTER SUGAR
4 EGG YOLKS
4½ tbsp GLUCOSE SYRUP

FOR THE TOFFEE PUDDING
140g (5oz) PITTED DATES,
  finely chopped
1 VANILLA POD, split and seeds
  scraped out
¾ tsp BICARBONATE OF SODA

40g (1¼oz) UNSALTED BUTTER,
  plus extra for greasing
140g (5oz) CASTER SUGAR
2 EGGS
140g (5oz) SELF-RAISING FLOUR

FOR THE TOFFEE SAUCE
50g (1¾oz) UNSALTED
  BUTTER
250ml (8fl oz) DOUBLE CREAM
2½ tbsp GLUCOSE SYRUP
125g (4½oz) LIGHT SOFT
  BROWN SUGAR
½ tbsp BLACK TREACLE

1 For the vanilla ice cream, combine all the ingredients in a bowl and whisk until smooth. Churn in an ice-cream machine, until set. Place in a plastic container with a lid in the freezer until serving. Alternatively, pour the mixture in a freezerproof container and freeze until mushy. Beat with a fork until the ice crystals are broken up. Return to the freezer and repeat the process twice.
2 For the sticky toffee pudding, preheat the oven to 150°C (300°F/Gas 2). Boil the dates, vanilla seeds and pod, and 150ml (5fl oz) water together in a small pan for 5 minutes until nearly all the water has evaporated. Remove the vanilla pod. Stir in the bicarbonate of soda.
3 Cream the butter and sugar until pale. Beat in the eggs.
4 Fold in the flour, then the dates until just combined. Don't overmix. Liberally butter four 200ml (7fl oz) dariole moulds. Divide the mixture between the moulds – no more than two-thirds full. Bake for 30 minutes until a skewer inserted into the centre comes out clean. Cool for a few minutes.
5 Meanwhile, put the ingredients for the toffee sauce in a pan, bring to the boil, stirring, and simmer for 5 minutes, until thick.
6 Turn the puddings out onto plates. Spoon the hot sauce over and add a scoop of vanilla ice cream to one side.

GREGG WALLACE

"Super, super yum. Flavours, tastes, textures: good. I'd say job well done."

HAWAIIAN POKÉ OF PINEAPPLE AND MACADAMIA NUTS, VANILLA AND RUM SAUCE AND COCONUT RICE PUDDING

Tim Anderson MasterChef 2011 champion

PREPARATION TIME
15 minutes

COOKING TIME
35 minutes

SERVES 4

"Doing something a little bit individual and outlandish might make me stand out more."

FOR THE RICE PUDDING
50g (1¾oz) JAPANESE SHORT-GRAIN RICE or ARBORIO RICE
40g (1¼oz) CASTER SUGAR
½ tsp GROUND CINNAMON
½ tsp freshly grated NUTMEG
finely grated zest of ½ ORANGE
finely grated zest of ½ LIME
300ml (½ pint) COCONUT MILK
300ml (½ pint) WHOLE MILK

FOR THE POKÉ
50g (1¾oz) MACADAMIA NUTS, roughly chopped

1 small supersweet PINEAPPLE, peeled, cored, and diced
3 tbsp desiccated COCONUT
shredded zest of ½ LIME
shredded zest of ½ ORANGE

FOR THE SAUCE
50g (1¾oz) BUTTER
75g (2½oz) LIGHT SOFT BROWN SUGAR
1 VANILLA POD, split and seeds scraped out
1 tbsp DARK RUM

1 First cook the coconut rice pudding. Combine the rice, sugar, cinnamon, nutmeg, orange and lime zests, coconut milk, and whole milk in a saucepan and bring to the boil. Reduce the heat and simmer gently, uncovered, for 25 minutes, stirring continuously until the rice is soft and creamy. Add a little extra milk if the pudding begins to dry out. Cover with a circle of wet greaseproof paper to prevent a skin forming. Set aside.
2 Make the poké. Toast the macadamia nuts in a dry frying pan for a few minutes, shaking the pan all the time until lightly golden. Remove from the heat immediately to prevent them burning and transfer them to a bowl. Add the diced pineapple. Toss together to mix well.
3 In the same dry frying pan, toast the desiccated coconut until golden brown, stirring all the time, being careful not to let it burn. Transfer immediately to a plate and set aside.
4 To make the vanilla and rum sauce, melt the butter over medium heat, then stir in the brown sugar and cook until the sugar has melted completely. Stir in the seeds from the vanilla pod, then remove from the heat. Add the rum and ignite. Gently swirl the pan until the flames subside.
5 Remove the paper from the rice pudding and transfer it into a glass bowl, then pour on the vanilla rum sauce. Top with the poké of pineapple and nuts, then the toasted coconut, and finish with the lime and orange zests sprinkled over the top.

TIM'S HAWAIIAN POKÉ SIMPLIFIED FOR **EVERY**DAY... ▶ PAGE 278

FUSION RICE PUD

GREGG WALLACE'S TRADITIONAL RICE PUDDING WITH A CHOICE OF TROPICAL TOPPINGS IS A CLEVER TAKE ON TIM'S HAWAIIAN-INFLUENCED DESSERT

PREP: 1 HR • COOK: 1½–2 HRS

RICE PUDDING

SERVES 6

100g (3½oz) PUDDING RICE
15g (½oz) BUTTER, softened
50g (1¾oz) CASTER SUGAR
1–2 tsp PURE VANILLA EXTRACT
1 litre (1¾ pints) WHOLE MILK
150ml (5fl oz) DOUBLE CREAM

1 Preheat the oven to 140°C (275°F/ Gas 1). Rinse the pudding rice under cold running water and leave to drain.
2 Use the butter to liberally grease the inside of 6 large ramekins on a baking tray, or a 1.4 litre (2½ pint) ovenproof dish. Add the rice to the dish along with the sugar,
3 Mix the vanilla in the milk, to taste. Pour half over the rice, stir well, cover and bake in the oven for 30 minutes.
4 Mix the remaining milk and cream together. Remove rice from the oven, stir in the milk and the cream mixture, and bake for a further 1 hr–1hr 20 minutes or until rice is soft and swollen, the mixture is thick and creamy, and the top is lightly golden. The pudding should wobble slightly when the dish is shaken. Serve warm.

"To get really creamy rice pudding, the trick is to use whole milk and cream, and bake it slowly. I love it!"

...CHOOSE FROM

DOUBLE COCONUT

1 x 400ml can COCONUT MILK
Flesh of ½ COCONUT, grated

1 Follow the rice pudding recipe, but substitute 400ml (14fl oz) of the whole milk for the coconut milk, and mix together with the remaining 600ml (1 pint) whole milk. Continue to cook as in the main recipe.
2 Toast the grated coconut in a dry, non-stick frying pan over medium heat until golden, shaking the pan to prevent burning. Tip out immediately. Scatter the coconut over the rice pudding and serve.

PINEAPPLE & CARDAMOM

2 CARDAMOM PODS, seeds removed and
  husks discarded
50g (1¾oz) CASTER SUGAR
250g (9oz) fresh PINEAPPLE, cut into small chunks

1 Finely grind the cardamom seeds in a pestle and mortar.
2 Heat the sugar and 4 tbsp water in a small saucepan over medium heat until the sugar has melted, then add the cardamom seeds and pineapple chunks. Cook for 10–15 minutes, stirring gently, until the pineapple has caramelized nicely. Serve the rice topped with the warm pineapple.

MANGO TOPPING

30g (1oz) PISTACHIO NUTS, chopped
1 small ripe MANGO, stoned and chopped
1 tbsp CASTER SUGAR
1 tbsp LIME JUICE

1 Toast the pistachio nuts in a clean, dry frying pan over a medium heat for 5–6 minutes then remove from the heat.
2 Place the ripe mango, sugar, and lime juice in a blender and whizz together until very smooth. Serve the rice with the mango purée spooned over, and the toasted pistachio nuts scattered on top.

CLEMENTINE CAKE WITH PASSION FRUIT AND LIMONCELLO ICE CREAM, ORANGE AND STAR ANISE SORBET, AND LIME CHANTILLY CREAM

Kirsty Wark journalist and presenter and 2011 Celebrity finalist

PREPARATION TIME
40 minutes

COOKING TIME
4 hours 10 minutes

SERVES UP TO 8

FOR THE CAKE
375g (13oz) CLEMENTINES (4–5)
SUNFLOWER OIL, for greasing
6 EGGS
225g (8oz) CASTER SUGAR
250g (9oz) GROUND ALMONDS
1 heaped tsp BAKING POWDER

FOR THE SYRUP
juice of 2 CLEMENTINES
50g (1¾oz) CASTER SUGAR
1 tbsp ORANGE MARMALADE

FOR THE ICE CREAM
2 PASSION FRUITS
300ml (10fl oz) DOUBLE CREAM
300ml (10fl oz) WHOLE MILK
3 tbsp LIMONCELLO
100g (3½oz) CASTER SUGAR

FOR THE ORANGE SORBET
5 ORANGES, squeezed; you will
    need 300ml (10fl oz) of juice
100g (3½oz) CASTER SUGAR
2 STAR ANISE

FOR THE ORANGE STICKS
ORANGE PEEL, reserved from
    the oranges
150g (5½oz) GRANULATED SUGAR

FOR THE CHANTILLY CREAM
200ml (7fl oz) DOUBLE CREAM
50g (1¾oz) ICING SUGAR
1 VANILLA POD, split and seeds
    scraped out
1 tsp LIME JUICE

1 Put the clementines into a pan of cold water, bring to the boil, and cook for 2 hours. Drain and, when cool enough to handle, cut each clementine in half and remove the pips. Then blitz everything – skins, pith, and fruit – in a food processor.
2 Preheat the oven to 190°C (375°F/Gas 5). Grease and line a 20cm (8in) round springform cake tin with baking parchment.
3 Beat the eggs in a mixing bowl. Mix in the sugar, almonds, and baking powder, then add the clementine pulp and mix until smooth.
4 Pour the cake mixture into the prepared tin and bake for 1 hour, until golden and cooked through, covering the tin loosely with foil after 40 minutes to stop the top from over-browning. Test the cake with a skewer – if it is ready, the skewer will come out clean.
5 Remove from the oven and leave to cool in the tin on a wire rack. Once cooled, remove from the tin.
6 For the syrup, put all the ingredients into a small pan and bring to the boil. Simmer for 3–4 minutes until sticky, then remove from the heat and spoon over the cake.
7 Meanwhile, make the ice cream. Halve the passion fruits and scoop the pulp into a bowl. Clean the shells and set aside for later.
8 Mix the passion fruit pulp with the remaining ingredients and churn in an ice-cream machine until set. Alternatively, pour the mixture in a freezerproof container and freeze until mushy.

Simplify for **EVERY**DAY

• Use boules of bought passion fruit ice cream and drizzle with limoncello in small serving dishes on the plate. • Use bought orange sorbet instead of the home-made orange and star anise sorbet and decorate with chocolate orange sticks.

Whisk until the ice crystals are broken up. Return to the freezer and repeat the process twice.

9 If serving just 4, scoop some ice cream back into the passion fruit shells and put them into the freezer until ready to use (or put all in a plastic container with a lid and freeze until needed).

10 For the sorbet, place the orange juice, caster sugar, and star anise in a pan and bring to the boil, stirring until the sugar has dissolved. Remove from the heat and leave to cool completely. Strain, then churn or freeze as for the ice cream.

11 Meanwhile, make the orange sticks. Preheat the oven to 130°C (250°F/Gas ½). Cut the reserved orange peel into little sticks 2cm (¾in) long and 3mm (⅛in) thick.

12 Boil the sugar with 100ml (3½fl oz) water until the sugar has completely dissolved. Add the orange sticks and simmer for 10 minutes. Drain, then transfer to a baking tray lined with baking parchment. Cook in the oven for 1 hour until crisp.

13 For the Chantilly cream, beat the double cream to soft peaks, then beat in the sugar, vanilla seeds, and lime juice.

14 Slice the cake and plate with the ice cream, Chantilly cream, and sorbet. Top the sorbet with a few orange sticks and serve.

Clementines are almost seedless and have delicate inner membranes, making them easy to handle. When buying, check for firm, heavy fruit with a fresh fragrance and unblemished skin with no soft or wrinkled areas.

APPLE TARTE TATIN
Nick Pickard actor and 2011 Celebrity finalist

PREPARATION TIME
10 minutes

COOKING TIME
10 minutes

SERVES 4

FLOUR, for dusting
375g pack ALL BUTTER
   PUFF PASTRY
2 tsp LIQUID GLUCOSE
4 tbsp CASTER SUGAR
100g (3½oz) UNSALTED BUTTER
3 PINK LADY APPLES, peeled,
   cored, and quartered

TO SERVE
4 tbsp CRÈME FRAÎCHE
ICING SUGAR, to garnish
GROUND CINNAMON, to garnish

1 Preheat the oven to 200°C (400°F/Gas 6). Lightly dust the work surface with flour, then roll out the puff pastry to a thickness of 5mm (¼in). Cut out four 13cm (5½in) discs from the pastry – they need to be slightly larger than the size of the blini pans you will be using. Place the pastry discs on a baking tray and refrigerate until needed.

2 Put ½ tsp glucose, 1 tbsp sugar, and 25g (scant 1oz) butter into each blini pan and heat gently until the butter has melted and the sugar begins to dissolve. Gently tilt and rotate the pans as the sugar begins to caramelize – do not stir the mixture or the sugar will crystallize. Cook until the mixture starts to turn a light caramel colour, then remove from the heat and leave to cool slightly.

3 Add 3 apple quarters to each pan, rounded-side down. Top the apples with a disc of pastry, making sure the pastry fits snugly inside the pan.

4 Bake in the oven for 10 minutes or until the pastry is risen and golden. Remove from the oven and leave to cool for 5 minutes on a wire rack. Turn out onto a flat serving plate and leave to rest for a further 5 minutes.

5 Serve with a spoonful of crème fraîche on top and dusted with icing sugar and cinnamon.

CHOCOLATE-ORANGE BREAD AND BUTTER PUDDING

Phil Vickery MBE England rugby player and 2011 Celebrity champion

PREPARATION TIME
25 minutes

COOKING TIME
30–35 minutes

SERVES 6–8

115g (4oz) UNSALTED BUTTER,
 softened, plus extra
 for greasing
8 EGG YOLKS
50g (1¾oz) DEMERARA SUGAR,
 plus extra for sprinkling
pinch of SALT
250ml (8fl oz) MILK
250ml (8fl oz) DOUBLE CREAM
zest of 2 large ORANGES

1 VANILLA POD, split
 and seeds scraped out
1½ x 400g (14oz)
 BRIOCHE, sliced
100g (3½oz) DARK
 CHOCOLATE CHIPS
230g tub CORNISH
 CLOTTED CREAM

1 Preheat the oven to 180°C (350°F/Gas 4). Grease a shallow 3 litre (5¼ pint) baking dish.

2 For the custard, whisk the egg yolks with the demerara sugar and salt in a large bowl until all the sugar is dissolved.

3 Place the milk, cream, orange zest, and vanilla seeds in a saucepan and bring to the boil. Remove from the heat and leave for 2 minutes to infuse.

4 Slowly pour the milk mixture into the egg mixture, whisking until combined.

5 Butter the brioche slices and cut into triangles. Layer a third of the brioche slices in the greased baking dish followed by a third of the chocolate chips, then repeat twice.

6 Pour the custard over the bread and sprinkle the extra sugar over the top. Bake in the oven for 25–30 minutes until golden brown.

7 Serve the bread and butter pudding hot with a spoonful of clotted cream.

JOHN TORODE

"I really like the flavour of the chocolate, the richness of the custard, and the orange running all the way through it."

LEMON POSSET WITH FRESH FRUIT AND SHORTBREAD

Linda Lusardi actress and 2011 Celebrity semi-finalist

PREPARATION TIME
15 minutes

COOKING TIME
25 minutes, plus cooling

SERVES 4

GREGG WALLACE

"Mmm. Creamy, sharp with lemon, enough sweetness in there. Really good shortbread biscuit, that's really good. That's a good pud, John."

FOR THE POSSET
750ml (1¼ pints) DOUBLE CREAM
200g (7oz) CASTER SUGAR
juice of 3 LEMONS

FOR THE SHORTBREAD
200g (7oz) UNSALTED
   BUTTER, softened
60g (2oz) ICING SUGAR
1 tsp VANILLA EXTRACT
200g (7oz) PLAIN FLOUR

½ tsp SALT
150g (5½oz) DARK CHOCOLATE,
   broken into small pieces

TO FINISH
250g (9oz) fresh fruit:
   STRAWBERRIES, RASPBERRIES,
   and BLACKBERRIES

1 Preheat the oven to 180°C (350°F/Gas 4). For the posset, put the cream and sugar into a saucepan and bring to the boil. Simmer for 6 minutes, then remove from the heat. Whisk in the lemon juice, then leave to cool.

2 Divide the mixture between 4 serving glasses, then chill in the fridge for at least 2 hours until set.

3 Meanwhile make the shortbread. Using an electric hand whisk, cream the butter and sugar together until pale and fluffy, then stir in the vanilla extract. Sift the flour and salt into the mixture and stir until combined.

4 Wrap the dough in cling film, then chill in the fridge for 1 hour.

5 Remove the dough from the fridge, unwrap, and place on a lightly floured surface. Roll out to a thickness of 5mm (¼in), then cut out with a heart-shaped cookie cutter. Transfer to a non-stick baking tray, then chill in the fridge for 30 minutes.

6 Bake the shortbread for 8–10 minutes until lightly golden, then transfer to a wire rack to cool.

7 Put the chocolate into a heatproof bowl and set it over a pan of gently simmering water. Stir until the chocolate has melted, then remove from the heat.

8 Put the chocolate in a paper piping bag with the point snipped off, or use a teaspoon, and drizzle the chocolate over the shortbread biscuits in a zigzag pattern. Leave to set.

9 When ready to serve, top the possets with the mixed fruits and serve with the shortbread biscuits.

TRIO OF ITALIAN DESSERTS – PANNA COTTA, PASSION FRUIT MOUSSE, AND LEMON AND ROSEMARY ICE CREAM

Sara Danesin Medio MasterChef 2011 finalist

PREPARATION TIME
1 hour 40 minutes, plus
chilling and freezing

COOKING TIME
30 minutes

SERVES 4

"I wanted to try
and do something
that really showed
effort in my
desserts – to
show you that
I can set all
those things,
and make them
look beautiful."

Panna cotta with berry compôte

FOR THE PANNA COTTA
2 GELATINE LEAVES
120ml (4fl oz) MILK
250ml (8fl oz) DOUBLE CREAM
1 VANILLA POD, split
50g (1¾oz) CASTER SUGAR

FOR THE COMPÔTE
250g (9oz) fresh MIXED BERRIES,
   such as STRAWBERRIES,
   RASPBERRIES, BLACKBERRIES
85g (3oz) CASTER SUGAR
3 tbsp KIRSCH

1 Make the panna cotta. Soften the gelatine leaves in ice cold water for about 5 minutes.
2 Put the milk, double cream, vanilla pod, and sugar into a saucepan and heat to 80°C (176°F) – do not let it boil.
3 Strain into a jug and discard the vanilla pod. Remove the soaked gelatine from the water, squeeze out any excess water, and whisk into the milk and cream mixture until dissolved.
4 Divide the mixture between four 100ml (3½fl oz) dariole moulds and transfer to the fridge for 2–3 hours until set.
5 For the compôte, put the berries and sugar in a heavy-based pan and cook gently until soft and syrupy, about 15 minutes. Add the Kirsch and leave to cool.

Passion fruit mousse with sablé biscuit

FOR THE MOUSSE
2 GELATINE LEAVES
150ml (5fl oz) DOUBLE CREAM
200g (7oz) PASSION FRUIT PURÉE
60g (2oz) ICING SUGAR

FOR THE GLAZE
1/2 GELATINE LEAF
75g (2½oz) PASSION FRUIT PURÉE
2 tsp SUGAR

FOR THE SABLÉ BISCUIT BASE
125g (4½oz) PLAIN FLOUR
100g (3½oz) cold BUTTER
pinch of SALT
100g (3½oz) ICING SUGAR
1 EGG YOLK
FLOUR, for dusting

1 Soften the gelatine leaves in ice cold water for about 5 minutes. In a bowl whip the cream to soft peaks.
2 Gently heat the passion fruit purée and sugar in a pan until dissolved. Add the squeezed gelatine and stir until dissolved. Leave to cool until the consistency of egg white.
3 Fold the passion fruit purée mixture into the whipped cream and use to fill a piping bag fitted with a 1cm (½in) nozzle.
4 On a baking tray, line 4 food rings, each 5cm (2in) in diameter and 6cm (2½in) in height, with cling film, ensuring the bottoms are sealed tight. Pipe the mousse mixture into the lined moulds, leaving a gap of 3mm (⅛in) at the top of each.
5 Chill in the fridge for 2–3 hours until completely set.
6 Prepare the glaze. Soften the gelatine leaves in ice cold water for about 5 minutes.
7 Gently heat the passion fruit purée and sugar in a pan until dissolved. Add the squeezed gelatine and stir until dissolved. Leave to cool until the consistency of egg white, then pour on top of the set mousses. Return to the fridge for 30 minutes or until set.
8 Preheat the oven to 180°C (350°F/Gas 4). Make a well in the flour. Add the butter, salt, and sugar, and slowly incorporate the flour until you have a paste.
9 Add the egg yolk and slowly incorporate until a smooth dough is formed. Work as little as possible.
10 Wrap in cling film and place in the fridge for 30 minutes.
11 When ready to use, roll out very thinly and cut rounds 5cm (2in) in diameter. Place on a baking tray, lined with baking parchment, and bake for 6–8 minutes until golden. Cool slightly then transfer to a wire rack to cool completely. Store unused biscuits in an airtight container.

Lemon and rosemary ice cream

FOR THE ICE CREAM
3 tbsp LEMON JUICE
zest of 1 LEMON
100g (3½oz) CASTER SUGAR
10cm (4in) sprig of ROSEMARY
300ml (10fl oz) DOUBLE CREAM
pinch of SALT

FOR THE CARAMEL FLOWERS
100g (3½oz) CASTER SUGAR
finely grated zest of ½ LEMON

TO DECORATE
PHYSALIS, for decoration

1 Make the ice cream. Mix the lemon juice, zest, and sugar in a bowl. Strip the leaves from the rosemary sprig and put in the mixture. Leave to infuse for 30 minutes, stirring occasionally.
2 Strain into a jug and whisk in the cream, and a pinch of salt. Pour into an ice-cream machine and churn until set. Transfer to the freezer until serving. Alternatively, place the mixture in a freezerproof container and freeze until mushy. Whisk until the ice crystals are broken up. Return to the freezer and repeat the process twice.
3 Meanwhile make the caramel flowers. Put 3 tbsp water in a small, heavy-based pan. Sprinkle in the sugar and slowly dissolve over low heat, stirring occasionally. Add the zest.
4 Bring to the boil and, using a wet pastry brush, brush any sugar crystals off the sides of the pan. Boil without stirring until a light golden colour. Pour immediately onto a baking tray lined with baking parchment.
5 Whilst still warm, cut out flower shapes, using a 1.5cm (⅔in) fluted cutter, from the caramel. Leave to harden.

TO SERVE
To assemble the dish, place a sable biscuit on each of 4 serving plates and turn out the mousses on top of the biscuits. Turn out the panna cotta, and top with the compôte. Put a scoop of ice cream in 4 shot glasses. Push a caramel flower in each, add to plates. Decorate the plates with physalis and serve straight away.

DREAM OF A CREAM

GREGG WALLACE TAKES SARA'S DESSERT AND MAKES
IT SIMPLE WITH DELICIOUS FRUITY ACCOMPANIMENTS

PREP: 25 MINS • CHILL: 3 HRS • COOK: 10–15 MINS

SERVES 4

600ml (1 pint) DOUBLE CREAM
4 tbsp CASTER SUGAR
1 VANILLA POD
1 sachet POWDERED GELATINE
SUNFLOWER OIL, for greasing

1 Split the vanilla pod with a sharp knife and scrape out the seeds with the knife or a teaspoon.
2 Combine the cream, sugar, vanilla pod, and scraped seeds in a saucepan over medium heat and slowly bring to a simmer, stirring with a whisk or wooden spoon, until the sugar has dissolved. Remove from the heat and set aside for 10 minutes to infuse.
3 Place 4 tablespoons of cold water into a small heatproof bowl, sprinkle the gelatine over, and leave to soften for 3–5 minutes. Stand the bowl in a pan of hot water. Stir well until completely dissolved.
4 Remove the vanilla pod from the cream, then whisk in the dissolved gelatine until completely combined.
5 Pour the vanilla-flavoured cream into 4 lightly oiled ramekin dishes and leave to cool completely. Cover with cling film, and chill for at least 3 hours to set.
6 Turn out onto serving plates. Spoon the topping of your choice over and serve.

"You can get away with pure vanilla extract for speed, but it's best to use fresh pods for va va voom flavour."

Carefully split the vanilla pod using a small, sharp knife. Hold the pod down at one end and, with the blade facing away from you, split the pod.

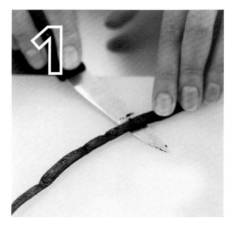

Whisk the pod and the scraped seeds with the cream and sugar. Heat in a saucepan over a medium heat, allowing the flavours to blend together.

STRAWBERRY AND RASPBERRY COMPÔTE

50g (1¾oz) STRAWBERRIES,
  hulled and halved
50g (1¾oz) RASPBERRIES
3–4 tbsp VANILLA CASTER SUGAR

1 Place the strawberries, raspberries and vanilla sugar in a saucepan and cook for 2–3 minutes or until the fruit has softened.but still holds its shape.
2 Leave to cool before serving
3 Gently pull away the edges of the panna cottas from the ramekins.

PASSION FRUIT AND LEMON SAUCE

3 large PASSION FRUIT
200ml (7fl oz) ORANGE JUICE
1 tbsp LEMON JUICE
2 tbsp CASTER SUGAR
1 tsp ARROWROOT

1 Using a teaspoon, remove all the pulp and juice from the passion fruit and place in a pan.
2 Add the fruit juices and simmer together for 6 minutes.
3 Sieve the sauce to remove the seeds. Blend the arrowroot with 2 tsp cold water. Stir in, bring to the boil, stirring, until thickened and clear. Cool before serving.

FIGGY PUDDING SERVED WITH FIG SAUCE AND CREAM

Ruth Goodman social historian and 2011 Celebrity contestant

PREPARATION TIME
20 minutes, plus soaking

COOKING TIME
1 hour

SERVES 4

200g (7oz) soft, ready-to-eat
    DRIED FIGS, roughly chopped
splash of DRY SHERRY
finely grated zest and juice
    of 1 LEMON
50g (1¾oz) BUTTER, plus extra
    for greasing
50g (1¾oz) SELF-RAISING FLOUR

100g (3½oz) fresh
    BREADCRUMBS
60g (2oz) SOFT LIGHT BROWN
    SUGAR
2 EGGS, lightly beaten
2 tbsp DOUBLE CREAM, plus
    extra to serve

1　Soak the figs in the sherry and lemon zest and juice for at least 30 minutes.

2　Rub together the butter and self-raising flour. Add to the breadcrumbs with the brown sugar.

3　Add half of the soaked figs along with half the steeping liquid to the breadcrumb mixture. Add the beaten eggs and a dash of the cream. Mix well.

4　Butter 4 dariole moulds. Divide the mixture between the moulds. Place a piece of buttered greaseproof paper over each one, cover with pleated foil, and fasten with string, or twist and fold under the rim of the moulds to secure. Place in a steamer and steam for 1 hour, topping up the steamer with boiling water as necessary.

5　Place the remaining soaked figs along with their steeping liquid into a small blender or food processor. Blend until smooth. Add water to thin to desired consistency – a thick paste or a pouring sauce. Place in a pan and simmer for 2 minutes.

6　Serve the figgy puddings with the sauce and a dash of cream.

GREGG WALLACE

"Flavours are wonderful. The fig is deep, not too sweet – I find that very nice indeed."

TRIO OF BRITISH DESSERTS
Tim Anderson MasterChef 2011 champion

PREPARATION TIME
1 hour, plus chilling
and freezing

COOKING TIME
1 hour 15 minutes

SERVES 4

Preparation

FOR THE CUSTARD BASE
250g (9oz) SUGAR
8 EGG YOLKS

250ml (8fl oz) MILK
250ml (8fl oz) SINGLE CREAM

Beat together the sugar and egg yolks until pale and thick. Simmer the milk and cream together in a saucepan and pour over the egg yolks and sugar. Whisk to combine, then strain into a clean pan. Heat gently, stirring, until the mixture thickens to the point where it coats the back of a spoon evenly. Remove from the heat and transfer immediately to a large bowl.

Sticky toffee crème brûlée

FOR THE CRÈME BRÛLÉE
100ml (3½fl oz) DOUBLE CREAM
100g (3½oz) MUSCOVADO SUGAR
4 STONED DATES
4 STONED PRUNES
1 VANILLA POD, split and seeds
  scraped out
2 EGG YOLKS
3 tbsp PLAIN FLOUR

100ml (3½fl oz) prepared
  CUSTARD BASE
CASTER SUGAR, for topping

FOR THE SAUCE
250ml (8fl oz) BLACKCURRANT
  ALE, such as Lindemans Cassis
3 tbsp CRÈME DE CASSIS
100ml (3½fl oz) STOUT
50g (1¾oz) SUGAR
3 tbsp DOUBLE CREAM

Simplify for **EVERY**DAY

• Use bought fresh custard instead of making your own.
• Use drained, canned rhubarb and add a splash of rosé wine, if available, or just a little of the rhubarb juice. • Freeze the rhubarb and custard mixture in a small, rectangular container and cut into squares when frozen. Use these to make blocks instead of the spheres to fry.
• Use plain white breadcrumbs for the crumble with the oats.

1 Preheat the oven to 180°C (350°F/Gas 4). Place the cream and sugar in a pan over medium heat and stir continuously until the sugar has completely dissolved. Add the dates, prunes, and vanilla seeds and simmer until the dates have softened.
2 Add the egg yolks and flour to the custard base and whisk until smooth. Pour the toffee mixture onto the custard and whisk to combine. Transfer to a food processor and blitz until smooth.
3 Divide the mixture between mini ramekins, 50ml (2fl oz) in volume, and place them in a roasting tray. Add hot water to the tray until it comes halfway up the sides of the ramekins, then bake in the oven for 20–25 minutes until set. Leave to cool, then transfer to the fridge to chill.

4 Once completely chilled, sprinkle the top of each crème brulée with caster sugar and glaze with a blowtorch. Refrigerate until ready to serve.

5 For the sauce, combine all the ingredients in a saucepan, bring to the boil, then simmer until reduced to 100ml (3½ fl oz). Keep the sauce warm until needed, then transfer to small jugs before serving.

Rhubarb crumble with custard

FOR THE RHUBARB COMPÔTE
2 RHUBARB sticks, diced
100g (3½oz) SUGAR
100ml (3½fl oz) PINK CHAMPAGNE

FOR THE CUSTARD
250ml (8fl oz) prepared CUSTARD
  BASE
1 VANILLA POD, split and seeds
  scraped out

FOR THE CRUMBLE
50g (1¾oz) PLAIN FLOUR
1 EGG
50g (1¾oz) ROLLED OATS
50g (1¾oz) PANKO BREADCRUMBS
VEGETABLE OIL, for deep frying
ICING SUGAR, for dusting
1 RHUBARB stick

1 Put all of the rhubarb compôte ingredients in a saucepan, bring to the boil, then simmer until the rhubarb is very soft. Transfer to a food processor and blitz until smooth. Place in a bowl and chill.

2 Combine the custard base and vanilla seeds in a small bowl, cover with cling film, and chill.

3 To assemble, place the rhubarb compôte and vanilla custard base in a bowl and stir gently to create a rippled effect. Fill 8 hemispheric tbsp measures, or eight 15ml (½fl oz) hemispheric moulds, with the mixture and transfer to the freezer to set.

4 When frozen solid, dip the back of the spoons briefly in warm water to loosen the frozen mixture, then turn out onto a chilled baking tray. Brush the flat surface of 1 of the half spheres with a little warm water, then press 2 halves together to make a complete sphere. Immediately return to the freezer and freeze until solid. Repeat the process to make 1 sphere per serving.

5 To make the crumble, whisk the flour, 4 tsp water, and the egg into a thick batter, then set aside. Combine the oats and panko breadcrumbs and blitz in a food processor. Set aside in a separate bowl.

6 Heat the oil for deep frying to 160°C (325°F). Dip each frozen rhubarb sphere in the batter, shake off any excess, then roll in the oat and panko mixture. Fry for 2 minutes until the outside is golden and the inside is completely molten. Drain on a rack set over a roasting tray. When dry, dust with icing sugar.

7 Cut the rhubarb into very thin strips and wrap around the base of each rhubarb crumble sphere. Serve immediately.

Cheddar cheesecake with whisky jelly

FOR THE CHEESECAKE BASE
2 DIGESTIVE BISCUITS
2 tsp chopped WALNUTS
1 tbsp FLOUR
1½ tbsp SUGAR
1 tbsp OATS
40g (1¼oz) BUTTER

FOR THE CHEESECAKE FILLING
100ml (3½fl oz) MILK
30g (1oz) SUGAR
20g (¾oz) very MATURE CHEDDAR CHEESE, finely grated
20g (¾oz) MASCARPONE CHEESE

2 tbsp AGAR-AGAR FLAKES
100ml (3½fl oz) prepared CUSTARD BASE

FOR THE WHISKY JELLY
3 tbsp plus 1 tsp HIGHLAND WHISKY
100ml (3½fl oz) LOWLAND WHISKY
3 tbsp GINGER BEER
50g (1¾oz) SUGAR
1 tbsp AGAR-AGAR FLAKES

TO DECORATE
12 BLACKCURRANTS
4 MINT leaves

1 For the base, preheat the oven to 180°C (350°F/Gas 4). Blitz all the ingredients to a coarse powder in a food processor. Roll out to a thickness of 8mm (⅓in) on a non-stick baking sheet. Bake for 12 minutes until golden. Remove from the oven and leave to cool.
2 Line four 4cm (1½in) diameter cooking rings with acetate and use to cut discs out of the biscuit base mixture, retaining the disc of biscuit base inside the ring. Transfer the rings to a baking tray lined with greaseproof paper.
3 For the filling, put the milk and sugar into a small pan and bring to the boil. Add the cheeses and stir to combine. Sprinkle the agar-agar into the pan and boil for 4 minutes until dissolved. Remove from the heat and whisk into the custard base. Pour the mixture inside the lined cooking rings on top of the biscuit base to a depth of 5mm (¼in). Transfer to the fridge and chill until set.
4 To make the whisky jelly, put all the ingredients in a saucepan and bring to the boil. Boil for 5–6 minutes until the agar-agar has dissolved completely. Pour into a small plastic container to a depth of 5mm (¼in). Chill for 20 minutes or until set.
5 Just before serving, cut out 4cm (1½in) circles of the jelly. Place the cheesecakes on 4 serving plates, loosen the edges, and lift off the rings. Top each with a disc of whisky jelly. Decorate each cheesecake with 3 blackcurrants and a mint leaf.

TO SERVE
Place the cheesecakes on 4 serving plates, loosen the edges, and lift off the rings. Top each with a disc of whisky jelly. Decorate each cheesecake with 3 blackcurrants and a mint leaf. Arrange the brulées, crumble spheres and jugs of sauce alongside.

RASPBERRY CRÈME BRÛLÉE, RASPBERRY AND MÛRE SORBET, AND MADELEINES SPRINKLED WITH RASPBERRY DUST

Kirsty Wark journalist and presenter and 2011 Celebrity finalist

PREPARATION TIME
30 minutes, plus freezing

COOKING TIME
50 minutes

SERVES 4

FOR THE CRÈME BRÛLÉES
3 EGG YOLKS
50g (1¾oz) CASTER SUGAR
1 VANILLA POD, split
  and seeds scraped out
300ml (10fl oz) DOUBLE CREAM
150g (5½oz) RASPBERRIES
2 tbsp DEMERARA SUGAR

FOR THE RASPBERRY SORBET
125g (4½oz)
  GRANULATED SUGAR
200g (7oz) RASPBERRIES
½ tbsp LEMON JUICE
1 tsp CRÈME DE MÛRE LIQUEUR

FOR THE MADELEINES
50g (1¾oz) UNSALTED BUTTER,
  plus extra for greasing
60g (2oz) CASTER SUGAR
1 EGG
1 EGG YOLK
finely grated zest and juice of ½
  LEMON
pinch of SALT
60g (2oz) SELF-RAISING
  FLOUR, sifted
RASPBERRY DUST, to decorate

1 For the crème brûlée, preheat the oven to 160°C (325°F/Gas 3). Put the egg yolks, caster sugar, and vanilla seeds in a bowl and whisk until pale and creamy.
2 Scald the cream in a saucepan (heat to the point where tiny bubbles form around the edges and some skin forms on the surface, but do not boil). Take off the heat and whisk into the egg mixture. Pass the mixture through a fine sieve to trap any large vanilla seeds.
3 Place a layer of the raspberries in the base of four 120ml (4fl oz) ramekins. Using a jug, pour the custard mixture into the ramekins. Place the ramekins in a baking tin. Pour in boiling water until it is halfway up the sides of the ramekins, then transfer them to the oven and cook for 30 minutes until set. Leave the custards to cool, then transfer to the fridge to chill.
4 When chilled, sprinkle each ramekin with demerara sugar. Place under a very hot grill or use a blow torch to melt the sugar until golden brown. Leave to cool completely before serving.
5 For the raspberry sorbet, place the sugar and 200ml (7fl oz) water in a saucepan and bring to the boil. Boil for 5 minutes until the sugar has completely dissolved, then set aside and leave to cool.
6 Purée the raspberries with the lemon juice in a food processor, then pass through a fine sieve. Combine the raspberry purée with the sugar syrup and crème de mûre. Churn in an ice-cream maker until set, then transfer to a plastic container with a lid and store

in the freezer until ready to serve. Alternatively, place the mixture inside a freezerproof container and freeze until mushy. Whisk until the ice crystals are broken up. Return the mixture to the freezer and repeat twice.

7 For the madeleines, preheat the oven to 180°C (350°F/Gas 4). Generously grease a madeleine tray with butter. Melt the remaining butter in a saucepan and leave to cool slightly.

8 Beat the caster sugar, egg, and egg yolk in a food mixer or with an electric hand whisk at medium speed until the mixture has tripled in volume. Add the lemon and salt and beat to combine. Fold in the flour, being careful not to overwork the mixture, then fold in the cooled, melted butter until fully combined.

9 Spoon the batter into the madeleine moulds until they are two-thirds full. Place in the oven and bake for about 10–12 minutes until the edges are golden brown and the centres spring back when lightly pressed. Allow to cool.

10 Sprinkle the madeleines with raspberry dust and serve with the crème brulées and sorbet.

Raspberries are now available for most of the year, but the best are the seasonal ones in summer and early autumn. Check the punnets carefully – if they are stained with juice, the berries are past their best. If you do not eat them on the day of purchase, pat dry with kitchen paper and store in the fridge in a paper bag for 1–2 days.

WARM TREACLE TART WITH PECAN BRITTLE AND VANILLA ICE CREAM
Nick Pickard actor and 2011 Celebrity finalist

PREPARATION TIME
30 minutes, plus resting
and freezing

COOKING TIME
1 hour

SERVES 8

GREGG WALLACE

"That's really really good. That's really, really warm and cosy."

FOR THE PASTRY
225g (8oz) PLAIN FLOUR
pinch of SALT
25g (scant 1oz) CASTER SUGAR
115g (4oz) very cold
    UNSALTED BUTTER, diced

FOR THE ICE CREAM
500ml (16fl oz) DOUBLE CREAM
2 VANILLA PODS, spit and
    seeds scraped out
3 EGG YOLKS
75g (2½oz) CASTER SUGAR

FOR THE FILLING
350g (12oz) GOLDEN SYRUP
1 heaped tbsp BLACK TREACLE
finely grated zest and juice of
    1 LEMON
4 EGGS, beaten
25g (scant 1oz) fresh
    BREADCRUMBS

FOR THE BRITTLE
100g (3½oz) CASTER SUGAR
25g (scant 1oz) PECAN NUTS,
    roughly chopped

1 Preheat the oven to 180°C (350°F/Gas 4). To make the pastry, place the ingredients in a food processor. Blitz until resembling breadcrumbs. With the food processor running, slowly add 150ml (5fl oz) water until the mixture forms a ball. Knead gently until smooth. Wrap in cling film, and rest in the fridge for 30 minutes.
2 Roll out the pastry thinly and line a 23cm (9in) tart tin, set on a baking tray, leaving the edges folded over. Rest again in the fridge for 30 minutes. Line with baking parchment and fill with baking beans. Trim the edges. Bake for 12 minutes. Remove the beans and parchment. Bake a further for 5 minutes to dry out.
3 For the ice cream, heat the cream with the split vanilla pod and seeds to the boil, then set aside for 2 minutes. Remove the pod. Whisk the eggs and sugar until thick and pale. Whisk in the cream, whisking all the time. Let it cool. Pour the mixture into an ice-cream machine and churn until set. Transfer to a plastic container with a lid and store in the freezer until serving. Alternatively, pour the mixture in a freezerproof container and freeze until mushy. Whisk until the ice crystals are broken up. Return to the freezer and repeat the process twice.
4 For the tart filling, mix the syrup, treacle, lemon juice, and zest. Whisk in the eggs and breadcrumbs. Pour into the pastry case. Bake for 35–40 minutes until set. Set aside, keep warm.
5 For the brittle, slowly heat the sugar in a small frying pan until golden brown. Add the nuts, mix in, and pour onto a baking tray lined with baking parchment. Leave until hard. Roughly crush.
6 With a warm knife, cut slices of the warm tart and serve on plates with a ball of ice cream with some brittle sprinkled on top.

TRIFLE
Aggie MacKenzie journalist and 2011 Celebrity semi-finalist

PREPARATION TIME
15 minutes

COOKING TIME
20 minutes, plus chilling

SERVES 8–10

FOR THE CUSTARD
600ml (1 pint) DOUBLE CREAM
1 VANILLA POD, split and
   seeds scraped out
6 EGG YOLKS
100g (3½oz) CASTER SUGAR
2 tsp CORNFLOUR

FOR THE TOPPING
30g (1oz) flaked ALMONDS
1 tbsp ICING SUGAR

FOR THE SPONGE MIXTURE
8 TRIFLE SPONGES
4 tbsp LEMON CURD
100ml (3½fl oz) PEDRO
   XIMENEZ SHERRY
300g (10oz) RASPBERRIES
2 BANANAS, sliced
4–5 soft RATAFIA BISCUITS
300ml (10fl oz) DOUBLE CREAM

1 Preheat the oven to 160°C (325°F/Gas 3). To make the custard, place the cream and vanilla in a saucepan, bring to the boil, then remove from the heat. In a bowl, beat the egg yolks with the sugar and cornflour until pale, then pour the cream over and whisk to combine.
2 Transfer the mixture to a clean pan and put over low to medium heat, stirring all the time until thickened enough to coat the back of a spoon, then immediately remove from the heat and pour into a jug. Leave to cool completely.
3 For the topping, put the almonds in a sieve and rinse under the tap. Transfer to a plate and sprinkle some icing sugar over them. Spread out on a baking tray lined with baking parchment or silicone and bake in the oven for about 12–15 minutes until nicely browned.
4 Split the trifle sponges and spread with a little lemon curd, then lay them in a single layer in a shallow dish. Douse with half of the sherry. Crush the raspberries a little so that they start to yield some juice and scatter them over the sponges. Cover with a layer of banana, crumble over the ratafias, then add the rest of the sherry.
5 Pour the cooled custard over the sponge and fruit mixture. Whisk the cream to soft peaks, then spoon over the custard. Scatter the almonds over the top to finish. Chill until ready to serve.

QUINCE COMPÔTE CROUSTADES WITH A CARAMEL CAGE, PISTACHIO KULFI, COCONUT SORBET, AND BERRY COULIS

Jackie Kearney MasterChef 2011 final 4

PREPARATION TIME
1 hour 15 minutes, plus freezing and cooling

COOKING TIME
40 minutes

SERVES 4

FOR THE CROUSTADES
8 sheets of FILO PASTRY
100g (3½oz) UNSALTED
  BUTTER, melted

FOR THE QUINCE COMPÔTE
2 QUINCES, peeled, cored, and
  cut into 1cm (½in) cubes
pinch of freshly grated NUTMEG
2 CLOVES
1 CINNAMON STICK
1 GREEN CARDAMOM POD
3 tbsp CASTER SUGAR
3 tbsp PORT

FOR THE PISTACHIO KULFI
250ml (8fl oz) EVAPORATED MILK
pinch of SAFFRON STRANDS,
  soaked in 2 tbsp hot water
25g (scant 1oz) UNSALTED,
  SHELLED PISTACHIOS, plus
  extra for decorating

25g (scant 1oz) whole
  peeled ALMONDS
125ml (4fl oz) DOUBLE CREAM

FOR THE BERRY COULIS
200g (7oz) BLUEBERRIES
2 tbsp CASTER SUGAR
2 tbsp KIRSCH

FOR THE COCONUT SHARDS
flesh from ½ COCONUT

FOR THE SORBET
75ml (2½fl oz) AGAVE SYRUP
75ml (2½fl oz) WATER
juice of 1½ LIMES
200ml (7fl oz) COCONUT MILK

FOR THE CARAMEL CAGE
250g (9oz) CASTER SUGAR
2 tbsp GLUCOSE SYRUP

Simplify for **EVERY**DAY

• For the croustades, use 3 filo sheets sandwiched with melted butter. Cut in quarters then press a square into each of 4 buttered individual tartlet tins so the points stick up. Brush with more butter and bake as in the recipe until golden. Remove from the tins. • Use bought toasted coconut chips. • Use diced canned pears heated with the spices, instead of quinces.
 • Use bought coconut ice cream for the sorbet. • Use vanilla ice sprinkled with chopped nuts for the kulfi.

1 For the croustades, preheat the oven to 190°C (375°F/Gas 5). Trim the filo pastry sheets slightly, then cut each sheet into four 10cm (4in) squares. Cut each square diagonally in half to form 2 small triangles.

2 Grease the outside of four 10cm (4in) tartlet tins with melted butter and place them upside-down on a baking tray.

3 Drape the triangles of the filo pastry over each mould so that the corners are separate and resemble flower petals, brushing with melted butter between each piece of the pastry. Keep adding them until the "petals" are evenly layered around the moulds (you need 16 triangles per mould).

4 Bake for 6–8 minutes until golden brown (don't overcook). Leave to cool, then gently lift off the moulds and turn the croustades up the right way.

5 For the quince compôte, put all the ingredients into a heavy-based saucepan with 100ml (3½fl oz) water and bring to the boil. Simmer for 15 minutes or until the quinces are soft but still hold their shape. Remove the whole spices from the pan. Set aside the mixture to cool.

6 For the pistachio kulfi, combine the evaporated milk, saffron water, and nuts in a large bowl. In a separate bowl, whisk the cream to soft peaks, then carefully fold into the milk mixture. Transfer to an ice-cream machine and churn until set. Transfer to a plastic container with a lid and store in the freezer. Alternatively, place the mixture in a freezerproof container and freeze until mushy. Whisk until the ice crystals are broken up. Return to the freezer and repeat the process twice.

7 Meanwhile, line four 100ml (3½fl oz) dariole moulds with cling film. Divide the mixture between the moulds and transfer to the freezer for 1 hour until set.

8 For the berry coulis, put the blueberries in a small pan with the sugar and Kirsch. Bring to the boil and simmer for 2–3 minutes until the sugar has completely dissolved and the fruit begins to break down. Pass the mixture through a sieve into a bowl and set aside until needed.

9 Preheat the oven again, if necessary, to 190°C (375°F/Gas 5) For the coconut shards, thinly slice the coconut using a mandolin, then scatter over a non-stick baking tray. Bake for 8–10 minutes until the shards start to turn golden. Take care not to overcook or they will burn. Cool completely before serving.

10 For the agave and coconut sorbet, combine all the ingredients in a large jug, then freeze as for the pistachio kulfi.

11 For the caramel cages, put the sugar into a heavy-based pan and heat gently. Tilt and rotate the pan to move the sugar as it melts, but do not stir. Once the sugar has melted, add the glucose syrup and continue to cook until the mixture turns a light caramel colour. The temperature should reach 160°C (325°F) on a sugar thermometer.

12 Allow the caramel to cool for a few seconds, and then using 2 forks, scoop out the caramel and drizzle quickly back and forth over the back of a lightly greased ladle. Change directions to create the lattice effect.

13 Remove immediately and set aside to cool. Repeat to make 3 more cages.

TO SERVE
Use oblong serving plates, place a filo croustade in the centre of each, and fill with the quince compôte. Cover each with a caramel cage. Turn out the kulfi on one side, and decorate with the whole pistachios. Place a scoop of sorbet on a pool of blueberry sauce on the other side of the croustades.

SPICED CUSTARD POT WITH BLACKBERRY COMPÔTE AND CARDAMOM SHORTBREAD

Annie Assheton MasterChef 2011 final 6

PREPARATION TIME
20 minutes, plus infusing
and chilling

COOKING TIME
1 hour

SERVES 4

FOR THE CUSTARD
200ml (7fl oz) DOUBLE CREAM
200ml (7fl oz) MILK
1 STAR ANISE
1 CINNAMON STICK
2 CARDAMOM PODS,
   crushed lightly
2 ALLSPICE BERRIES
7 EGG YOLKS
75g (2½oz) CASTER SUGAR

FOR THE COMPÔTE
325g (11oz) BLACKBERRIES
60g (2oz) CASTER SUGAR

FOR THE SHORTBREAD
5 CARDAMOM PODS
125g (4½oz) PLAIN FLOUR
25g (scant 1oz) RICE FLOUR
50g (1¾oz) CASTER SUGAR
100g (3½oz) BUTTER

1 First make the custard by combining the cream, milk, star anise, cinnamon stick, cardamom pods, and allspice berries in a saucepan and bringing up to boiling point. Remove from the heat and leave to infuse for 15 minutes.

2 Meanwhile, put the yolks in a bowl with the sugar. Whisk together until light and frothy. Whisk in the infused milk, until well blended. Strain the mixture back into the saucepan and stir over a gentle heat until the custard begins to thicken. Once thickened, transfer to a jug and leave to cool, stirring now and then so that a skin doesn't form on top.

3 Put the blackberries in a saucepan with the sugar, cover and cook gently until the blackberries start to soften and the juices run. Remove the lid, bring to the boil, reduce the heat and simmer for 5 minutes. Leave to cool. Spoon some compôte into 4 serving glasses and chill. When the custard is cool, pour carefully onto the compôte and chill again to firm slightly.

4 For the biscuits, preheat the oven to 160°C (325°F/Gas 3). Crush the cardamom pods lightly, tip the seeds into a mortar and grind with a pestle. Add to a food processor with the flours, sugar, and butter, and blitz to combine. Press the mixture into a greased Swiss roll tin and chill for 20 minutes. Bake for about 20 minutes until just golden. Remove from the oven, cut into rectangles, cool for 5 minutes in the tin, then transfer to a wire rack until cold. Store unused biscuits in an airtight container.

5 To serve, place the pots of custard and compôte on serving plates and place a biscuit across the top of each pot.

SEASHORE AND HEDGEROW
Tom Whitaker MasterChef 2011 finalist

PREPARATION TIME
1 hour

COOKING TIME
40–45 minutes

SERVES 6

"I want the pudding to be a little bit of a shocker in some ways."

FOR THE BISCUIT CRUMBLE
100g (3½oz) PLAIN FLOUR
1 tsp BAKING POWDER
pinch of SALT
100g (3½oz) JUMBO OAT FLAKES
40g (1¼oz) GROUND ALMONDS
40g (1¼oz) DEMERARA SUGAR
75g (2¼oz) UNSALTED BUTTER,
  softened
3 EGG YOLKS

FOR THE PUDDING
3 large GELATINE LEAVES
25g (scant 1oz) DRIED
  CARRAGEEN MOSS, washed
250ml (8fl oz) DOUBLE CREAM
1 VANILLA POD, split open
6 EGG YOLKS
100g (3½oz) CASTER SUGAR
100ml (3½fl oz) WHOLE MILK
3 tbsp AGAR-AGAR FLAKES
250ml (8fl oz) BUTTERMILK
175ml (6fl oz) CONDENSED MILK

FOR THE ELDERFLOWER JELLY
300ml (10fl oz) SPARKLING
  ELDERFLOWER JUICE
100g (3½oz) ELDERFLOWERS,
  washed
50g (1¾oz) CASTER SUGAR
4 tbsp AGAR-AGAR FLAKES

FOR THE SAUCE
100g (3½oz) dried ROSEHIPS
100ml (3½fl oz) WATER
30g (1oz) CASTER SUGAR
3 tbsp QUINCE JELLY

TO DECORATE
18 MINT leaves
1 EGG WHITE, whisked
50g (1¾oz) CASTER SUGAR
2 tbsp PUMPKIN SEEDS
12 BLACKBERRIES

1 To make the crumble, preheat the oven to 180°C (350°F/Gas 4). Sift the flour, baking powder, and salt into a bowl and add the oats. Mix the almonds and sugar together and add to the bowl. Rub the softened butter into the mixture, then add the egg yolks and mix until well combined. Line a baking tray with a silicone mat and sprinkle the mixture over. Bake for 15–20 minutes until crisp and golden, then set aside to cool.
2 For the carrageen moss pudding, soak the gelatine leaves in cold water for 10 minutes. Place the carrageen moss in a pan with the cream and vanilla pod and simmer for 2–3 minutes.
3 Meanwhile, whisk the egg yolks and sugar together until smooth and creamy. Pour the infused cream through a sieve into the egg mixture and whisk to combine. Pour the mixture into a clean pan and heat very gently until thickened, being careful not to overheat the mixture. As soon as a thick custard consistency is reached, remove the pan from the heat and immediately transfer the mixture to a jug or bowl.

4 Heat the milk in a small pan until simmering, then add the agar-agar. Simmer without stirring for 2 minutes, then whisk the mixture and simmer until smooth and the agar-agar has melted. Combine this mixture with the custard, then squeeze the excess water from the gelatine leaves and whisk into the mixture.

5 In a separate bowl, whisk together the buttermilk and condensed milk, then whisk into the custard mixture until smooth and fully combined. Divide the mixture between six 100ml (3½fl oz) dariole moulds and chill in the fridge until set.

6 Meanwhile, paint the mint leaves for decoration with egg white and then dust each side with caster sugar. Transfer to a baking tray lined with baking parchmentand leave to dry in a warm place until crisp.

7 For the elderflower jelly, place the elderflower juice, elderflowers, and sugar in a heavy saucepan and simmer for 10 minutes until the sugar has completely dissolved. Strain the liquid into a clean pan and sprinkle the agar-agar over the surface. Simmer without stirring for 2 minutes then whisk and simmer for a further 2–3 minutes until the agar-agar has completely dissolved. Pour the mixture into a small plastic container to a depth of 1.5cm (½in) and transfer to the fridge for 30 minutes to set. Just before serving, turn the jelly out onto a clean chopping board and cut into 1cm (½in) cubes.

8 For the quince and rosehip sauce, bring the rosehips, sugar, water, and quince jelly to a simmer in a small pan and cook for 10 minutes. Remove from the heat and blitz in a food processor until smooth. Pass through a fine sieve and leave to cool. If the mixture is still a little grainy, add a dash of water and pass through a sieve for a second time.

TO SERVE

Remove the moss puddings from the moulds and place at one side of each plate. Pour some of the coulis at an angle across the plate and scatter pieces of the crumble and the pumpkin seeds in and around it. Arrange the cubes of jelly at the other side of the plate and top them and the pudding with the crystallized mint leaves. To finish, arrange 2 blackberries on each plate.

RHUBARB AND STRAWBERRY SOUFFLÉ
Danny Goffey musician and 2011 Celebrity semi-finalist

PREPARATION TIME
15 minutes, plus macerating

COOKING TIME
28 minutes

SERVES 6

FOR THE RHUBARB REDUCTION
500g (1lb 2oz) RHUBARB,
  roughly chopped
200g (7oz) CASTER SUGAR
2 tbsp CORNFLOUR
2 tbsp FRAMBOISE or other
  RASPBERRY LIQUEUR

FOR THE SOUFFLÉS
6 fresh STRAWBERRIES, hulled
  and cut in thirds
3 tbsp STRAWBERRY LIQUEUR
25g (scant 1oz) UNSALTED
  BUTTER, melted
150g (5½oz) CASTER SUGAR
3 EGG WHITES
200ml (3½fl oz) reserved
  RHUBARB REDUCTION

1 For the reduction, place the rhubarb in a saucepan with 100g (3½oz) of the sugar. Bring to the boil, cover, reduce the heat, then simmer for 10 minutes until soft and sticky.
2 Mix the cornflour with the framboise liqueur and stir into the rhubarb until thick. Purée with a hand-held blender. Transfer to a bowl.
3 Mix 100ml (3½fl oz) water and the remaining sugar in a pan and simmer for 5 minutes until the sugar has completely dissolved. Cook for a further 2–3 minutes until the mixture turns pale gold. Remove from the heat immediately or the mixture will caramelize and become hard. Pour the sugar syrup into the rhubarb and stir well.
4 For the soufflés, combine the strawberries with the strawberry liqueur in a bowl. Leave to macerate for 10 minutes and then drain.
5 Preheat the oven to 180°C (350°F/Gas 4). Butter the ramekins using upward strokes, dust them with 3 tbsp of the sugar, and then chill in the fridge until needed.
6 Place the egg whites in a bowl, whisk with an electric whisk until you have soft white peaks, then add the remaining sugar, a little at a time, continuing to whisk until stiff and glossy.
7 Pour 100ml (3½fl oz) of the rhubarb reduction into a large bowl and whisk in a third of the egg whites to loosen. Gently fold in the remaining whites with a metal spoon until just mixed.
8 Half-fill the ramekins with the mixture, then place 3 pieces of soaked strawberries in the middle. Fill with the mixture to the top. Flatten with a palette knife. Run your thumb around the edge of each to make a ridge. Cook in the oven for 10 minutes.
9 Immediately place on serving plates and serve with a little of the remaining rhubarb reduction in tiny jugs on the side.

Simplify for **EVERY**DAY

• Use a drained, large can of rhubarb (add a few drops of pink food colouring if it is not a good colour). • You could omit the macerated strawberries and just put a few sliced ones in the base of the dishes and top with a splash of liqueur if you wish.

CORNISH JUNKET WITH STEWED RHUBARB
Phil Vickery MBE England rugby player and 2011 Celebrity champion

PREPARATION TIME
10 minutes

COOKING TIME
30 minutes, plus cooling

SERVES 4

"I don't think anyone will know what it is, but it's something I ate a lot of as a young kid. It means an awful lot to me."

FOR THE JUNKET
400ml (14fl oz) WHOLE MILK
150ml (5fl oz) WHIPPING CREAM
50g (1¾oz) CASTER SUGAR
1 VANILLA POD, split and
   seeds scraped out
2–3 parings of LEMON zest
pinch of freshly grated NUTMEG,
   plus extra for sprinkling
1 tsp RENNET

FOR THE RHUBARB
3 sticks of RHUBARB
50g (1¾oz) CASTER SUGAR,
   or to taste
finely grated zest of 1 LEMON

1 For the junket, place the milk, cream, sugar, vanilla pod and seeds, and lemon zest into a saucepan and gently heat to 37°C (98.6°F).
2 When up to temperature, remove the zest and vanilla pod and pour the mixture into a large jug with a pinch of grated nutmeg. Add the rennet and stir.
3 Pour into serving dishes and leave to set at room temperature. Once set, place in the fridge to cool for 45 minutes. Just before serving, sprinkle a little more freshly grated nutmeg over the top.
4 Cut the rhubarb into 5cm (2in) lengths and put into a pan with a splash of water. Add half the caster sugar and the lemon zest. Cook until tender, ensuring that the rhubarb retains its shape as much as possible. Taste and add more sugar if necessary – you need to keep some sharpness in the rhubarb to contrast with the junket. Leave to cool, then chill in the fridge until needed.
5 Serve the junket topped with the rhubarb.

Nutmeg is valued for its warm aroma and bittersweet, woody flavour. Whole nutmeg will keep almost indefinitely in an airtight container to be freshly grated when required.

LIQUORICE-POACHED PEARS WITH A SABLÉ BISCUIT AND PRALINE-COATED MILK AND HONEY ICE CREAM
Tom Whitaker MasterChef 2011 finalist

PREPARATION TIME
1 hour 15 minutes, plus
chilling and freezing

COOKING TIME
30 minutes

SERVES 4

Ice cream

FOR THE ICE CREAM
600ml (1 pint) WHOLE MILK
2 tbsp CLEAR HONEY
1½ tsp LIQUID GLUCOSE
5 tbsp CONDENSED MILK
4 tbsp DOUBLE CREAM

FOR THE PRALINE
100g (3½oz) CASTER SUGAR
25g (scant 1oz) toasted,
  flaked ALMONDS

FOR THE MINT LEAVES
12 large MINT leaves
1 EGG WHITE
CASTER SUGAR

1 Make the milk and honey ice cream. Put the milk and honey into a pan, bring to the boil, and reduce by half. Strain into a jug and leave to cool. When cooled, whisk in the glucose, condensed milk, and double cream.
2 Pour the mixture into an ice-cream machine and churn until set. Transfer to a plastic container with a lid and store in the freezer until serving. Alternatively, pour the mixture in a freezerproof container and freeze until mushy. Whisk until the ice crystals are broken up. Return to the freezer and repeat the process twice.
3 Meanwhile, make the praline. Line a baking tray with baking parchment. Put the sugar into a wide pan and heat, without stirring, until it caramelizes and turns a deep golden brown, about 140–150°C (275–300°F) on a sugar thermometer. Remove from the heat and add the flaked almonds.
4 Pour the mixture on to the prepared baking tray and spread out with a spatula. Allow to cool until hard and brittle, then break into smaller pieces and place in a food processor. Blitz until crumbly.
5 Meanwhile, prepare the crystallized mint leaves. Wash the leaves and pat dry on kitchen paper. Beat the egg white lightly with a fork on a plate and dip the leaves in it. Drain off excess egg white, sprinkle liberally with caster sugar. Place on baking parchment on a baking tray and leave to dry in a warm place.

Poached pears

FOR THE POACHED PEARS
300g (10oz) CASTER SUGAR
1 LIQUORICE STICK
2 tsp LIQUORICE ESSENCE
4 tsp CRÈME DE CASSIS
2 WILLIAMS PEARS

FOR THE SABLÉ BISCUITS
30g (1oz) ICING SUGAR,
  plus extra for dusting
125g (4½oz) UNSALTED
  BUTTER, cubed

1 VANILLA POD, seeds only
125g (4½oz) PLAIN FLOUR

FOR THE BRANDY CREAM
120ml (4fl oz) DOUBLE CREAM
1 tsp ICING SUGAR
4 tsp reserved POACHING
  SYRUP REDUCTION
1 tsp BRANDY

TO SERVE
4 tsp reserved POACHING
  SYRUP REDUCTION
1 tsp BRANDY

1 First, make the poaching syrup for the pears. Put 50g (1¾oz) of the sugar in a pan, melt on high heat until it is a rich, dark caramel. Do not stir. Add 500ml (16fl oz) hot water (take care, it may splutter), the remaining 250g (9oz) sugar, the liquorice stick, liquorice essence, and crème de cassis. Stir until dissolved, then leave to infuse for 20 minutes.
2 Bring the mixture back to the boil, peel, core and halve the pears, add to poaching syrup. Immediately remove from the heat, cover, and leave to infuse for 15–20 minutes until translucent. Remove the pears with a slotted spoon. Set aside to cool.
3 Pour half of the poaching liquid into a separate pan and reduce until syrupy. Set aside the poaching syrup reduction to cool.
4 Meanwhile, make the sablé biscuits. Sift the icing sugar into a bowl, add the butter and vanilla seeds, and stir to combine. Sift in the flour and rub in with the fingertips to form a smooth dough. Using a large sheet of cling film, roll the dough into a log shape and chill in the fridge until firm.
5 Preheat the oven to 180°C (350°F/Gas 4). Slice the dough into 5mm (¼in) thick rounds and place well apart on a baking tray lined with baking parchment. Bake for 10–12 minutes until pale gold. Dust with icing sugar. Transfer to a wire rack to cool.
6 Whisk the brandy cream ingredients until peaking. Chill.

TO SERVE
Lay 3 frosted mint leaves in a three-cornered star on each serving plate. Quickly coat 4 scoops of the ice cream in the praline crumbs and place in the centre of the mint leaves. Add a poached pear half to one side of each plate. Mix the poaching syrup reduction with the brandy and spoon a little in each pear cavity. Top each with a quenelle of the brandy cream. Lay a sablé biscuit to one side of the pears and serve immediately.

SUMMER COMFORT

GREGG WALLACE'S NO-NONSENSE TAKE ON TOM'S DESSERT LOOKS GREAT AND TASTES SENSATIONAL

PREP: 30 MINS + FREEZING

ICE CREAM

SERVES 4

600ml (1 pint) WHOLE MILK
1 VANILLA POD, split open
6 EGG YOLKS
6 tbsp CLEAR HONEY
2 tsp CORNFLOUR

1 Bring the milk and vanilla to just below the boil. Then remove from the heat and leave to cool slightly.
2 Whisk the egg yolks, honey, and cornflour together, then slowly pour on the milk, whisking constantly. Strain back into the saucepan. Cook gently, stirring, until thickened slightly. Do not boil or the custard will curdle. Pour into a jug. Set aside to cool. Stir often.
3 Pour the cold custard into an ice cream machine and churn until set. Transfer to a plastic container with a lid and put in the freezer until serving. Alternatively, pour the mixture in a freezerproof container and freeze until mushy. Whisk to break up ice crystals. Freeze again. Repeat twice more.

"A simple custard ice cream with sticky toffee sauce is a marriage made in taste-heaven! Absolutely divine."

POACHED PEARS

200g (7oz) CASTER SUGAR
2 whole STAR ANISE
1 VANILLA POD, split open
4 small DESSERT PEARS, peeled, but left whole

1 Place the sugar and 300ml (10fl oz) water in a saucepan with the star anise and vanilla, and heat gently until sugar has dissolved. Bring to the boil and boil for 6 minutes.
2 Add the pears to the syrup and poach for 5–10 minutes, turning once. This will depend on the size of your fruit, but cook until the fruit look translucent and are tender but still hold their shape. Remove with a slotted spoon.

STICKY TOFFEE SAUCE

75g (2½oz) UNSALTED BUTTER
75g (2½oz) SOFT DARK BROWN SUGAR
100ml (3½fl oz) DOUBLE CREAM
1 tbsp TOASTED FLAKED ALMONDS
   and tiny MINT SPRIGS, to decorate

1 Melt the butter and sugar together over low heat until the sugar has dissolved.
2 Slowly stir in the cream and boil, stirring, for 3–4 minutes until you have a smooth, thick sauce.
3 Stand the pears on plates with scoops of ice cream. Top with the sauce, almonds, and mint.

BANANA COFFEE PIE AND PEAR PUDDING WITH CUSTARD

Linda Lusardi *actress and 2011 Celebrity semi-finalist*

PREPARATION TIME
40 minutes

COOKING TIME
50 minutes

SERVES 4

FOR THE PASTRY
200g (7oz) PLAIN FLOUR
100g (3½oz) BUTTER, cubed
50g (1¾oz) CASTER SUGAR
2 EGG YOLKS, beaten
1 tsp PURE VANILLA EXTRACT

FOR THE PIE FILLING
100g (3½oz) DARK CHOCOLATE,
   70% cocoa solids
100g (3½oz) MILK CHOCOLATE
2 large BANANAS
100ml (3½fl oz) SKIMMED MILK
1 tsp GROUND CINNAMON
40g (1¼oz) CASTER SUGAR
300ml (10fl oz) DOUBLE CREAM
1 tbsp CAMP COFFEE
   FLAVOURING
30g (1oz) DARK CHOCOLATE,
   grated

FOR THE PEAR PUDDING
75g (2½oz) PLAIN FLOUR
2 tbsp ICING SUGAR, plus extra
   for dusting
1 tsp GROUND CINNAMON
1 EGG
120ml (4fl oz) SEMI-SKIMMED
   MILK
50g (1¾oz) CASTER SUGAR
4 small DESSERT PEARS, peeled
   and thinly sliced
100g (3½oz) SULTANAS
2 tsp OLIVE OIL

FOR THE CUSTARD
2 EGG YOLKS
2 tbsp CASTER SUGAR
1 tsp CORNFLOUR
250ml (8fl oz) WHOLE MILK
1 tsp PURE VANILLA EXTRACT

1 For the pastry, preheat the oven to 200°C (400°F/Gas 6). Sift the flour into a bowl, then add the butter and rub together with your fingertips until the mixture resembles breadcrumbs.
2 Stir in the sugar, egg yolks, vanilla extract, and 1–2 tbsp water to form a firm dough. Knead gently until smooth.
3 Wrap in cling film and chill in the fridge for 30 minutes.
4 Once chilled, remove from the fridge and roll out thinly. Use the pastry to line 4, individual, 12cm (5in) round tart tins and chill in the fridge for a further 30 minutes.
5 Line the pastry cases with greaseproof paper and fill with baking beans. Bake for 10 minutes. Remove the baking beans and paper and bake for a further 5 minutes until the pastry is cooked through. Transfer to a wire rack and leave to cool completely.
6 For the pie filling, break the dark and milk chocolates into small pieces, then put into a bowl set over a pan of simmering water. Stir until melted, then remove from the pan and cool.
7 Put 1 of the bananas in a blender with the milk, cinnamon, and 20g (¾oz) of the sugar and blend until smooth.
8 Heat the remaining sugar in a small frying pan until brown and bubbling. Stir in the banana mix. Cook for 2 minutes, stirring.

9 Divide the mixture between the pastry cases and place the cases in the fridge for 15 minutes. Once cooled, slice the other banana and top each tart with the slices.

10 Whisk the cream and coffee extract to soft peaks, spoon over the top of the tarts, and sprinkle with the grated chocolate. Chill until ready to serve.

11 To make the pear puddings, first preheat the oven to 200°C (400°F/Gas 6). Sift the flour, icing sugar, and cinnamon into a bowl, then make a well in the centre, add the egg, and whisk. Gradually add the milk, whisking continuously until you have a smooth batter.

12 Heat 3 tbsp water and the sugar together in a frying pan until the sugar has dissolved. Cook for a further 2–3 minutes until the sugar starts to caramelize, then add the pears and sultanas. Cook for 2 minutes until the pears start to soften, then remove the pan from the heat.

13 Pour a little oil into 4 of the holes of a deep 6-hole muffin tin. Place the tray in the oven for 5 minutes until the oil is hot.

14 Divide the pears and sultanas between the muffin tins, then pour the batter over the top, ensuring that the fruit is completely covered. Bake for 20 minutes until risen and golden.

15 Remove from the oven and leave to cool slightly.

16 Meanwhile, make the custard. Beat together the egg yolks, caster sugar, and cornflour until pale.

17 Heat the milk in a pan until nearly boiling, then remove from the heat and pour onto the yolk mixture. Whisk until smooth, then return to a clean pan. Add the vanilla extract and cook over low heat until thickened, stirring all the time. Remove from the heat and pour into 4 small jugs.

18 To plate, place a banana coffee pie on each of 4 plates. Carefully turn out the pear puddings and place one on each plate alongside. Dust with sifted icing sugar. Stand the jugs of custard on the plates and serve straight away.

MANGO PARFAIT AND PASSION FRUIT GLAZE WITH A LIME AND VODKA SORBET

Sara Danesin Medio MasterChef 2011 finalist

PREPARATION TIME
1 hour, plus chilling
and freezing

COOKING TIME
10–30 minutes

SERVES 6

FOR THE LIME SORBET
250ml (8fl oz) WATER
225g (8oz) SUGAR
200ml (7fl oz) fresh LIME JUICE
1 tsp grated LIME zest
80ml (2½fl oz) VODKA

FOR THE PARFAIT
3 large EGG YOLKS
75g (2½oz) CASTER SUGAR
250g (9oz) ALPHONSO
  MANGO PURÉE
175g (6oz) DOUBLE CREAM

FOR THE GLAZE
2 GELATINE LEAVES
5 fresh PASSION FRUIT, split
20g (³/₄oz) CASTER SUGAR

TO SERVE
1 large, ripe ALPHONSO MANGO,
  thinly sliced, with six
  6cm (2½in) squares cut
6 sprigs of MICRO RED AMARANTH
3 VANILLA PODS, halved and split

1 First make the sorbet. Heat the water and sugar in a saucepan until the sugar has dissolved. Transfer to a jug and combine with the lime juice and zest and vodka. Leave to cool, then pour into an ice-cream machine and churn until set. Transfer to a plastic container with a lid, store in the freezer until ready to serve. Alternatively, place the mixture in a freezerproof container and freeze until mushy. Whisk until the ice crystals are broken up. Return to the freezer and repeat the process twice.
2 Next, make the parfait. Wrap cling film around the bases of six 6cm (2½in) square metal mousse moulds, each 3cm (1¼in) deep, to create a tight seal. Place the moulds on a baking tray.
3 Place the egg yolks and sugar in a heatproof bowl and beat lightly to mix. Set the bowl over a pan of lightly simmering water, making sure the base does not touch the water. Whisk the mixture until it triples in volume and is thick and pale. When you lift the beaters, the mixture should be thick enough to leave a ribbon trail across the surface. Fold in the mango purée.
4 In a separate bowl, whip the cream to soft peaks then fold carefully into the mango mixture. Divide the mixture between the lined moulds and transfer to the freezer for 2 hours until firm.
5 Soak the gelatine in cold water for 10 minutes, or until soft. Place the passion fruit juice and seeds in a small pan with the sugar. Gently heat to a simmer, then remove from the heat. Drain the gelatine, squeezing out any excess water, then whisk into the passion fruit until dissolved. Transfer to a bowl and refrigerate for 1 hour, until almost set. Spoon over the parfaits. Chill to set.
6 Lay the mango squares in dishes and top with sorbet and a sprig of amaranth. Unmould the parfaits alongside. Decorate each with a slice of mango and a split vanilla pod.

AMERICAN LUNCHBOX
Tim Anderson MasterChef 2011 champion

PREPARATION TIME
1 hour 45 minutes, plus
chilling and freezing

COOKING TIME
30 minutes

SERVES 4

Peanut Butter and Jelly "Sandwich"

FOR THE CAKE
75g (2½oz) UNSALTED BUTTER
50g (1¾oz) SMOOTH PEANUT
  BUTTER
100g (3½oz) CASTER SUGAR
5 tbsp CRÈME FRAÎCHE
2 EGGS
100g (3½oz) SELF-RAISING FLOUR

FOR THE BANANA BUTTER
3 very ripe BANANAS, peeled and
  roughly chopped

50g (1¾oz) UNSALTED BUTTER
100g (3½oz) CASTER SUGAR
freshly grated NUTMEG, to taste

FOR THE STRAWBERRY JELLY
120ml (4fl oz) GERMAN
  WHEAT BEER
250g (9oz) STRAWBERRIES,
  hulled, and quartered
125g (4½oz) CASTER SUGAR
1 tsp AGAR-AGAR FLAKES

1 For the cake, preheat the oven to 180°C (350°F/Gas 4).
Grease and line a 25 x 15cm (10 x 6in) non-stick baking tin.
2 Cream the butter together with the peanut butter, sugar,
and crème fraîche until smooth and creamy. Gradually add
the eggs and mix until smooth. Fold in the flour, pour into the
lined tin, and bake for 20–25 minutes until golden. Transfer
to a wire rack and leave to cool completely.
3 Once cool, trim the edges of the cake, then cut into four
10 x 6cm (4 x 2½in) rectangles. Cut each piece through
the middle to make 4 "sandwiches". Set aside until needed.
4 For the banana butter, put all the ingredients in a pan and
simmer gently for 10 minutes until the bananas are completely
soft. Rub the mixture through a sieve and chill until serviing.
5 For the strawberry jelly, put all the ingredients in a pan,
bring to the boil, and simmer gently until the strawberries
are completely soft. Cool to set.
6 Just before serving, spread 4 slices of cake with the banana
butter, add the strawberry jelly, and top with the remaining
slices of cake to make 4 sandwiches.

Mochi Sorbet "Apple"

FOR THE SORBET
250ml (8fl oz) APPLE JUICE
juice of ½ LIME
4 tbsp GOLDEN SYRUP

FOR THE MOCHI
pinch of SAFFRON
2 tbsp CASTER SUGAR
4 tbsp BEETROOT JUICE
4 tbsp CRANBERRY JUICE

1 tbsp GOLDEN SYRUP
185g (6½oz) MOCHIKO
  (Japanese rice flour)
pinch of SALT
PLAIN FLOUR, for dusting
25g (scant 1oz) UNSALTED
  BUTTER, for frying

1 For the sorbet, mix together the juices and syrup, then churn in an ice-cream machine until set. Transfer to a plastic container with a lid and place in the freezer until serving. Alternatively, place the mixture in a freezerproof container and freeze until mushy. Whisk until the ice crystals are broken up. Return to the freezer and repeat the process twice.
2 For the mochi, grind the saffron together with the caster sugar in a pestle and mortar until powdered. Put in a pan with the juices, 3 tbsp water, and syrup. Heat gently, stirring, until dissolved.
3 While still warm, whisk in the mochiko and salt until a sticky dough is formed. Wrap in cling film and chill for 1 hour until firm.
4 On a well-floured surface, roll out the mochi to 3mm (⅛in) thick, then cut out four 10cm (4in) circles.
5 Melt the butter in a frying pan and fry the discs for 8 minutes, turning often, until golden brown. Remove from the pan, drain on kitchen paper, and leave to cool completely. Serve underneath the sorbet as a platform.

Filo "Crisps"

3 sheets FILO PASTRY
100g (3½oz) UNSALTED
  BUTTER, melted

50g (1¾oz) ICING SUGAR,
  plus extra for dusting
50g (1¾oz) dry-roasted PEANUTS
1 tsp GROUND CINNAMON

1 Preheat the oven to 200°C (400°F/Gas 6). For the "crisp packets", brush 1 sheet of filo pastry with butter and dust with icing sugar. Cut the sheet into quarters and fold each piece in half. Fold 4 pieces of foil to fit inside the filo flaps to support the openings and make loose crisp-bag shapes. Place on a baking tray and bake for 5–6 minutes until golden. Cool, then remove the foil.

2 For the filo "crisps", brush the remaining 2 filo sheets with butter and dust with icing sugar. Use a 5cm (2in) biscuit cutter to press out circles of pastry. Roll up 2 or 3 sausage shapes of foil and place on a baking tray. Drape the pastry discs over the foil to form curled crisp shapes. Bake for 4–5 minutes until crisp and golden. Carefully remove from the foil. Cool on a wire rack.
3 Blitz the icing sugar, peanuts, and cinnamon in a food processor until powdered, then sift over the filo "crisps" whilst still hot.
4 Serve the "crisps" spilling out of the filo "packets".

"Chocolate Milk"

250ml (8fl oz) OATMEAL STOUT
  (e.g. Samuel Smith's or
  Mackeson's)
50ml (1¾fl oz) COCONUT MILK

1½ tsp PURE VANILLA EXTRACT
2–3 tsp brewed ESPRESSO

1 Blend ingredients together until well blended, then chill in the fridge until ready to serve, poured in glasses.

TO SERVE
Arrange the sandwich, apple, and crisps on each of 4 plates. Serve with the "chocolate milk" alongside.

AMERICAN ICE – NICE!

GREGG WALLACE CAPTURES ALL THE FLAVOURS OF TIM'S AMERICAN LUNCHBOX, CREATING THE PERFECT FAMILY DESSERT **PREP: 30 MINS + FREEZING TIME**

APPLE SORBET

SERVES 4

50g (1¾oz) CASTER SUGAR
500ml (16fl oz) cloudy fresh APPLE JUICE
juice of ½ LEMON
4 ready made TRIFLE SPONGES

1 Heat 100ml (3½fl oz) water and the sugar gently until the sugar has melted, then boil for 3–5 minutes or until syrupy. Remove from the heat and cool.
2 Stir the syrup into the apple juice and add the lemon juice. Ideally, pour into an ice cream maker and churn until set.
3 Transfer to a freezerproof container and store in the freezer. Alternatively, pour the mixture into a shallow freezerproof container and freeze until mushy. Whisk to break up the ice crystals then return to the freezer. Repeat twice until the sorbet is softly frozen.

"This delicious sorbet is so easy to make! I love it with any one of the toppings scattered over. It's a really easy dessert to have to hand and you could put out all the toppings for a fun sharing experience."

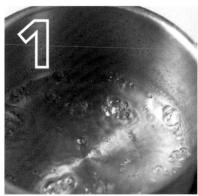

Heat the water and sugar in a pan until melted. Boil to form a syrup.

Pour the syrup into the apple juice in a bowl and stir to combine.

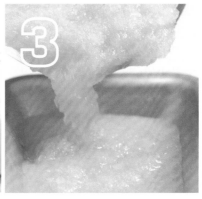

Freeze until the sorbet is mushy. Whisk, then freeze until softly frozen.

PEANUT AND JELLO TOPPING

75g (2½oz) smooth STRAWBERRY JAM
30g (1oz) SALTED PEANUTS, chopped to sprinkle

1 Melt the strawberry jam and 1–2 tsp water together in a small saucepan over a gentle heat until smooth and pourable, then leave until almost cold.
2 Spoon onto the sorbet (see To Assemble below) and sprinkle with chopped peanuts.

MAPLE SYRUP AND APPLE TOPPING

1 sweet DESSERT APPLE, cored and thinly sliced
2 tbsp MAPLE SYRUP
a sprinkling of chopped PECAN NUTS

1 Pile the apple slices on the sorbet (see to assemble below).
2 Drizzle the maple syrup over, and finish with a scattering of chopped pecan nuts.

BANOFFEE TOPPING

75g (2½oz) DULCE DE LÊCHE (readymade caramel such as Casa Argentina available from leading supermarkets)
1 BANANA, peeled and sliced

1 Heat the dulce de lêche in a small saucepan until pourable.
2 Pile the banana on the sorbet (see to assemble below) and spoon the dulce de lêche over.

TO ASSEMBLE
Place the sponges on individual serving plates. Top each with a few scoops of sorbet and then the topping of your choice.

WHAT'S IN MY FRIDGE?

FOR THOSE TIMES WHEN YOU OPEN YOUR FRIDGE AND THINK "WHAT CAN I MAKE WITH THAT?"

Here are four quick, easy, and delicious recipes for each **EVERY**DAY ingredient.

CHICKEN+

SOY SAUCE+HONEY+ NOODLES=SOY CHICKEN WITH NOODLES

SERVES 4 Cut 2 large (or 4 small) skinless CHICKEN BREASTS into slices. Stir-fry in 1 tbsp SUNFLOWER OIL for 3–4 minutes until cooked and golden. Add 1 tbsp SESAME OIL (optional), 2 tbsp SOY SAUCE, 1 tbsp CLEAR HONEY, a good pinch CHINESE FIVE-SPICE powder, 1 crushed GARLIC clove, and 300g (10oz) ready-to-wok (or freshly cooked), UDON or RICE NOODLES. Toss and stir until coated and hot. Add a handful of torn BASIL leaves and toss again. Serve straight away, on a bed of fresh wilted SPINACH.

LEMON+HONEY= GRILLED LEMON AND HONEY CHICKEN

SERVES 4 In a large, shallow dish, mix 1½ tbsp CLEAR HONEY with 1 large crushed GARLIC clove, juice of 1 small LEMON, 2 tbsp SOY SAUCE, 2 tbsp OLIVE OIL, 3 tbsp BALSAMIC VINEGAR, and some SALT and freshly ground BLACK PEPPER. Score one side of 4 skinless CHICKEN BREASTS in a criss-cross pattern. Add to the dish and turn to coat in the marinade. Cover and chill for 2 hours. Cook under a preheated grill for 15–20 minutes, turning and basting occasionally with any remaining marinade. Serve sliced with MAYONNAISE, flavoured with a little DIJON MUSTARD, LEMON JUICE, and some chopped BASIL.

SERENA CRUMP MASTERCHEF 2011 CONTESTANT
"I love to buy whole chicken legs then take the thigh bone out, and stuff and roll before roasting. Slice the stuffed chicken before serving. Very easy but looks impressive!"

CHILLI+CORIANDER=
CHICKEN AND CHILLI BURGERS

SERVES 4 Put a quartered ONION, 4 skinless CHICKEN BREASTS, 2 halved GARLIC cloves, 2 deseeded RED CHILLIES, and a handful of chopped CORIANDER in a food processor. SEASON to taste, and pulse until combined – be careful not to turn the mixture into a paste. Tip the mixture out into a bowl and mix in 1 tbsp PLAIN FLOUR and 1 beaten EGG. Using your hands, scoop a small handful of the mixture, roll, then flatten into a burger. Repeat until all the mixture has been used. Chill for 30 minutes to firm up. Preheat the grill. Brush the burgers with OIL. Grill for 8–10 minutes on each side until golden and cooked through. Serve in buns with LEMON-FLAVOURED MAYONNAISE and sliced TOMATOES.

PEANUT BUTTER+LIME+
COCONUT MILK=
CHICKEN SATAY

SERVES 4 Soak 12 wooden skewers in water for 30 minutes. Slice 4 skinless CHICKEN BREASTS into 3 strips lengthways. Mix 1 tbsp GROUNDNUT OIL, 2 tbsp SOY SAUCE, 1 tsp THAI FISH SAUCE, 2 crushed GARLIC cloves, and 2 tsp LIME JUICE, in a shallow dish. Add the chicken, coat, and chill. In a small pan, mix 2 tbsp CRUNCHY PEANUT BUTTER with 2 tsp LIME JUICE, 1 tbsp CLEAR HONEY, 1 tbsp SOY SAUCE, 120ml (4fl oz) COCONUT MILK, and ¼ tsp CHILLI POWDER. Simmer, stirring, until the sauce thickens. Add a little WATER if too thick. Preheat the grill. Thread the chicken concertina-style onto the skewers. Grill for 8 minutes, turning occasionally, until cooked through. Serve with satay sauce, for dipping.

BACON+

FRISÉE LETTUCE+EGGS= BISTRO SALAD

SERVES 4 Make the dressing first. Whisk 2 tbsp CIDER VINEGAR with 1 tsp WHOLEGRAIN MUSTARD, 1 tbsp chopped TARRAGON, 6 tbsp EXTRA VIRGIN OLIVE OIL, and some SALT and freshly ground BLACK PEPPER. Break up a FRISÉE LETTUCE into small sprigs and place in 4 bowls, with some halved CHERRY TOMATOES, 85g (3oz) WALNUT PIECES, and ¼ diced CUCUMBER. Dry-fry 175g (6oz) BACON LARDONS until crisp. Scatter over. Poach 4 EGGS and transfer to the bowls with a slotted spoon. Drizzle over the dressing and serve immediately, while the eggs are still warm.

EGGS+CHEESE+ BREADCRUMBS=SAVOURY CHEESE AND BACON MUFFINS

SERVES 4 Preheat the oven to 190°C (375°F/Gas 5). Fry 5 BACK BACON RASHERS over medium-high heat until cooked but not too crisp, then cut into bite-sized pieces. Mix together 200g (7oz) diced CHEDDAR CHEESE with 125g (4½oz) fresh BREADCRUMBS, ½ bunch of finely chopped SPRING ONIONS, 3 beaten EGGS, and 100ml (3½fl oz) MILK. Stir through the BACON and a handful of snipped CHIVES. SEASON to taste, then spoon into buttered, individual pudding moulds or ramekins. Bake for about 25 minutes until risen and golden.

CHORIZO+LENTILS=
SPANISH LENTILS

SERVES 4 Fry 2 sliced GARLIC cloves in 1 tbsp OLIVE OIL, stirring for 30 seconds. Remove from the pan. Add a slice of BREAD and brown on both sides. Process the bread and garlic to coarse crumbs in a food processor. Tip into a saucepan and stir in 2 drained 400g (14oz) cans BROWN LENTILS and 120ml (4fl oz) VEGETABLE STOCK. Add a BAY LEAF and heat through. Fry 175g (6oz) thick, diced STREAKY BACON or TOCINO, a finely chopped ONION and 115g (4oz) thickly sliced CHORIZO in 1 tbsp OLIVE OIL, stirring, for about 4 minutes until golden. Stir in 1 tsp SMOKED PAPRIKA. Add to the lentils, stir and simmer gently for 5–10 minutes until hot through, adding a little more stock, if necessary. Taste and re-season. Serve with CRUSTY BREAD.

BREAD+LETTUCE+
TOMATOES=BLT

SERVES 4 Grill or fry 12 SMOKED BACK BACON rashers until crisp. Drain on kitchen paper. Lightly toast 8 slices of BREAD on both sides, then spread with BUTTER. Spread 4 slices with MAYONNAISE. Top with some shredded ICEBERG LETTUCE, 3 bacon rashers per slice, more lettuce, then 2 ripe, sliced TOMATOES. Top with the remaining 4 buttered toast slices, press down and cut each in half. Secure each sandwich with a cocktail stick and serve straight away.

FISH+

RICE+GREEN BEANS+ARTICHOKES=FISH AND ARTICHOKE PILAF

SERVES 4–6 In a large frying pan or wok, gently fry 1 finely chopped ONION and 200g (7oz) GREEN BEANS, cut in short lengths, in 2 tbsp OLIVE OIL for 5 minutes to soften. Stir in ½ tsp GROUND TURMERIC, 2 crushed GARLIC cloves, and 400g (14oz) BASMATI RICE, until glistening. Add 1.4 litres (2½ pints) hot VEGETABLE STOCK, bring to the boil, reduce the heat to low, stir, cover, and simmer for 15 minutes. Add 280g (10oz) jar ARTICHOKE HEARTS, drained and halved, 4 chopped TOMATOES, a pinch of HOT PAPRIKA, and 675g (1½lb) any meaty FISH FILLET, skinned, and cut in chunks. Stir gently and SEASON. Cover and cook for a further 5 minutes or until the fish and rice are cooked. Add 2 tbsp chopped PARSLEY and the juice of a LEMON. Fluff up with a fork and serve.

SOY SAUCE+PINEAPPLE JUICE=SWEET AND SOUR FISH

SERVES 4 Mix 1 tbsp each of WHITE WINE VINEGAR, SOY SAUCE, TOMATO PURÉE, and SUGAR with 1 tsp CORNFLOUR, and 2 tbsp PINEAPPLE JUICE. Cut 675g (1½lb) skinned WHITE FISH or SALMON FILLETS into thin strips, and toss in 2 tbsp SEASONED CORNFLOUR. In a wok, heat 1 tbsp SUNFLOWER OIL, add the fish, and stir-fry for 5 minutes until golden, and then remove. Wipe the wok clean, add 1 tbsp OIL, and stir-fry 1 chopped ONION until soft. Add 2 chopped GARLIC cloves, 1 tsp grated FRESH GINGER, and a large handful of MANGETOUT or ¼ CUCUMBER, cut in strips. Stir-fry 1 minute. Pour in the sweet and sour sauce, cook, stirring, until thickened. Return the fish to the wok. Toss, until hot. Serve with RICE.

ANNIE ASSHETON MASTERCHEF 2011 FINAL 6
"Use leftover fish to make your children home-made fish fingers – use pesto to stick the breadcrumbs on. It's quick and easy and absolutely yummy."

TOMATOES+PASTRY=
TARTE AU POISSONS

SERVES 4 Preheat the oven to 200°C (400°F/Gas 6). Line a 20cm (8in) flan dish with shortcrust pastry, greaseproof paper and baking beans. Bake for 10 minutes. Remove the paper and beans and bake for a further 5 minutes to dry out. Set aside. Reduce the oven temperature to 160°C (325°F/Gas 3). Cook 1 finely chopped ONION in 45g (1½oz) BUTTER for 5 minutes to soften. Add 4 skinned and chopped TOMATOES, and 1 crushed GARLIC clove. Cool slightly. Stir in 2 tsp chopped THYME, some freshly grated NUTMEG, 150ml (5fl oz) SINGLE CREAM, and 2 beaten EGGS. SEASON to taste. Put 175g (6oz) any flaked, cooked FISH, or PRAWNS, into the pastry case. Top with the tomato mixture. Sprinkle with 1 tbsp grated GRUYÈRE CHEESE. Bake for 30 minutes or until set and golden.

NOODLES+SPRING ONIONS
=FISH AND NOODLE SALAD

SERVES 4 Cook 250g (9oz) UDON NOODLES. Drain and rinse with cold water, and put in a bowl. Add 300g (10oz) cooked flaked SALMON (or TUNA), a few sliced SPRING ONIONS, and 2 tbsp chopped BASIL leaves. Add some raw sliced MUSHROOMS too, if you have any. Whisk together 3 tbsp EXTRA VIRGIN OLIVE OIL, 1 tbsp WHITE WINE VINEGAR, 2 tsp LIME JUICE, a pinch each of SUGAR, GROUND GINGER, and DRIED CHILLI FLAKES, and a splash of THAI FISH SAUCE. SEASON to taste. Pour over the fish and noodles, and toss gently. Pile onto plates and garnish with a few extra torn BASIL leaves. Serve with SWEET CHILLI SAUCE to drizzle over.

EGGS+

BUTTER=
THE PERFECT OMELETTE

SERVES 1 Lightly whisk 2 EGGS with a splash of WATER and season with SALT and freshly ground BLACK PEPPER. Heat a small frying pan until hot and add a knob of BUTTER. Once the butter is melted and foaming, pour in the egg mixture, and pull the edges away from the side of the pan towards the centre using a spatula or fish slice. Keep doing this so that any uncooked mixture runs to the edge. After about 30 seconds, most of the egg will be set. It will be still soft and creamy in the middle. Sprinkle a handful of grated CHEESE (optional) down the centre of the omelette, then fold one half of the omelette over the top of the other. Slide onto a plate, and serve immediately, garnished with ROCKET.

POTATOES+ONIONS=
TORTILLA

SERVES 4 Heat 4 tbsp OLIVE OIL in a large non-stick frying pan. Add 2 large, diced POTATOES, and 1 finely chopped ONION. Fry gently, stirring frequently, until soft but not brown (or use cooked leftover potatoes and add when onion is soft). Add some cooked, leftover BROCCOLI, cut in small florets, and PEAS (optional). Beat 6 EGGS with some SEASONING and pour into the pan. Stir gently. Continue to cook over gentle heat for 20–25 minutes, until the omelette is golden underneath, and almost set. Loosen the edge, invert onto a plate then slide back into the pan. Cook for a further 5 minutes to brown the other side. Cut into wedges, and serve warm or cold.

ELIZABETH ALLEN MASTERCHEF 2011 CONTESTANT
"Always let eggs come to room temperature before using.
This helps prevent mayonnaise or emulsions from splitting."

TOMATOES+CREAM=
BAKED EGGS WITH TOMATOES

SERVES 4 Preheat the oven to 180°C (350°F/Gas 4). Spoon 1 tbsp DOUBLE CREAM into each of 4 ramekins, then break an EGG into each one, taking care not to break the yolks. Top each egg with another tbsp double cream and 1 tbsp chopped skinned or canned TOMATOES. Sprinkle with SALT and freshly ground BLACK PEPPER. Sit the ramekins in a roasting tin, and pour in hot water to come just halfway up their sides. Cover the roasting tin with foil, then carefully slide into the oven. Cook for about 15 minutes or until cooked to your liking. Serve immediately.

SPINACH+CHEESE SAUCE
=EGGS FLORENTINE

SERVES 4 Whisk 4 tbsp PLAIN FLOUR with 300ml (10fl oz) MILK in a saucepan. Add 30g (1oz) BUTTER, cook, whisking all the time, until thick and smooth. SEASON to taste and whisk in 2 EGG YOLKS, 2 tbsp SINGLE CREAM and 85g (3oz) grated GRUYÈRE CHEESE. Soften 2 chopped SHALLOTS in 30g (1oz) BUTTER for 2–3 minutes. Add 450g (1lb) SPINACH, cover, and cook for a few minutes, stirring occasionally until wilted. Drain well and divide among 4 ramekins. Poach 4 EGGS in gently simmering water with a splash of VINEGAR added, for 3–5 minutes until cooked to your liking. Drain with a slotted spoon and place on the spinach. Spoon the sauce over. Sprinkle with 30g (1oz) grated GRUYÈRE CHEESE. Cook under a preheated grill until golden and bubbling. Serve hot with BUTTERED TOAST.

CHEESE+

EGGS=CHEESE SOUFFLÉ

SERVES 4 Melt 45g (1½oz) BUTTER in a small saucepan. Stir in 45g (1½oz) PLAIN FLOUR and cook for 1 minute, stirring. Whisk in 250ml (8fl oz) MILK until blended, then bring to the boil, stirring constantly, until thick and smooth. Remove the pan from the heat, SEASON, and stir in 125g (4½oz) grated CHEDDAR CHEESE and ½ tsp DIJON MUSTARD. Preheat the oven to 190°C (375°F/Gas 5). Separate 5 EGGS. Whisk the egg whites until stiff. Whisk the yolks into the cheese mixture. Beat 1 tbsp of whites into the cheese mixture to slacken, then gently fold in the remainder with a metal spoon. Transfer to a greased 1.2 litre (2 pint) soufflé dish. Dust with 1 tbsp finely grated PARMESAN CHEESE. Bake for 25–30 minutes until the soufflé is puffed and golden brown. Serve straight away with a GREEN SALAD.

PUFF PASTRY= CHEESE STRAWS

MAKES 28 Preheat the oven to 190°C (375°F/Gas 5). Roll out 375g (13oz) PUFF PASTRY on a lightly floured surface into a 25 x 35cm (10 x 14in) rectangle. Spread 2 tsp ENGLISH MUSTARD over the top half of the pastry, leaving a 1cm (½in) gap all round. Top with 60g (2oz) grated MATURE CHEDDAR CHEESE and 30g (1oz) grated PARMESAN CHEESE. Beat 1 EGG YOLK with 2 tbsp MILK and use to brush the edges of the pastry. Fold the uncovered half of the pastry over the cheese. Press the edges together to seal. Lightly roll out to a 20 x 35cm (8 x 14in) rectangle. Cut the pastry into strips 1cm (½in) wide, then, holding both ends of a strip, twist into a spiral. Place well apart on lightly greased baking trays. Bake for 12–15 minutes until puffed and golden. Cool slightly on a wire rack. Best eaten warm but can be served cold.

JACKIE KEARNEY MASTERCHEF 2011 FINAL 4
"I make a leftover cheese pie, using shortcrust pastry – mixing cheese with potato and onion for the filling."

WINE+KIRSCH=SWISS CHEESE FONDUE

SERVES 4 Rub the cut side of a GARLIC clove around the inside of a fondue pot and discard. Add 360ml (12fl oz) DRY WHITE WINE, bring it to the boil, reduce the heat, and add 200g (7oz) each of grated GRUYÈRE and EMMENTAL CHEESES, a handful at a time. Stir until melted. Mix 2 tsp CORNFLOUR with 3 tbsp KIRSCH, and 1 tbsp LEMON JUICE, and blend in. Cook over low heat for 2–3 minutes, stirring, until thick and creamy. Remove from the heat. SEASON with freshly ground BLACK PEPPER. If the mixture is too thin, add more cheese or stir in a little more cornflour, blended with wine. If it's too thick, stir in a little warmed white wine. Transfer the pot to a burner on the table. Stirring often, to keep the fondue smooth. Spear cubes of BAGUETTE on fondue forks and dunk.

BEER+TOAST= WELSH RAREBIT

SERVES 4 Preheat the grill and position the rack 10cm (4in) from the heat. Toast 4 slices of BREAD until golden brown, then turn over and toast the other side. Leaving the grill on, remove the toast from the grill and place the slices on a baking tray. Meanwhile, melt 30g (1oz) BUTTER in a pan over low heat. Add 225g (8oz) grated MATURE CHEDDAR, or LANCASHIRE CHEESE, 1 tbsp ENGLISH MUSTARD POWDER, and 3 tbsp BROWN ALE or LAGER. Heat until creamy, stirring often. Spread the sauce over the toast and splash a few drops of WORCESTERSHIRE SAUCE on each. Return the cheese-covered toast to the grill for just a few minutes, or until the cheese is bubbling and golden. Cut each slice in half and serve straight away.

BEEF STOCK+CHEESE=
FRENCH ONION SOUP

SERVES 4 Gently fry 675g (1½ lb) thinly sliced ONIONS, in a little OLIVE OIL and BUTTER, stirring occasionally in a covered pan for 10 minutes, until soft but not brown. Turn up the heat, add 1 tsp SUGAR, and fry until a rich golden brown, stirring all the time. Add 120ml (4fl oz) RED WINE. Boil until almost evaporated, stirring. Sprinkle with 2 tbsp PLAIN FLOUR and stir for 2 minutes. Pour in 1.5 litres (2¾ pints) BEEF STOCK, and bring to the boil, stirring. Reduce the heat, cover, and simmer for 30 minutes. SEASON to taste. Meanwhile, preheat the grill. Toast 8 slices of BAGUETTE. Top with 115g (4oz) grated GRUYÈRE or EMMENTAL CHEESE. Grill until golden and bubbling. Divide the soup between 4 flameproof bowls and stir 1 tbsp BRANDY into each. Float 2 cheese toasts in each bowl of soup and serve straight away.

BREAD MIX+CREAM
CHEESE+BACON=
TARTE FLAMBÉ

SERVES 4 Mix ½ a 500g (1lb 2oz) packet WHITE BREAD MIX with ½ quantity of warm WATER given on packet, and knead. Leave in a warm place until doubled in bulk. Preheat the oven to 200°C (400°F/Gas 6). Knock back the dough, roll out, and press into an oiled Swiss roll tin. Meanwhile, soften 2 large, sliced ONIONS in 1 tbsp OLIVE OIL and a knob of BUTTER. Increase the heat, and fry until golden. Beat 100g (3½oz) CREAM CHEESE, with 1 tbsp CORNFLOUR, 1 EGG, some SEASONING, and 1 tbsp MILK. Spread over the dough, leaving a small border all round. Scatter over the onions and 2 rashers of SMOKED BACON, snipped in pieces. Bake for 30 minutes until the base is crisp and golden.

SARA DANESIN MEDIO MASTERCHEF 2011 FINALIST
"Old onions are just as good if baked skin-on in a hot oven for 35 minutes, drizzled with olive oil, and a generous pinch of sea salt."

+FLOUR TORTILLAS+ CHEESE=SWEET ONION QUESADILLA

SERVES 1 Gently fry 2 thinly sliced RED ONIONS in 1 tbsp OLIVE OIL with a good pinch of DRIED SAGE for 10 minutes, stirring, until soft and sweet. Heat a large non-stick frying pan. Lay 1 flour TORTILLA in the pan. Spread with the onion mixture. Sprinkle with 50g (1¾ oz) grated CHEDDAR CHEESE, and SEASON to taste. Cover with another TORTILLA, press down with a fish slice, and cook gently for 1–2 minutes until browned underneath. Carefully turn it over, and cook the other side until the cheese has fully melted. Serve hot, cut into quarters.

GRAM FLOUR+SPICES= ONION BHAJIS

SERVES 4 In a large bowl, mix together 225g (8oz) chopped ONIONS, 115g (4oz) GRAM FLOUR, 2 tsp CUMIN SEEDS, 1 tsp, GROUND TURMERIC, 1 tsp GROUND CORIANDER, and 1 finely chopped GREEN or RED CHILLI. Add enough cold WATER (about 8 tbsp) to bind the mixture together to make a thick batter. Deep-fry spoonfuls of the mixture, roughly the size of golf balls, in hot VEGETABLE OIL, turning occasionally, until all sides are golden. Remove the bhajis from the oil using a slotted spoon, and drain on kitchen paper. Reheat the oil. Return the bhajis to the oil and quickly fry a second time until crisp and golden brown all over. Drain on kitchen paper and serve hot with raita – PLAIN YOGURT flavoured with chopped MINT and a little SEASONING.

POTATOES+

ONIONS+FETA=
POTATO CAKES

SERVES 4 Boil 450g (1lb) peeled and quartered FLOURY POTATOES in a pan of salted water for 15–20 minutes until soft. Drain, then mash. Mix with 1 grated ONION, a handful of finely snipped CHIVES, 125g (4½ oz) grated FETA CHEESE, and 1 lightly beaten EGG. Season with plenty of SALT and freshly ground BLACK PEPPER. Heat 1 tbsp OLIVE OIL in a non-stick frying pan over medium heat. Using floured hands, scoop up large balls of the potato mixture, roll, and flatten slightly. Carefully add to the hot oil and fry for 2–3 minutes on each side until golden, adding a little more oil, if needed. Drain on kitchen paper. Serve hot with SALAD.

CREAM+CHEESE+EGGS=
POTATO GRATIN

SERVES 4 Preheat the oven to 180°C (350°F/Gas 4). Peel 900g (2lb) POTATOES and thinly slice. Layer in a buttered, shallow 2.3 litre (4 pint) ovenproof dish with 2 finely chopped GARLIC cloves, 175g (6oz) grated GRUYÈRE or EMMENTAL CHEESE, and some SALT and freshly ground BLACK PEPPER, finishing with a layer of cheese. Beat 300ml (10 fl oz) SINGLE CREAM with 2 EGGS and pour over. Cover the dish with foil, then bake for 1 hour. Remove the foil and cook for a further 30 minutes, or until set, the top is golden, and the potatoes are tender. Serve with SALAD or as a side dish.

ANNELIESE KIELY MASTERCHEF 2011 CONTESTANT

"Add potato to ground almonds, sugar, and lemon rind for a delicious marzipan."

SOURED CREAM+PARMA HAM=POTATO SALAD WITH PARMA HAM

SERVES 4–6 Boil 675g (1½lb) small halved NEW POTATOES in SALTED WATER until tender. Drain and set aside. Meanwhile, heat a small frying pan over medium-high heat. Add 1 tbsp CARAWAY SEEDS and lightly toast, stirring frequently, for 2 minutes. Set aside. To make the dressing, whisk together 2 finely chopped SPRING ONIONS, 150ml (5fl oz) SOURED CREAM, 1 tsp DIJON MUSTARD, 1 tbsp RED WINE VINEGAR, 1 crushed GARLIC clove, and 3 tbsp EXTRA VIRGIN OLIVE OIL. SEASON to taste. In a salad bowl, mix the potatoes with 6 thinly sliced strips of PARMA HAM, and the CARAWAY SEEDS. Pour the dressing over, toss gently, and then garnish with some chopped FLAT-LEAF PARSLEY. Just before serving, lay a sprig of parsley on top.

OLIVE OIL=CHUNKY POTATO WEDGES

SERVES 4–6 Preheat the oven to 200°C (400°F/Gas 6). Quarter lengthways 900g (2lb) all-purpose POTATOES, such as Maris Piper, unpeeled. If large, slice them again lengthways. Put them in a large roasting tin, add 2 tbsp OLIVE OIL, and toss well with your hands. Sprinkle with plenty of SALT, and a pinch of HOT PAPRIKA or CAJUN SPICES (if you would like them a little spicy). Roast in the oven for 40 minutes, or until they are crisp and golden, turning once. Serve with MAYONNAISE, or GUACAMOLE, or as an accompaniment to any meat, fish, or chicken dish.

BREAD+BLUE CHEESE=
BREAD SALAD

SERVES 4 Toast 3 thick slices of CIABATTA or other rustic bread, and cut into cubes. Put in a large bowl and add 2–3 tbsp EXTRA VIRGIN OLIVE OIL, a handful of torn BASIL, some SALT, and plenty of freshly ground BLACK PEPPER. Toss together, with your hands and leave to stand for 10 minutes. Add 4–6 ripe, roughly chopped TOMATOES, ½ a 190g (6½oz) jar ROASTED PEPPERS, drained and sliced, a handful of toasted PINE NUTS, and 125g (4½oz) cubed DOLCELATTE or other creamy blue cheese. Toss gently and transfer to plates.

POTATOES+SOURED
CREAM=POTATO SKINS
WITH TOMATO SALSA

MAKES 8 Preheat the oven to 200ºC (400ºF/Gas 6). Prick 4 large BAKING POTATOES, rub with OLIVE OIL, and bake for about 1 hour until soft when squeezed. Cool slightly then quarter. Scoop out most of the flesh, leaving a thin layer. (Use the soft potato seasoned and fried in cakes with bacon or eggs). Place on a baking tray, skin sides down. Drizzle with 2 tbsp OLIVE OIL and sprinkle with SALT. Mix together 6 chopped TOMATOES, a good pinch of DRIED CHILLI FLAKES, 2 tbsp chopped CORIANDER or PARSLEY, and some SEASONING. Spoon onto the skins. Bake for 20 minutes until crisp at the edges. Transfer to a plate. Top with spoonfuls of SOURED CREAM and a sprinkling of DRIED OREGANO.

TOM WHITAKER MASTERCHEF 2011 FINALIST

"If you have spare tomatoes, slice in half, remove seeds, season with salt, pepper, oil, and herbs, and then place in a warm oven, for 4–5 hours. They can be kept in oil for up to a month and are great for salads and pizzas."

ONIONS+BASIL=
FRESH TOMATO SAUCE

MAKES 600ML (1 PINT) Gently fry 1 chopped ONION, 2 crushed GARLIC cloves and 1 BAY LEAF in 2 tbsp OLIVE OIL for 5 minutes until soft. Add 675g (1½lb) skinned and roughly chopped ripe TOMATOES, 2 tbsp TOMATO PURÉE, and 2 tsp SUGAR. Bring to the boil and cook 5 minutes, stirring. Add 175ml (6fl oz) WATER, bring to the boil, reduce the heat, and simmer for about 20 minutes or until thick, rich, and pulpy, stirring occasionally. Discard the bay leaf, stir in a handful of torn BASIL, and SEASON to taste. Serve tossed with PASTA or cooked MEDITERRANEAN VEGETABLES, with grilled CHICKEN or FISH, or as a base sauce for PIZZA.

BORLOTTI BEANS+
COURGETTES=TOMATO,
BEAN AND COURGETTE STEW

SERVES 4 Gently fry 1 large, finely chopped ONION in 3 tbsp OLIVE OIL in a large saucepan, stirring, for 3 minutes. Add 2 diced COURGETTES, and cook for a further 5 minutes, stirring. Add 2 chopped GARLIC cloves, a 400g can drained and rinsed BORLOTTI BEANS, 4 roughly chopped TOMATOES, 1 tsp SMOKED PAPRIKA, 1 tsp dried OREGANO, a pinch of SUGAR, and some SEASONING. Bring to the boil, reduce the heat, and simmer for about 10 minutes, until the courgettes are tender. Taste and re-season. Spoon into bowls, and drizzle with a little CHILLI OIL, if liked. Serve with CRUSTY BREAD.

CARROTS+

POTATOES+CURRY PASTE +PASTRY=CURRIED VEGETABLE PASTIES

SERVES 4 Preheat the oven to 200ºC (400ºF/Gas 6). Boil 2 large diced CARROTS and 1 large diced POTATO together in salted water until tender. Drain. Cut 450g (1lb) SHORTCRUST PASTRY in quarters. Roll out, and cut each into a 15–18cm (6–7in) circle using a small plate as a guide. Gently mix the cooked vegetables with 2 chopped SPRING ONIONS, 1 tbsp CURRY PASTE, 1 chopped GARLIC clove, 1 tsp grated FRESH GINGER, handful of chopped CORIANDER, 1 tbsp LEMON JUICE, and SEASON. Spoon onto the centres of the pastry circles, and brush edges with water. Fold over to make half-moon shapes. Pinch the edges together to seal. Transfer to a baking tray. Slash the tops with a knife. Brush with beaten EGG. Bake for 20–30 minutes until golden. Good hot or cold.

BUTTER+BROWN SUGAR= GLAZED CARROTS

SERVES 4 Place 450g (1lb) thinly sliced CARROTS into a saucepan with the thinly pared zest and juice of 1 ORANGE, 30g (1oz) BUTTER, 1 tbsp LIGHT BROWN SUGAR, 1 crushed GARLIC clove, some SALT and freshly ground BLACK PEPPER, and ½ tsp chopped THYME. Just cover with water. Bring to the boil, cover and cook over medium heat for 8–10 minutes until tender. Remove the lid and boil until the liquid has evaporated, and the carrots are glazed and golden at the edges, shaking the pan occasionally to prevent sticking. Sprinkle with a few thyme leaves. Serve as an accompaniment to grilled MEAT or FISH or try sprinkling with crumbled FETA CHEESE and toasted PUMPKIN SEEDS for a light meal.

ORANGE JUICE+
VEGETABLE STOCK=
CARROT AND ORANGE SOUP

SERVES 4 In a large saucepan, cook a sliced LEEK, and 500g (1lb 2oz) sliced CARROTS in 2 tsp SUNFLOWER OIL, and a knob of BUTTER, over low heat for 5 minutes. Stir frequently. Add a chopped POTATO, ½ tsp each ground CORIANDER and CUMIN, and fry for 30 seconds. Pour in 300ml (10fl oz) ORANGE JUICE and 500ml (16fl oz) VEGETABLE STOCK. Add a BAY LEAF, bring to the boil, reduce the heat, cover, and simmer for 40 minutes, or until the vegetables are very tender. Purée in a blender or food processor. Return to the saucepan and add a little more stock if too thick. Reheat, ladle into bowls, and serve topped with a spoonful of PLAIN YOGURT and some chopped CORIANDER.

EGGS+TARRAGON=CARROT
AND TARRAGON TIMBALES

SERVES 4 Preheat the oven to 200°C (400°F/Gas 6). BUTTER 4 ramekins and line the bases with baking parchment. Coarsely grate 350g (12oz) CARROTS. Plunge into a pan of boiling water for 30 seconds. Drain and rinse with cold water. Squeeze out excess moisture and place in a bowl. Stir in 2 beaten EGGS, 175g (6oz) grated GRUYÈRE CHEESE, ½tsp ENGLISH MUSTARD, 2 tbsp CRÈME FRAÎCHE, 2 tbsp finely chopped TARRAGON, and freshly ground BLACK PEPPER. Stand the ramekins in a roasting tin with enough boiling water to come halfway up the sides. Cover the tin loosely with foil. Bake for 25 minutes, or until just firm. Turn out onto serving plates. Serve with tomato salad.

CABBAGE+

APPLES+VINEGAR=
BRAISED RED CABBAGE WITH APPLE

SERVES 4 Heat a knob of BUTTER and 2 tbsp OLIVE OIL in a flameproof casserole. Add a thinly sliced red ONION and cook for 3 minutes, stirring until softened but not browned. Add a large diced COOKING APPLE, a handful of RAISINS, and 1 small shredded RED OR WHITE CABBAGE. Mix thoroughly, then stir in 4 tbsp RED WINE VINEGAR, 3 tbsp LIGHT BROWN SUGAR, and 150ml (5fl oz) WATER. SEASON to taste. Bring to the boil, reduce the heat, cover, and simmer very gently for about 1 hour or until the cabbage is very tender. Add a little more water, if necessary to prevent drying out. Taste and re-season if necessary. Serve hot with GAMMON, PORK, DUCK, or grilled GOAT'S CHEESE.

CARROTS+MAYONNAISE=
COLESLAW

SERVES 4 Finely shred ½ small WHITE CABBAGE, discarding the thick core. Place in a bowl. Coarsely grate 2 large CARROTS into the bowl. Thinly slice 2 SPRING ONIONS, diagonally, or finely grate ½ small ONION, and add. Finely slice 2 CELERY sticks and add (optional). Blend 120ml (4fl oz) MAYONNAISE with 4 tsp MILK and the juice of 1 small LEMON. Add to the coleslaw with 2 tbsp chopped flat-leaf PARSLEY and 1 tbsp snipped CHIVES. Mix well and SEASON to taste. Chill, if time, to allow the flavours to develop. Serve with CHEESE, HAM, or HARD-BOILED EGGS, in JACKET POTATOES, or as an accompaniment to BURGERS or grilled CHICKEN.

MATTHEW DRIVER MASTERCHEF 2011 CONTESTANT
"Old fashioned, but never forget bubble and squeak –
a meal by itself or fabulous with cold, leftover meat. "

MUSHROOMS+TOMATO SAUCE=CABBAGE ROLLS

SERVES 4 Gently fry a finely chopped ONION, 115g (4oz) chopped MUSHROOMS, and a finely chopped CELERY stick in 2 tbsp OLIVE OIL for 5 minutes, stirring. Remove from the heat and stir in 115g (4oz) BROWN BREADCRUMBS, a beaten EGG, 2 tbsp chopped PARSLEY, a pinch of ground CORIANDER and a squeeze of LEMON JUICE. SEASON well. Cut out the thick stalks from 8 large SAVOY CABBAGE leaves. Blanch the leaves in boiling water for 2 minutes. Drain. Divide the filling among the leaves and roll up, folding in the sides to form parcels. Pack into a flameproof casserole dish. Pour over 150ml (5fl oz) VEGETABLE STOCK. Cover, and simmer gently for 30–40 minutes until tender. Heat 400g (14oz) PASSATA with ONION and GARLIC. SEASON to taste. Spoon onto plates, top with the rolls. Serve hot with SAUTÉED POTATOES.

CARROTS+PEANUTS= THAI-STYLE SHREDDED CABBAGE WITH PEANUTS

SERVES 4 To make the dressing, put 1 tbsp LIGHT SOY SAUCE, 1 tbsp THAI FISH SAUCE, 1 FRESH GREEN CHILLI, deseeded and finely chopped, 1 grated or finely chopped GARLIC clove, the juice of 2 LIMES, 1–2 tsp CASTER SUGAR, and a handful of finely chopped CORIANDER, in a small bowl. Mix thoroughly until the sugar has dissolved. Season to taste. Quarter, core, and chop 2 EATING APPLES. Put in a bowl with 4 grated CARROTS, 1 small, shredded WHITE CABBAGE, and a handful of SUNFLOWER SEEDS. Toss well. Drizzle the dressing over and toss together until well mixed. Transfer to a serving dish and scatter a handful of SALTED or DRY-ROASTED PEANUTS over the top. Serve as a light lunch.

CHOCOLATE+

EGGS+CREAM=
CHOCOLATE MOUSSE

SERVES 6 Break up 200g (7oz) DARK CHOCOLATE. Melt in a bowl over a pan of simmering water. Stir gently to melt. Remove from the heat. Meanwhile, separate 3 EGGS. Whisk the egg whites until stiff. Whisk in 2 tbsp CASTER SUGAR. Whip 150ml (5fl oz) DOUBLE CREAM until softly peaking. Stir the egg yolks and 2 tbsp BRANDY into the melted chocolate. Add to the whipped cream and gently fold them together with a metal spoon. Add the whisked egg whites and gently fold in, using the metal spoon. Spoon into coffee cups and decorate with GRATED CHOCOLATE. Chill for at least 2 hours or until ready to serve. Stand the cups on coffee saucers and lay a teaspoon on each saucer to eat the mousse with.

BUTTER+CREAM=
CHOCOLATE MARQUISE

MAKES 10–12 SLICES Line a 900g (2lb) loaf tin with cling film. Break up 400g (14oz) DARK CHOCOLATE and place in a saucepan with 175g (6oz) BUTTER, 175g (6oz) CASTER SUGAR, and 4 tbsp COCOA POWDER. Melt over a very low heat, stirring. Beat 6 EGG YOLKS (use the whites for meringues) in a bowl. Pour in the chocolate mixture, stirring constantly. Whip 500ml (16fl oz) DOUBLE CREAM and fold in. Transfer to the prepared tin. Chill at least 2 hours or overnight until set. Turn out, remove the cling film and, using a hot knife, cut into slices. Serve dusted with a little cocoa, with mixed fresh BERRIES and POURING CREAM.

NEIL BALDWYN MASTERCHEF 2011 CONTESTANT
"Try not to store chocolate in the fridge – as it warms it will form condensation, which will spoil the finish of your desserts."

BUTTER+BISCUITS=
CHOCOLATE BISCUIT CAKE

MAKES 8–10 PIECES Melt 250g (9oz) DARK CHOCOLATE, broken into pieces, 150g (5oz) BUTTER and 2 tbsp GOLDEN SYRUP in a saucepan, stirring. Remove from the heat and stir in 450g (1lb) roughly-crushed (not too finely) PLAIN BISCUITS (a mixture of broken ones from the tin or bought broken ones are fine), a good handful of RAISINS (or other DRIED FRUIT), and a handful of roughly chopped BLANCHED ALMONDS (or other NUTS). Mix well and press into a greased 18cm (7in) square baking tin. Cool, then chill overnight to firm. Serve cut into pieces.

NUTS+DRIED CHERRIES=
CHOCOLATE TRUFFLES

MAKES 12–14 Break 125g (4½oz) DARK CHOCOLATE into pieces and place in a microwave-safe bowl. Microwave on Medium for 1–2 minutes or until melted, then stir until smooth (or melt in a bowl over gently simmering water). Stir in a splash of IRISH CREAM LIQUEUR or BRANDY, then add 25g (scant 1oz) finely chopped BRAZIL NUTS and 50g (1¾oz) chopped DRIED CHERRIES or RAISINS. Leave to cool for 30 minutes. Meanwhile, finely grate 30g (1oz) DARK CHOCOLATE. Scoop up a generous teaspoonful of the chocolate mixture and form into balls. Roll in about 30g (1oz) finely GRATED CHOCOLATE, or COCOA POWDER, then place on greaseproof paper and chill for 30 minutes or until set. Serve as a sweet treat with coffee.

STEM GINGER+CREAM+ LEMON=STEWED APPLE WITH GINGER, AND LEMON CREAM

SERVE 4 Peel, core, and slice 1.35g (3lb) EATING APPLES such as Cox's, or COOKING APPLES. Put in a pan with 150ml (5fl oz) APPLE JUICE or WATER, and 1 tbsp STEM GINGER SYRUP from the jar. Bring to the boil, reduce the heat, cover, and simmer gently, stirring occasionally, until tender. Remove from the heat and beat well. Stir in 3 pieces finely chopped STEM GINGER. Add a splash of LEMON JUICE or SUGAR, to taste. Cool, then chill. Meanwhile, whip 150ml (5fl oz) DOUBLE CREAM with 2 tsp CASTER SUGAR, and the finely grated zest of a small LEMON. Transfer the apple to 4 serving glasses. Top with the LEMON CREAM and decorate with STEM GINGER.

WALNUTS+GROUND CINNAMON=SPICED BAKED APPLES

SERVES 4 Preheat the oven to 180°C (350°F/Gas 4). Put 85g (3oz) WALNUT PIECES, 1 tbsp RAISINS, 1 tbsp LIGHT BROWN SUGAR, 30g (1oz) BUTTER, ¼ tsp GROUND CINNAMON, and a splash of LEMON JUICE into a food processor. Pulse to produce a coarse-textured mixture. Carefully cut a 2.5cm (1in) slice from the top of each of 4 large GOLDEN DELICIOUS APPLES (or similar), and set aside. Using an apple corer, or a small sharp knife, core each apple. Place in an ovenproof dish. Pile the nut mixture into the apples, and replace the reserved tops. Add about 1cm (½in) water. Bake in the oven for 30 minutes, or until the flesh is tender when pierced with the point of a knife. Serve with CREAM or CUSTARD.

JAMES PERRY MASTERCHEF 2011 FINAL 5
"Apples are the pride of Britain and a great partner for many flavours. Soak thin slices in apple juice, to increase the flavour – great in a salad with mackerel or braised red cabbage."

FLOUR+BUTTER+SUGAR =APPLE CRUMBLE

SERVES 4 Preheat the oven to 190°C (375°F/Gas 5). Peel, core, and thinly slice 500g (1lb 2oz) EATING APPLES, such as Cox's. Put the apples in an ovenproof dish with 1 tbsp LEMON JUICE, and toss until well coated. Sprinkle with a pinch of GROUND CLOVES or MIXED SPICE (optional). Place 115g (4oz) PLAIN FLOUR and 75g (2½oz) BUTTER in a mixing bowl, and rub together until the mixture resembles coarse breadcrumbs. Stir in 60g (2oz) ROLLED OATS and 75g (2½ oz) DEMERARA SUGAR. Spoon over the apples and press down gently. Bake for 45 minutes until crisp and golden on top and the apples are tender. Serve hot with CREAM, ICE CREAM, or CUSTARD.

PASTRY+ALMONDS+ MAPLE SYRUP=CARAMEL APPLE AND ALMOND TART

SERVES 6 Preheat the oven to 190°C (375°F/Gas 5). Line 6 flan cases, set on a baking tray, with 250g (9oz) SWEET SHORTCRUST PASTRY. Line with greaseproof paper and fill with baking beans. Bake for 12 minutes. Remove the paper and bake for a further 5 minutes. Remove from the oven and cool. Whisk 4 EGGS with 300ml (10fl oz) CRÈME FRAÎCHE, 2 tbsp MAPLE (or GOLDEN) SYRUP, 115g (4oz) LIGHT BROWN SUGAR, 1 tsp VANILLA EXTRACT, and 115g (4oz) GROUND ALMONDS. Transfer to the cases. Peel, core, and slice 3 tart EATING APPLES, such as Granny Smiths. Arrange over the tops, and sprinkle each with ½ tsp CASTER SUGAR. Bake for 20 minutes, until set. Serve with CREAM or ICE CREAM.

London, New York, Munich, Melbourne, and Delhi

First published in Great Britain in 2012
by Dorling Kindersley Limited
80 Strand, London WC2R 0RL

Penguin Group (UK)

Principal recipe editors Carolyn Humphries, Diana Vowles
Additional recipe editing Amanda Wright
Proofreader Claire Tennant-Scull

Editor Kajal Mistry
Project Art Editor Collette Sadler
Editorial Assistant David Fentiman
Design Assistant Jade Wheaton
Managing Editor Dawn Henderson
Managing Art Editor Christine Keilty
Senior Creative Nicola Powling
Jacket Design Assistant Rosie Levine
Production Editor Clare McLean, Sarah Isle
Senior Production Controller Claire Pearson
Creative Technical Support Sonia Charbonnier
Art Director Peter Luff
Publisher Mary Ling

DK India
Editors Kokila Manchanda, Nidhilekha Mathur,
Ekta Sharma, Arani Sinha
Art Editors Divya PR, Mansi Nagdev
DTP Designer Rajdeep Singh
Managing Editor Glenda Fernandes
Managing Art Editor Navidita Thapa
DTP Manager Sunil Sharma

Recipe photography Stuart West
Photography art direction Kat Mead
Food stylists Jane Lawrie, Valerie Barrett
Food stylist assistant Paul Jackman
Prop stylist Jessica Georgiades

Cover photography Noel Murphy
Fashion styling Boo Attwood
Clothing Paul Costello, Paul Smith
Grooming Katie Reedman

Printed and bound by Firmengruppe APPL,
aprinta druck, Wemding, Germany

Acknowledgements

Shine would like to thank

David Ambler, Juliette Bidwell, Laura Biggs, Martin Buckett, Jo Carlton, Bev Comboy, Clare Elliot, Elizabeth
Fisher, Simone Foots, John Gilbert, Jessica Hannan, Lori Heiss, Victoria Howarth, Ozen Kazim, Digby Lewis,
Eva Lofvenberg, Alex Mahon, Maya Maraj, Jamie Munro, Elisabeth Murdoch, Lou Plank, Lyndsey Posner, Franc
Roddam, Karen Ross, Rosemary Scoular, Donna Stevenson, Caroline Stott, John Torode, Will Vaughan, Sophie
Walker, Gregg Wallace, and Heidi Wallace.

MasterChef 2011 contestants whose recipes and quotes are included in this book:

Elizabeth Allen, Tim Anderson, Annie Assheton, Neil Baldwyn, Darren Campbell MBE, Margi Clarke, Serena
Crump, Sara Danesin Medio, Matthew Driver, Paul Elder, Nicky French, Danny Goffey, Ruth Goodman, Ricky
Groves, Ondine Hartgroves, Claudia Huxtable, Shobu Kapoor, Jackie Kearney, Anneliese Keily, Kennedy Leitch,
Tim Lovejoy, Fiona Luck, Linda Lusardi, Aggie MacKenzie, Sharon Maughan, Colin McAllister, Michelle Mone
OBE, Polly Oxby, James Perry, Nick Pickard, Justin Ryan, Peter Seville, Alice Taylor, Phil Vickery MBE, Kirsty
Wark, and Tom Whitaker.

Dorling Kindersley would like to thank

Laura Nickoll, Tia Sarkar, Alastair Laing, and Sarah Fassnidge for editorial help; Sylvain Jamois, Ann Reynolds,
Jane Bamforth, and Paul Jackman for recipe testing; Zaklya Bishton at Shine for help with supplying images;
Wayne Holder for couriering, and Hilary Bird for indexing.